*The Cooperstown Symposium on Baseball
and American Culture* 1997 *(Jackie Robinson)*

The Cooperstown Symposium on Baseball and American Culture

1997 (Jackie Robinson)

Edited with an Introduction by
  Peter M. Rutkoff

Series Editor: Alvin Hall

McFarland & Company, Inc., Publishers
Jefferson, North Carolina, and London

"A Story in Black and White: Baseball and Racism in 1938" by Chris Lamb was previously published as "L'affaire Jake Powell: The Minority Press Goes to Bat Against Segregated Baseball," *Journalism and Mass Communication Quarterly*, Vol. 76, No. 1, pp. 21–34. Used by permission of *Journalism and Mass Communication Quarterly*.

"Something to Cheer About: The Negro Leagues at the Dawn of Integration" by James E. Overmyer was previously published in James E. Overmyer, *Queen of the Negro Leagues: Effa Manley and the Newark Eagles* (Lanham MD: Scarecrow, 1998). Used by permission of the Scarecrow Press.

"Nine Principles of Successful Affirmative Action: Branch Rickey, Jackie Robinson, and the Integration of Baseball" by Anthony R. Pratkanis and Marlene E. Turner was previously published in *NINE: A Journal of Baseball History and Social Policy Perspectives* (1993): pp. 36–61. Used by permission of *NINE*.

"The Great Experiment Fifty Years Later" by Jules Tygiel was previously published as "Afterword" in Jules Tygiel, *Baseball's Great Experiment: Jackie Robinson and His Legacy*, 2d ed., © 1997 by Jules Tygiel. Used by permission of Oxford University Press, Inc.

ISBN 0-7864-0831-6 (softcover : 50# alkaline paper) ∞

Library of Congress cataloguing data are available

British Library cataloguing data are available

Manufactured in the United States of America

McFarland & Company, Inc., Publishers
  Box 611, Jefferson, North Carolina 28640
  www.mcfarlandpub.com

To the Gambier Board of Rabbis:
Jim Lubetkin, Tracy Schermer, Will Scott, and David Lynn

Acknowledgments

Thanks to Al Hall of the Union Institute, and Jim Gates and Tim Wiles of the National Baseball Hall of Fame and Museum. Special thanks to Jean Demaree, my colleague and administrative assistant whose work made this volume possible. Thanks, too, to Sarah Demaree for the index.

Table of Contents

PART 3: THE LEGACY OF ROBINSON

Preface

Al Hall

Just as 1989 seemed to be a good year to organize a conference in Cooperstown, New York, entitled "Baseball and American Culture," 1997 seemed an equally good year to dedicate the Cooperstown Symposium on Baseball and American Culture to Jackie Robinson, baseball, and race relations in the United States. Nineteen hundred and eighty-nine marked the fiftieth anniversary of the National Baseball Hall of Fame and Museum, Inc. Nineteen hundred and ninety-seven celebrated a half-century passed since Jackie Robinson broke the color barrier in major league baseball and changed, forever, not only the complexion of sport but also many other aspects of American life.

From its beginning in 1989, the Cooperstown Symposium on Baseball and American Culture has been co-sponsored by the State University of New York at Oneonta and the National Baseball Hall of Fame. As the dean of continuing education at Oneonta State, I had the honor of developing an idea first proposed by Tom Heitz, then librarian at the Hall. At the same time the Hall of Fame was celebrating its fiftieth birthday, we wanted to bring a group of scholars together to examine the impact of baseball on American culture. We planned a one-time event, but the first proved so successful that subsequent symposiums have been held every June.

Until 1997, the symposium was a multi-disciplinary meeting that examined baseball's impact on American life from many perspectives. There was no single theme. Each year, speakers, drawn largely from the faculties and staffs of the country's colleges and universities, presented papers in diverse disciplines from art history to women's studies, and many in between. The presenters shared two things — a passionate love for the national pastime and a solid grounding in the scholarship of an academic discipline.

The Ninth Cooperstown Symposium was somewhat different. Because 1997 marked the fiftieth anniversary of Jackie Robinson joining the Brooklyn Dodgers, the Hall of Fame would mark the occasion by opening a new permanent exhibit on "Baseball and African Americans." The Symposium invited Jules Tygiel, author of *Baseball's Great Experiment: The Legacy of Jackie Robinson*, to deliver the keynote address. Abstracts were solicited on Robinson, race relations and African Americans. Of the thirty papers presented, well over half were on these topics. The highlight of the conference was the opening of the new exhibit with Rachel Robinson present, along with others including Larry Doby, Sam Lacey, Buck O'Neill, and Joe Morgan.

This volume, the third in the history of the Symposium, contains the best of the papers presented on the central themes. These papers, along with nearly three hundred others presented over the years, confirm that virtually any aspect of American history can be told using baseball as the vehicle. They confirm Ken Burns' words, in his keynote address to the Sixth Cooperstown Symposium: "There's a rich and evocative history hidden in our deceptively simple national pastime. The story of baseball is the story of America. It's a startling mirror of American life."

Introduction —
Jackie Robinson: Baseball, Brooklyn, and Beyond

Peter Rutkoff

As a youngster, Art Rust, Jr., one of New York's first prominent black sportscasters, lived on St. Nicholas Avenue, a stone's throw equally from Minton's and Monroe's, the after-hours clubs where Charlie Parker and Thelonious Monk created bebop, and the Polo Grounds, home of the New York Giants. Rust remembered the day in the 1930s when "Billy the Cop," just off duty, told Rust's father that Giant manager Bill Terry, the last National League player to hit over .400, complained to the precinct commander that he didn't want any "nigger cops" patrolling the Polo Grounds, at least not near the executive entrances.[1]

Almost twenty years later, in the early 1950s, George Weiss, the general manager of the New York Yankees, a team whose Ruthian dominance prevailed in the Stadium, built with intentional perversity within eyesight of the Polo Grounds just across the East River in the South Bronx, responded to charges that the Yankees had failed to sign black players. In private, Weiss said, "I will never allow a black man to wear a Yankee uniform. Boxholders from Westchester don't want that sort of crowd. They would be offended to have to sit with niggers."[2] Publicly, in the spring of 1952, he responded that the team had been looking long and hard for a black player, "good enough to make the Yankees." Weiss' accuser, Jackie Robinson, then entering his sixth season with the Brooklyn Dodgers, rejoined, "Bullshit."[3]

On April 18, 1946, Robinson had made his professional debut, playing for Montreal, the Dodgers' highest minor league team, against the Jersey City Giants at Roosevelt Stadium in Jersey City. A minor-league-record
52,000 fans came to see the historic event. There had also been nine lynchings in the American South in 1946.[4] The African American experience, by
the end of the Second World War, had become an integral part the "national
game" of baseball.

Professional baseball mirrored the fundamental tensions of urban
American life. A game played by boys about to be men, baseball — like
theater — provided a sunshiny, pastoral contrast to the dark reality of city
life. Its precision, statistical uniformity, and team centeredness all testified
to its modernity. Yet "the Game," as many called it, played to the imagination, producing larger-than-life heroes whose individualism and mythic
proportions transcended team, or community discipline. Despite baseball's obsession with statistical measurement, until the 1960s, each park and
then stadium possessed its own unique spatial, architectural, and social
character. In New York, moreover, each of the three teams possessed complex cultural and social histories whose lore belonged to the residents of
the neighborhoods in which they played and, in many cases, resided. New
York City baseball was a city game but most importantly it was a neighborhood game. Like the environs in which it existed, baseball could not
remain immune to the demographic, economic, and political changes of
the postwar era. The years 1945–1957 were truly golden for New York's
professional teams, but they were sadly tragic as well.

If baseball's inherent poetry suspended disbelief, it has also served as
a unique social and cultural mirror. Its organization into major and minor
leagues, the issuance of contracts, and its hierarchy reflected the increased
stratification and professionalization of America. With cities at its hub,
players moved up to the majors following apprenticeship in the towns and
villages of the nation's hinterlands, bringing with them the vulnerable
innocence of their background and experience. "Shoeless Joe" Jackson fell
prey, in the end, to the temptations and manipulations of city folk, prompting the child's response of "say it ain't so," a cry of lost simplicity. But it
was also a statement of the need for contemporary heroism in an age of
uniformity. Baseball provided the males of America with heroes aplenty,
heroes like Babe Ruth, larger than life itself, like Joe Jackson, whose naive
corruptibility lent itself to disillusionment and then redemption, or like
Casey Stengel, whose clowning spirit masked a master strategist and
manipulator. A game where fathers passed along skills and lore to their
sons, baseball's masculine ethos brought women to the ballpark to witness
but not share the rituals. Even the innovation of "Ladies Day," attributed

to the Dodgers, only opened the public spectacle of baseball to the distaff sex. The dugout, locker room, and road remained enclaves closed to all save the male participants who guarded the secrets of sweat, liniment, tobacco, and philandering. Baseball could not remain immune from the culture of which it was a part, but its images were carefully constructed and its secrets painstakingly preserved. In New York during the fifteen years following the Second World War, baseball told many stories and created new heroes appropriate to the age.

The story of Jackie Robinson, from his first conversations with Brooklyn Dodger general manager Branch Rickey to his retirement more than a decade later, dominated the social and symbolic history of baseball in New York between 1945 and 1957. Without Robinson, only the Yankees would have emerged as a dominant team. Yet, with him, baseball, and its impact on New York and postwar America, changed as never before. Not only did Robinson represent the hopes of African Americans in their struggle to achieve equality, and not only did his presence create the first truly integrated team in the history of American sports, but most of all Robinson played with a verve, energy, and competitive intensity unmatched in the long history of the game. As Leo Durocher, Robinson's first manager and, after 1947, his arch rival, said, "This guy didn't just come to play. He came to beat ya. He came to stuff the goddamn bat up your ass."[5]

Roy Tucker, star center fielder of the pre–World War II Brooklyn Dodgers, awakened one morning in occupied France with his leg shattered. Tucker had bailed out after his plane had been hit by German anti-aircraft fire. Known as the "Kid from Tompkinsville," Tucker realized that the Resistants gathered around him, one of them a Jew, were ordinary people who "risked their lives all day, every day."[6] Months later, a recovered Tucker rejoined his team to reclaim his old position from the talented rookie, Lester Young, who exclaimed, "Say you're a white guy to help me when I'm grabbing your spot on the team." Tucker's teammates, the wily pitcher Bones Hathaway, the stocky and Jewish catcher Jocko Klein, "just about the best catcher in baseball ... he's got guts," and Highpockets Kellton, the phenomenon from the mountains of Appalachia, made these Dodgers a kind of cross section of American democratic virtue.

These fictional Brooklyn Dodgers — Roy Tucker, Jocko Klein, and Bones Hathaway — were the creation of juvenile writer John Tunis, whose series of baseball books from 1937 through 1950 chronicled the process of overcoming that his heroes embodied as they sought to win but only at a human price. Victorious only with virtue, defeated when confused over the meaning of success, the fictional Dodgers proved that their virtues, and the corresponding triumph of good over evil, could surmount all obstacles. Even when they were behind in the crucial game of a pennant drive, two runs down in the bottom of the ninth, they were sure to win if they had cleaned up their moral house. Tunis's fictional team, although modeled on the actual Dodgers, had, however, no equivalent for Jackie Robinson. The Tunis Dodgers, even in the books he wrote after 1946, remained all white. Yet, to many New Yorkers, to root for the real and beloved Bums seemed an act of affirmation of nothing less than American democracy itself.[7] When Lewis Milstone, the director of *A Walk in the Sun*, introduced the GIs of his mythic company, he conformed to the convention of America's ethnic foxhole as the repository of the nation's diversity and strength: urban Americans, Italians, Jews, and Poles, fighting side by side with Southern squirrel hunters and New Hampshire farmers. Without Robinson, the lineup of Milstone's infantry soldiers could as easily have been that of the Dodgers themselves. Dixie Walker, Preacher Roe, Pee-Wee Reese, Carl Furillo, Cookie Lavagetto, Cal Abrams, and Jake Pitler were part of the Durocher-led teams of the postwar era. The historic signing of Jackie Robinson, in a sense, fulfilled the promise of the Dodger myth in American culture. With the major league's first black player, the Dodgers had, indeed, become emblematic of American society. In contrast to the Tammany-inspired Giants, whose dominance belonged to a New York of an earlier, Jim Crow era, and the Imperial Yankees, who exploited the city's traditional ethnicity as American corporations exploited the ethnic working class, the Dodgers, for a short time, embodied the values and pluralistic ideals of modern America, located in Brooklyn.

In 1913, Charlie Ebbets, whose team had joined the National League in 1890 and won pennants in that inaugural year as well as in 1899 and 1900, laid the cornerstone for his new "field." Completed in time for the 1913 season, over time Ebbets Field translated the idiosyncrasies of its structure to both its neighborhood and its players. Contained by the streets of the city, with Bedford Avenue flanking the left-field fence, Ebbets Field belonged to a family of urban ballparks whose intimacy and grace combined with its steel-and-concrete construction to express precisely the tensions inherent in the game of baseball. Modern in structure, individual in style and layout, from the notch in center field to the beveled fence in right, Ebbets Field evoked the memory of a pastoral park situated at the city's crossroads. In time, New York's two earliest subway systems, the IRT and BMT, as well as three bus lines and the famed trolley lines, all stopped within three blocks of Ebbets Field. Dodger publicists in the 1930s and 1940s claimed, however, that as many as one-third of those who came to watch the

"Bums," or the Dodgers (after the notorious trolley tracks) as the renamed Robins and Bridegrooms came to be known, arrived on foot.[8] More than either the Giants or the Yankees, the Dodgers belonged to their neighborhood.

The competitive Dodgers of the last decade of the "dead ball" era, however, soon gave way to a twenty-year span of failure. Between 1920 and 1941, the assemblage from Brooklyn, or the Daffiness Boys, played baseball as if winning games had become secondary to winning the hearts and minds of the neighborhood. "It was a peaceful, middle class life, and baseball seemed vitally important," one writer wistfully recalled.[9] Babe Herman, the team's slugger who endeared himself to the crowds, hit, it was said, like Ott but fielded like Solomon.[10] The creator of Berraisms avant, so to speak, la parole, Herman, whose lifetime average of .324, including an astounding .393 in 1930, once responded to a female fan who remarked that he looked cool by saying, "Thanks, you don't look so hot yourself."[11] Between 1921 and 1938, the team finished in the first division but four times, and clung to sixth with such tenacity that they finished in that position in five consecutive years, from 1925 through 1929. The onset of the Depression could hardly deflate the Dodgers' fortunes, and when Wilbert Robinson, the beloved manager whose tenure had matched that of his old friend and rival John McGraw with the Giants, was replaced by the omnipresent Casey Stengel, the Dodgers collapsed totally, finishing seventh in 1935 and again in 1937. Only the pitching of Van Lingo Mungo brought the Dodgers any distinction during these dismal years.

Owned not by a charismatic figure drawn from the captaincy of urban commerce, the Dodgers of record-breaking futility belonged to the Brooklyn Trust Company, a bank. By 1937, however, even the Brooklyn Trust had suffered enough. Acting quickly, the bank hired Larry MacPhail, a hard-drinking yet innovative executive from Cincinnati, as the new general manager. MacPhail set out to transform the team into a contender. He traded for the fiery Leo Durocher, still active as a shortstop for the aging Gas House Gang of St. Louis, and installed him as the team's player-manager. MacPhail refurbished Ebbets Field, installing lights just in time for Johnny Vander Meer's second no-hit game in 1938, brought the already noted broadcaster, Red Barber, over from Cincinnati, and simultaneously announced that the Dodgers would break New York's three-team ban on radio broadcasts. Dodger Blue replaced Dodger Green, as MacPhail hired Babe Ruth as a coach, traded for veteran stars like Dixie Walker and Ducky Medwick, and resurrected the moribund farm system.[12] The MacPhail-Durocher tandem, called by some the alliance of drinking and gambling, succeeded almost immediately. Between 1938 and 1941, the Dodgers finished third, second twice, and finally, in 1941, captured the National League championship, only to lose to the Yankees when catcher Mickey Owen, with two out in the ninth inning of the fourth game, let a strike get past him, allowing the Yankees to forge ahead in the game and the Series. Decimated by the war's "Spartan seasons," the Dodgers' mix of youthful exuberance, typified by Pee-Wee Reese, "Pistol" Pete Reiser, and the Cardinal veterans Medwick and Walker, the latter rechristened in Brooklynese as the "people's cherce," fell apart. To replenish its ranks, the team resurrected its old hero from the 1920s, Babe Herman, who in his first appearance in Ebbets Field in sixteen seasons "connected ... for a sharp single and then fell flat on his face rounding first base."[13] The Dodgers recovered from Herman's last season in the majors and regrouped to finish in a tie with the Cardinals in 1946 when they lost the league's first playoff. In 1947, they captured the National League pennant as their newest star, Jackie Robinson, won the Rookie of the Year Award.

The Dodgers captured, too, the social and cultural stability of Depression-bound Brooklyn. The borough that had once been a city continued to grow demographically, claiming close to three million residents by the eve of the Second World War. The neighborhoods of Crown Heights, Park Slope, and Flatbush blended into one another, creating a middle-, lower middle-, and working-class residential city within the county. Irish, Italian, and Jewish parents and children attended churches and synagogues, shopped on the busy thoroughfares, attended Erasmus Hall High School and Brooklyn College, took the new A train into Manhattan, frolicked in Prospect Park and Coney Island, and worshipped at Ebbets Field. "My God, it was like the Emerald City," recalled one resident from the late 1930s: "As you got closer you'd pick up your pace."[14] Nostalgia for a more peaceful time floods the memories of that Brooklyn generation. Aware that they lived in the third largest city in the world, Brooklynites were proud: "Three million people, and hardly a Mayflower descendent among them."[15] Ethnicity the norm, these immigrants and their children knew little of the more than 100,000 African Americans who continued to live around their extended neighborhoods in Bedford-Stuyvesant and Brownsville just to the North of Crown Heights and Flatbush. Far more than either the businesspeople and civil servants who continued to form the core of support for the Giants or the suburbanites who lavished their affection on the Yankees, the true Dodger fans — the men, women, and children of central Brooklyn — created a version of their culture even at the park itself.

When Larry MacPhail prevailed on Red Barber to join the Dodgers as a broadcaster following the 1938 season, he brought to Brooklyn one of the distinctive voices and personalities in sports journalism. Humane, literate,

Southern, Barber's wonderfully expressive phrases, "Well, he's sure sittin' in the catbird seat" and "Let's see, the bases are FOB ... [full of Brooklyns]" gave the team a special radio personality, one that Barber simultaneously recorded and created. When Wheaties paid the Brooklyn Trust $70,000 for the initial rights to the Dodgers' home games, Barber and MacPhail made sure that they were to be broadcast on WOR, one of the city's powerful 50,000-watt stations.[16] By the late 1940s, Barber and the Dodgers had become so intertwined in the public mind and ear that "the Old Redhead" came to play a very important role in the unfolding drama of Jackie Robinson.

Barber brought Ebbets Field to the neighborhood, and his persuasively sympathetic identification with the team no doubt accounted for the tenacity with which Brooklyn's Dodger fans clung to the mystique of their team. For many, actual attendance at the game mattered less than hearing Barber and, then, reading about the team in the *Brooklyn Eagle* (the purveyor of the infamous "Wait Till Next Year" banner headline that appeared following the 1941 debacle) and in the bulldog edition of the Daily News that appeared at newsstands as early as 8:00 P.M. Diehard fans recalled listening to Dodger games as they shopped along Prospect Avenue, each grocery, butcher, tailor, and repair shop radio tuned to WOR, making it possible for customers to hear daily every play as they moved up and down the bustling avenue. At the same time, Barber and the radio brought more fans to the ballpark than ever before. Between 1938 and 1939, Brooklyn attendance jumped by almost 50 percent, outdrawing the Yankees by more than 100,000 in Barber's first year of broadcasting.[17]

The folk culture that evolved at Ebbets Field reflected the popular enthusiasm kindled by Barber's broadcasts. Even during their worst years, the Dodgers' rivalry with the Giants brought screaming full houses to the intimacy of Ebbets Field. "The scene," wrote New York sportscaster Stan Lomax, "at Ebbets Field was one of riding the crest of a volcano."[18] When the Giants were not in town, and the volcanic disturbance gave way to a weekday game against another second-division team, the Dodger faithful could count on participating in a kind of urban ritual whose parameters established the rules of participation. Orchestrated by the sonorous voice of announcer Tex Richards, whose malapropisms descended directly from the presence of Babe Herman and Casey Stengel — "Will the fans along the railing in left field please remove their clothes?" — the music at Ebbets Field echoed throughout the ballpark. Somewhere behind the Schaeffer scoreboard resided Gladdis Goding, whose organ played to the crowd's mood and the game's situation, even though the two phenomena were not always congruent. When Gladdis found it difficult to whip the crowd into its normal state of animation, the favorite Dodger Sym-Phony could be counted on to provide a humorous interpolation. Directed by Lou Soriano, one of several band members who identified themselves as "Italians from Williamsburg," the Sym-Phony, seated behind the home dugout, disagreed with the obviously errant calls of the umpires with a rendition of "Three Blind Mice" and often sent opposing strikeout victims back to their dugouts to the refrain of "The Worm Crawls In."[19] Hilda Chester, a middle-aged woman armed with a cowbell, provided additional cheer, ringing loudly whenever the home team right fielder, Carl Furillo, in the late forties and fifties made an especially aesthetic grab of a carom off the beveled right-field fence, often directly in front of the famous sign by clothier and, later, Brooklyn Borough President Abe Stark, who advertised his store at 1514 Pitkin Avenue with the words, "HIT SIGN. WIN SUIT."[20] Before the Dodger home games, a rotund ex-clown, Happy Felton, presided over his "knothole" gang, a contest of sorts pitting several aspiring little leaguers against each other with a prize of asking one's favorite Dodger an important question, such as, "Pee-Wee, what do you think of the team's chances this year?" From the presence of Yong's Motors, just across the street from the chain-link extension of the right-field fence to the ornate marble rotunda that greeted visitors who arrived from the four corners of Brooklyn, the subculture of Dodger baseball provided a sense of camaraderie and permanence. As long as Hilda and Tex, Gladdis and the Sym-Phony, played their songs of affection, it seemed that the team and its environs remained impervious to the ravages of time.

The historic signing of Jackie Robinson by the Dodgers' general manager and part owner, Branch Rickey, signaled not just a change for baseball in Brooklyn; it served as a prophecy. The historic questions were, except to the most reactionary or pessimistic of observers, not whether baseball ought to end its adherence to the segregationist "gentleman's agreement" of Jim Crow, but where and when it would do so. The logic that dictated Brooklyn in the two years from 1945 to 1947 derived less from the two dominatingly strong personalities of Robinson and Rickey than from their mutual relationship with the very conditions that, a decade later, would compel what was arguably the game's most successful franchise to flee the changing city of its birth for greener and golden pastures in the West.

The reality of Robinson's role as the first African American player verified the myth that equated the Dodgers with American pluralist democracy. Branch Rickey, a deeply religious man who followed the teachings of Ghandi, at least to the extent that he acquired the nickname the Mahatma, arrived in Brooklyn in 1942 following a remarkable career with the Cardinals. In St. Louis, he had presided over the Cardinal dynasty of the late

1930s and early 1940s with proficiency, especially with regard to the extensive minor league system he had been credited with organizing. Rickey determined to follow the same course with the Dodgers. Earning well over $100,000 a year for his remarkable skills as negotiator and trader, like George Weiss, Rickey also took a percentage from the cash deals he engineered.[21] In May, 1947, Rickey traded pitcher Kirby Higby and four minor leaguers to the Pirates for utility outfielder Al Gionfriddo and $125,000. Gionfriddo played left in the Series that year, making one of the game's most renowned catches against DiMaggio, while Rickey pocketed his portion, estimated at 20 percent of the deal.[22]

A complexly motivated human being, Rickey, sometime in 1943 or 1944, clearly determined that the Dodgers would be his agent to end racial segregation in American baseball. Rickey acted alone in his program, but he could not have succeeded without the shift in public opinion due to World War II: the double "V" campaign of civil rights groups and activists during the war; the constant journalistic support from virtually all the African American and some segments of the New York press; the examples of Joe Louis and Jesse Owens; and the realities of money and demography coupled with the need to create a dynamic baseball franchise.[23] Each contributed to the Robinson-Rickey watershed. Operating under the cover of inaugurating a third Negro League, Rickey sent Dodger scouts to identify and sign Negro stars and in October 1945 signed Jackie Robinson, shortstop of the Kansas City Monarchs, to a contract with the Dodgers' northernmost AAA farm team, the Montreal Royals. That same winter, with less fanfare, the team also acquired the contracts of catcher Roy Campanella, a longtime star with the Baltimore Elite (pronounced e-light) Giants, and pitching prospect Don Newcombe.

In return for the historic role bestowed upon him, Robinson agreed to apply Rickey's version of passive resistance to the predictable range of racist acts that he would encounter on and off the field. He would, he concurred, let his performance speak for itself, abjuring other responses until the issue was settled. For three long seasons, Robinson endured, suffering slurs and threats, knockdowns and high spikes. In so doing, he reinforced his dominant characteristic: his burning and focused desire to compete, to win, to "stick the bat up your ass," as Leo Durocher put it. The exception to the daily physical and verbal torment that Robinson suffered was provided by pirate star Hank Greenberg, then in the twilight of his career and, as a Jew, no stranger to baseball's prejudice. Having knocked Robinson down in a collision at first base, Greenberg later asked if Robinson was all right. After the game, Robinson responded, "Class tells ... it sticks out all over Mr. Greenberg."[24] Greenberg, who had once threatened the Babe's record when he hit 58 home runs with the Tigers, played an important role in the early life of Joe Black, the hardballing Dodger pitcher of the early 1950s. As a teenager in New Jersey in the 1930s, Black, an African American high-school baseball star, came of racial age the day that a scout told him, "colored guys don't play baseball." In tears, Black went home and examined the scrapbook he had kept of his favorite major league players. Realizing that they were all white, Black destroyed his treasure, keeping only a picture of Greenberg. "All of us," he told Roger Kahn, "we had to wait for Jackie."[25]

The choice of Robinson, like that of Monte Irvin of the Giants, and Larry Doby who broke the "color" line in the American League with the Indians in 1948, had been calculated. Organized baseball had mirrored American society's racial attitudes since the 1870s, when the National League created the first "gentleman's agreement" to exclude "non-white" players, forcing Bud Fowler, an African American born in Cooperstown, New York, out of the league. By 1892, coincident with the hardening of Jim Crow nationally, all organized leagues prohibited non-whites from playing the American Game.[26] In response, African American business leaders, most notably Gus Greenlee, later the owner of the Pittsburgh Crawfords, the team of Satchel Paige and Josh Gibson, created first in 1920 and again in 1933 the Negro Leagues. Playing in the parks owned by major and minor league teams, the Negro National and American Leagues became, by the end of the Second World War, the single "biggest black dominated enterprise."[27] Negro League stars often played against major leaguers, as most found it necessary to supplement their "team" salaries with constant barnstorming and winter league play. Most echoed the sentiments of Roy Campanella, who for ten years played fifty weeks a year in the states and in the Caribbean: "Never once did it occur to me that I would someday be playing in the majors."[28] The standard argument used to justify the exclusion of African Americans from baseball insisted that black ball players lacked the ability to perform in the clutch. Moreover, white owners realized that the inclusion of black stars into the major leagues would likely spell the end to the income they derived from renting their ballparks to the Negro Leagues. When major league owners met in the early winter of 1947 to consider Rickey's plans to promote Robinson to Brooklyn, they voted 15–1 against the plan. Only Commissioner "Happy" Chandler, who gave Rickey the go-ahead, supported the Dodgers' plan.[29] For Rickey, it was critical that the first black player be a non–Southerner, possess a college education, and have experience and credentials in and out of baseball.

Jackie Robinson, born the son of a Georgia sharecropper in 1919, had grown up in Southern California, where his mother worked as a domestic and presided over an athletically inclined brood that included his older brother Mac, who had won the Silver Medal in the 1936 Berlin Olympic Games. A four-sport star at UCLA in 1940 and 1941, Robinson led the Pacific Coast Conference in scoring in both the seasons he played for the Bruins basketball team. As an Army lieutenant, Robinson had been brought to court-martial for refusing to move to the back of a military bus in 1944 while stationed at Fort Hood, Texas. Clearly he had earned his stripes.

Jackie Robinson's conquest of the Dodgers and then the major leagues proved the soundness of Rickey's strategy. When several Dodgers talked secretly of signing an anti–Robinson petition during spring training, the team leader and shortstop, Pee-Wee Reese from Kentucky, refused; instead, Reese put his arm around Robinson as the two of them left the field after practice.[30] When manager Durocher learned of the pending revolt, he said with characteristic directness, "I don't care if a guy is yellow or black, or if he has stripes like a fuckin' zebra, I'm the manager, and I say he plays."[31] For his role in the matter, hometown favorite Dixie Walker dispatched to the last-place Pirates. On the field, both the Phillies and the Cardinals specialized in tormenting Robinson during his inaugural season and, in each city, Robinson's teammates confronted opposing players who raised the specter of racism. When the Cardinals, who had beaten the Dodgers in the 1946 playoffs, threatened to strike, National League president Ford Frick, who had been auspiciously silent for most of the spring, forced himself to come to Robinson's defense. Similarly, Red Barber confronted his racial prejudices. Rickey had informed Barber of his plans earlier that year and Barber, to his chagrin, remained silent, believing that the "experiment" would fail. By midsummer, Barber acknowledged Robinson's ability and intense competitiveness, quietly championing the Dodger infielder's career, whose impact he later compared to that of Babe Ruth.[32] On September 23, 1947, a day after clinching the pennant against the Cardinals, the Dodgers proclaimed Jackie Robinson Day at Ebbets Field. At age 28, Jackie Robinson, a black rookie, had led his team to the league championship, hitting .297 and stealing 29 bases, earning him the league's Rookie of the Year Award.

In ten major league seasons, Robinson hit .311, including a .342 mark in his MVP year in 1949, while playing every position except center field and catcher. Intense, competitive, hot as his crosstown rival, Joe DiMaggio, was cool, Robinson's concentration and determination set the standard for the enormous success of the Dodgers in their glory days from 1947 through 1956. Bat held high, almost awkwardly, cocked behind his right ear, Robinson dared opposing pitchers to deal with or at him. Fast and daring on the basepaths with his signature pigeon-toed moves as he darted off third base, his number 42 a blur of motion, he challenged and distracted, winning games on audacity alone. A stinging line-drive hitter and master of the art of bunting, Robinson's home runs, although he never hit more than 19 in a season, provided a propitious charge in the Dodgers' drive to pennant after pennant. Often forgotten in the lore of the Giant's "miracle of Coogan's Bluff" victory over the Dodgers in 1951 was Robinson's remarkable play on the last day of the regular season, in which his great catch in the bottom of the 12th inning preserved an 8–8 tie with the Phillies. His home run two innings later brought the Dodgers back into a first place tie with the Giants. Between 1949 and 1954, only Stan Musial of the Cardinals could challenge Robinson's claim as the most dominant player in the National League. Jackie Robinson provided the Dodgers, the game of baseball, and Brooklyn with a vivid and dramatic symbol.

On February 5, 1947, Branch Rickey addressed a group of middle-class African Americans assembled at the Carlton Branch of the Brooklyn YMCA. Aware that Robinson's presence on the minor league Royals in 1946 had inspired blacks to attend baseball games as never before, Rickey asked for confidentiality as he cautiously admonished his audience. Unintentionally echoing Horace Stoneham's fears that, when Robinson played, "Negroes in Harlem ... would riot and burn down the Polo Grounds," Rickey warned that blacks might threaten Jackie's success unless they curbed their (drunken) celebrations.[33] Stoneham's and Rickey's fears never materialized, but even before Robinson set foot in Ebbets Field and the Polo Grounds, New York's white baseball establishment expressed the racial anxieties that ultimately led to their decision to abandon the city altogether. From the late 1940s on, the demographic revolution that transformed Brooklyn from a predominantly white ethnic satellite city of New York into the largest African American community in the nation provided "evidence" of the correctness of white anxiety and fear. The more successful the Dodgers became in the 1950s, the more baseball owners feared black urban dominance. No less than in the 1880s, baseball could not escape the social and cultural context in which it existed.

At the start of the 1949 season, just after Robinson arrived at the Dodgers' training camp in Vero Beach, Florida, he declared that the fans and the team would see a new Jackie Robinson.[34] The deal with Rickey was over and, for the next eight years, he felt free to speak his mind on and off the field. Argumentative, combative, and aggressive, Robinson led his team to greatness, as the Dodgers drove to the National League championships in 1947, '49, '52, '53, '55 and '56, tying the Giants in 1951 and, finally, winning the World Series against the Yankees in 1955, to the enormous relief of their fans, whose rabid attention made the franchise as successful at the gate as on the field. From opening day in 1947, when blacks made up an estimated 14,000 of the 26,623 who attended, the Dodgers claimed a special place in the hearts of African Americans.[35] In St. Louis, Philadelphia, and Chicago, blacks came to major league games as never before, on foot, by train, or chartered buses, from the downtowns and from the hinterlands of America's National League cities. For many in Brooklyn, the Robinson Dodgers became the first place that the traditional white ethnic population came into contact with their black neighbors and, for some of an older generation, Rickey's fears rang true. "Sure, first they get into baseball," said one union member, "and then they'll be taking my job." For others, however, white as well as black, Jackie Robinson was a pure American hero. Jews from Flatbush and Brighton Beach, who readily identified their struggle against discrimination with that of black Americans, cheered the Dodgers and Robinson as if they were attending a civil rights rally: "At some point everyone was yelling 'Jackie,' 'Jackie,' 'Jackie' and … suddenly I realized that someone was yelling 'Yonkel,' 'Yonkel,' which is Yiddish for Jackie."[36]

The team that Rickey assembled around Jackie Robinson — the Dodgers of Duke Snider, Carl Furillo, Roy Campanella, Pee-Wee Reese, Billy Cox, Gil Hodges, Don Newcombe, Joe Black, and Carl Erskine — provided Brooklyn with an exciting, powerful, yet humanly flawed team, heroes who won the pennant on the last inning of the last day of the season and who lost the last game of the World Series. The 1953 Dodgers, arguably the best team of their era, won 105 games, had five starting players batting over .300, and Cox played third with such magic in his glove that his batting average was beside the point. Campanella, Snider, and Furillo each drove in more than 100 runs; Furillo won the batting championship after suffering a broken hand in a melee with the Giants in early September; and Snider slammed 42 home runs, the first of five consecutive years in which he hit more than 40.[37]

Roy Campanella, who along with Don Newcombe joined the Dodgers in 1949 to become the team's second black star, drove in 142 runs in 1953 and earned the second of this three MVP Awards. Of black and Italian parentage, Campanella had grown up in Philadelphia as a "half-breed," but, despite a disposition that remained both accommodating and cheerful, a foil to Robinson's intense outspokenness, he also knew who he was: "I've had a struggle all my life. I'm a colored man."[38] After the 1953 season, Campanella rejoined his first minor league manager, Walt Alston, who had been brought to the parent club when current manager Chuck "Jolly Cholly" Dressen had the temerity to ask the organization, now dominated by Walter O'Malley, for a two-year contract. Campanella and Newcombe had played for Alston in Nashua, New Hampshire, in 1946. There, Campanella supplemented his $1,000 a year salary with the twenty or so chickens that the local fans provided for each of the home runs he smacked. Wonderfully direct and earthy, Campanella once admitted that he read the *Tribune* rather than the *Times* because "it is the onliest paper I can get delivered in time for me to read it in the shithouse in the morning."[39]

Campanella, along with Robinson, Newcombe, Black, and rookie Jim Gilliam, provided the Dodgers with a core of five black players, making it the most integrated team in baseball at a time when many major league teams, most notably the Yankees, had not a single black player on their roster. Led by the combative Robinson, who ordered his black player teammates to "spread out. Don't eat together at one table.... You all sit at the same table you look like a spot," the Dodgers set the standard for breaking the lingering traditions of Jim Crow that all black baseball players encountered on the road. Moreover, Robinson took the powerfully strong Don Newcombe under his wing and convinced the young pitcher, the son of a chauffeur from Madison, New Jersey, who had won the Rookie of the Year Award in 1949, that it was his sacred duty to protect the Dodgers' black hitters from the constant barrage of high and inside "head-hunting" pitches to which they were subject. In time, Newcombe became one of the most feared pitchers in the National League and his retaliation soon ended the harassment that Robinson and Campanella endured.[40]

Wary of becoming a "black" team, the Dodgers continued to play the ethnic card that endeared them to New York's traditional fans. Before he left the Dodgers to become a part owner of the Yankees, Larry MacPhail, like McGraw before him, desperately wanted a "Jewish presence" on the team. With as many as 1 million Jews in Brooklyn, MacPhail and the Dodger ownership, which after the war included team lawyer O'Malley, signed outfielders Goody Rosen and Cal Abrams and coach Jake Pitler.[41] Pitler had played in 111 games for the Pirates in 1917 and 1918, hitting .232, and had knocked around organized baseball for almost three decades, while Rosen, who had played part-time with little distinction for the team before the war, returned in 1945 to hit .325 for Durocher's second-place team. Abrams, from Brooklyn, appeared occasionally for the Dodgers in 1949, 1950, and 1951. Unexpectedly, in the first half of the 1951 season, Abrams went on a tear, leading the National League in hitting in July, when his average soared to .478. The *New York Post* celebrated the newest Dodger star with one of its famous back-page headlines, "Mantle, Schmantle, We Got Abie."[42] Abrams slumped in August, finishing the year at .280, and the Dodgers shipped him to Cincinnati in 1952. In 1956, Abrams finished his five-team, eight-year career with the White Sox. Sandy Koufax, graduate of Lafayette High School in Bensonhurst, and winner of nine games during his three years with Brooklyn, gave the Dodgers the great Jewish star they had searched for, but only after they had moved to Los Angeles.

Still, the Dodgers of the 1950s — the team of Robinson, Furillo, Campanella, Snider, and Reese; of Newcombe, Cox, Roe, and Erskine — embodied the dream of American pluralist democracy. The platoon of the Second World War returned to civilian life had been, appropriately and heroically, integrated by Jackie Robinson. They belonged to New York, and especially to Brooklyn, standing for the decency inherent in the complex racial and ethnic mix of the modern city. That the Dodger players understood this far better than their counterparts on the Giants and Yankees was revealed in the way they sought to weave themselves into the fabric of the community. Gil Hodges lived on Bedford Avenue, near Avenue M in the heart of Flatbush, and continued to reside there even when he became manager of the New York Mets in the 1960s.[43] Reese, Snider, Erskine, and substitute catcher Rube Walker lived in Bay Ridge, socializing with one another's families and playing stickball in the streets with local kids. Durocher, pitcher Johnny Podres, and Furillo lived in several small hotels in Brooklyn Heights; in 1948, Robinson moved to Flatbush, where, after encountering initial resistance, he was welcomed as a local hero. Like their fans, the Dodgers of Brooklyn walked or took public transportation to Ebbets Field.[44] Even as late as May 1956, Reese, the oldest regular on the team, having begun his career in 1941, remained convinced that the Dodgers would never move. The team made a million dollars a year, he reasoned, and he and his teammates loved their adopted city. Reese backed up his opinion and bet with Don Zimmer, his heir apparent at shortstop, that the Dodgers would stay in Brooklyn.[45] The players, the fans, and the team seemed bound to Brooklyn, to the residential middle- and working-class life that characterized postwar Brooklyn. Tree-lined streets, candy stores, and the rumble of the el combined with the closeness of extended families whose open emotionalism made for a rough congeniality, an animated spirit of camaraderie, that made Brooklyn and the Dodgers virtually interchangeable. The Dodgers of the late 1940s and early 1950s represented a powerfully strong cultural image. Their flawed, unpredictable success, their emblematic social idealism, enabled them to serve as a symbol for the aspirations of their city. As long as the Dodgers remained in Brooklyn, its people continued to believe that their world would continue to persist as a community.

Yet between 1940 and 1960, the aggregate population of Brooklyn declined by 60,000, its white population by 340,000, while its nonwhite residents increased by 270,000. The African American population of Brooklyn, from the American South and the West Indies, exploded from 107,000 in 1940 to 371,000 two decades later, making the expanded neighborhood of Bedford-Stuyvesant, and subsequently Brownsville–East New York, the most populous black community in the nation.[46] The immigration of rural and West Indian blacks to the area north and east of Crown Heights–Flatbush placed even more pressure on the traditional, Jewish, Italian, and Irish residents of central Brooklyn. Those whose modest incomes prohibited the trek to the suburbs moved a shorter distance east of Canarsie, bordering on Jamaica Bay, causing the population in that area to increase by 75 percent between 1950 and 1960. In the words of columnist Jimmy Breslin, "Men with cotton-bailing hooks in their pockets, and sad-faced women with their arms laden from hours spent jiggling small children in buses and railway cars from Greenville in South Carolina and Waycross in Georgia … pushed the poor and not so poor East."[47]

West Indians, in the years after the Second World War, moved into the area of the Brooklyn Children's Museum six blocks north of Ebbets Field. By 1960, Crown Heights itself contained a population that was approximately one-third non-white mixed with recently arrived Hasidic Jews, who had migrated to the neighborhood from Williamsburg. As middle-class Jews and Italians moved away from the neighborhood surrounding Ebbets Field, rents in the single-family houses and scattered apartments soared while investments and maintenance declined proportionally.[48] With virtually no parking, Ebbets Field became, by the mid–1950s, an increasingly inhospitable place to its traditional white middle-class fans who had abandoned Brooklyn for suburban Long Island. Blacks claimed the Robinson Dodgers as "their" team, and in the perception of many whites, including owner Walter O'Malley, their presence at the ballpark drove away white fans. "Puerto Ricans also brought change," said an Irish-American Brooklynite, Bill Reedy: "Now everything was at a local bodega…. Brooklyn was changing … who the hell ever heard of frying green bananas."[49] O'Malley, who had ousted Rickey in a bitter struggle for control of the Dodgers in 1950, claimed that he became concerned when his wife and mother-in-law complained of "hoodlums and purse snatchers," confirming private studies that showed that Ebbets Field, whose audience was about one-third women, would soon be "unsuitable" for night games.[50]

The O'Malley, as the owner of the Dodgers preferred to be called, not only bested Rickey for control of the team, but in 1953 ousted Red Barber in the same motion that swept Jolly Cholly Dressen from the manager's position. O'Malley's constant preoccupation with profits and competition, heightened on the one hand by his realization that more suburban New

Yorkers could travel and park at Aqueduct Race Track than at Ebbets Field, and challenged on the other by the astounding success of the 1953 Milwaukee Braves, who drew over two million fans in their first season in the West, drove him to demand that New York provide a new stadium for the Dodgers.[51] Consistently good attendance at Ebbets Field, averaging more than 1.2 million a year in the 1950s, combined with a lucrative broadcasting contract to make the Dodgers the most profitable team in baseball. Still, O'Malley feared that the combination of westward expansion, social and racial change, the emergence of the automobile, and the aging of his wonderfully coherent team would undermine the organization's financial stability.

But, four years later, only 6,702 fans came to see the Dodgers' final home game in Ebbets Field on September 24, 1957. Appropriately, Jackie Robinson had retired earlier that year rather than accept a trade to the cross-city Giants, while Sal Maglie, the great Dodger killer of the 1950s, plied his trade that last season for both the Dodgers and the Yankees.

The Brooklyn Dodgers belonged, perhaps too intimately, to Brooklyn. After decades of daffiness, Rickey and Durocher assembled a team of wondrous and coherent talent whose pluralist identity replicated the community that gave them their name. The historic addition of Jackie Robinson gave Ebbets Field, for all of its corners and crevices, cowbells and Sym-Phonys, a truly contemporary feel. A team that dared to integrate, Dodger success fit the rightness of its cause (to lose regularly only to the Yankees was an appropriate, though tragic, counterpoint to their claim to greatness). But the Dodgers of postwar New York were also the Dodgers of Walter O'Malley who lacked the will to transcend the complex forces that so dramatically changed the city that sustained them. The reciprocal movements of middle- and working-class whites from central Brooklyn, along the Robert Moses–built expressways to suburban Long Island, and the migration of black and Hispanic peoples to the virtual center of Crown Heights, became an excuse for the most profitable team in baseball to seek alternatives to preserve its economic health. The Robinson Dodgers who brought blacks to professional baseball became the O'Malley Dodgers, fearful of remaining in a racially mixed neighborhood. The most urban of the city's teams, the flight of the Dodgers to suburban California derived as much from their owner's racial fears, coupled with old-fashioned greed, as from financial exigency.

Yet Jackie Robinson's legacy, happily, did transcend the frailties and limitations of his human, social, and cultural context. And that is exactly what this volume of essays seeks to explore. The legacy and symbol of

Jackie Robinson for baseball and for the American cultural experience that surrounds him are the subjects of this book. The passing years, a decade following his retirement, a quarter-century after his death, and then a half-century beyond his historic signing have served as benchmarks by which we collectively pause and take the pulse of the nation's progress.

Jackie Robinson's remarkable life and person have become a standard by which Americans reflect on the issues of race and class, of equity and fairness that have informed and deviled this society from its inception.

Notes

1. Art Rust, Jr., *Get That Nigger Off the Field* (New York: Delacourt, 1974), 8.
2. Peter Golenbock, *Dynasty: The New York Yankees, 1949–1964* (Englewood Cliffs, N.J.: Prentice Hall, 1975), 139.
3. *Ibid.*, 92.
4. Jules Tygiel, *Baseball's Great Experiment: Jackie Robinson and His Legacy* (New York: Oxford University Press, 1983), 3–8.
5. *Ibid.*, 190.
6. John R. Tunis, *The Kid Comes Back* (New York: William Morris, 1946), 41.
7. Harvey Frommer, *New York City Baseball: The Last Golden Age, 1947–1957* (New York: Macmillan, 1980), 150.
8. David McCullough, *Brooklyn* (New York: Dial, 1983), 172.
9. Maury Allen, *Jackie Robinson* (New York: F. Watts, 1987), 72.
10. *Ibid.*, 165.
11. *Ibid.*, 135.
12. Neil Sullivan, *The Dodgers Move West* (New York: Oxford University Press, 1987), 12.
13. Allen, *Jackie Robinson*, 189.
14. Golenbock, *Bums*, 83.
15. *Ibid.*, 155.
16. Red Barber, *1947: When All Hell Broke Loose in Baseball* (New York: Doubleday, 1982), 18–20.
17. Golenbock, 185.
18. Frommer, *New York City Baseball*, 3.
19. *Ibid.*, 100–102.
20. Christopher Jennison, *Wait Till Next Year* (New York: Doubleday, 1974), 99.
21. Tygiel, *Baseball's Great Experiment*, 45–50.
22. Barber, *1947*, 172; and Golenbock, *Bums*, 98.
23. Tygiel, *Baseball's Great Experiment*, 45–50.
24. Barber, *1947*, 194. Robinson's story appeared in the first of his two autobiographies, *Jackie Robinson: My Own Story*, as told to Wendel Smith (New York: Greenberg, 1948) and *I Never Had It Made*, as told to Alfred Ducket (New York: Putnam, 1972).
25. Roger Kahn, *The Boys of Summer* (New York: Harper and Row, 1972), 258.
26. Tygiel, *Baseball's Great Experiment*, 10–15. See also Robert Peterson, *Only the Ball Was White* (New York: Oxford University Press, 1970).
27. Peterson, *Only the Ball*, 98.
28. Roy Campanella, *It's Good to Be Alive* (Boston: Little, Brown, 1959), 96.

29. Golenbock, *Bums*, 145.

30. *Ibid.*, 148.

31. Tygiel, *Baseball's Great Experiment*, 170.

32. Barber, *1947*, 155.

33. Golenbock, *Bums*, 145; and Tygiel, *Baseball's Great Experiment*, 161.

34. Tygiel, *Baseball's Great Experiment*, 324.

35. Golenbock, *Bums*, 158.

36. *Ibid.*

37. Kahn, *Boys of Summer*, 153.

38. Campanella, *It's Good*, 288.

39. Kahn, *Boys of Summer*, 183.

40. *Ibid.*, 230.

41. Golenbock, *Bums*, 260.

42. *Ibid.*, 265.

43. Kahn, *Boys of Summer*, 314.

44. Frommer, *New York City Baseball*, 35.

45. Sullivan, *Dodgers*, 12.

46. Ira Rosenwaike, *Population History of New York City* (Syracuse: Syracuse University Press, 1972), 138.

47. Cited in Jonathan Reider, *Canarsie: The Jews and Italians of Brooklyn Against Liberalism* (Cambridge: MIT University Press, 1985), 16.

48. New York City Planning Commission, *Plan for New York* (Cambridge: MIT University Press, 1969), 4 (Brooklyn): 97–98.

49. Golenbock, *Bums*, 428.

50. Frommer, *New York City Baseball*, 3.

51. Sullivan, *Dodgers*, 38–42.

Part 1

BEFORE ROBINSON

William Clarence Matthews: "The Jackie Robinson of His Day"

Karl Lindholm

It is very probable that [William Clarence Matthews] will become a member of the Boston Nationals very soon.— Boston Traveler, *July 15, 1905*

A negro is just as good as a white man and has just as much right to play ball.... I think it is an outrage that colored men are discriminated against in the big leagues. What a shame it is that black men are barred forever from participating in the national game. I should think Americans should rise up in revolt against such a condition.... If the magnates forget their prejudices and let me into the big leagues, I will show them that a colored boy can play better than lots of white men, and he will be orderly on the field.— William Clarence Matthews, 1905

[Matthews] was the Jackie Robinson of his age.— Harold Kaese, Boston Globe, *January 17, 1965*

Harold Kaese was a sports columnist for the *Boston Globe* from 1945 to 1973. At least twice in the 1960s, he explicitly compared Jackie Robinson to William Clarence Matthews, a sports hero at Harvard decades before Robinson made his historic entry into Major League baseball.

Kaese's first column, on January 17, 1965, appeared under the headline, "Harvard Nine Defied South 60 Years Ago." It was inspired by the refusal of 21 "Negro" football players to play in the American Football League's All Star game in New Orleans that year as a "stand against racial prejudice." For Kaese, this action was reminiscent of the decision made sixty years earlier by the Harvard baseball team in support of their black shortstop, Matthews, to call off their spring trip. "Appreciating that the popular colored player could not make the trip without suffering humiliation from Southern prejudices," he wrote, "the Harvard team stayed in the North." In introducing Matthews at the beginning of this column, Kaese declares: *"He was the Jackie Robinson of his age."*[1]

Three years later, Kaese also cited Matthews in another column while relating anecdotes about the Harvard-Yale football rivalry. This time, Kaese reflected on Matthews gridiron exploits for Harvard in 1904. One of Matthews' teammates explained his prep background before entering Harvard and celebrated his athletic versatility: "Matthews was the first Negro to captain the Andover football team. He was a ten-letter man, *the Jackie Robinson of his day.*"[2]

In both articles, Kaese made particular note of Matthews' character and integrity. In the '65 piece, he quoted a teammate of Matthews' on the Harvard baseball team, who said "he was a damn good player and a very decent fellow." A classmate added: "We held him in the greatest respect and admired the way he undertook his duties, his athletic prowess, and his stand on social matters."[3]

So just who was this William Clarence Matthews? And how does his life justify comparisons to the impeccable Jackie Robinson, the hero of baseball's integration, whom we celebrate on this fiftieth anniversary of his dramatic breakthrough, the man that filmmaker Ken Burns asserts belongs with Thomas Jefferson and Abraham Lincoln in the forefront of American heroes?

Washington, DuBois, Garvey — and Matthews

The life of William Clarence Matthews, taken whole, is a fascinating story of American accomplishment set against bigotry and its constraints. Before we even consider his extraordinary baseball career, we encounter a man in Matthews whose life intersects with the archetypal responses of African-Americans to the realities of post–Civil War America. In fact, he was immediately connected to the great figures, the archetypes themselves, who embodied these responses.

As a young man, who was born in 1877 in Selma, Alabama, and raised in Montgomery, Matthews lived the up-from-slavery values of Booker T. Washington. He attended Tuskegee Normal and Industrial Institute and trained there under Washington. He showed such promise that he was sent North to continue his education, first at Phillips Andover Academy and then at the Harvard of W.E.B. DuBois, a bastion of progressive thinking at that time and home to the intellectual activism of William Munroe Trotter and other young black intellectuals who demanded that America address its deplorable racial record and values. In 1903, while Matthews was at Harvard, DuBois published his classic text on race, *The Souls of Black Folk*, attacking Washington's appeasement and archly forecasting: "the problem of the Twentieth Century is the problem of the color line."[4]

Later in his life, as a lawyer, Matthews joined forces with the black nationalist movement of the charismatic Jamaican, Marcus Garvey, and served in the early 1920s as his legal adviser. After Garvey was incarcerated for mail fraud, Matthews turned to mainstream Republican politics, serving as Chair in the negro community of the Coolidge campaign for the Presidency in 1924. The million black votes he helped turn out were crucial to the election of the taciturn Vermonter to the Presidency.

At the time of his premature death at the age of 51 in 1928, Matthews was established in the U.S. Attorney General's Office, working on an "important water adjudication matter"[5] in San Francisco. His death was reported in all the major East Coast newspapers. In the black press, it drew page one headlines. *The Pittsburgh Courier* ran a banner headline on its front page which proclaimed: "William Clarence Matthews Dies Suddenly at Capital/ Political Leader's Death a Shock."[6]

The above, however, does not explain Kaese's references to Jackie Robinson, except to note their affinity as prominent African-Americans. The fact is that Matthews, in addition to his prominence in politics and law in the latter half of his life, was an extraordinary athlete as a young man, one of the very best college baseball players in America in the first decade of the century and a talented all-round athlete. Furthermore, he was rumored to be headed to the major leagues in 1905 in defiance of baseball's color ban. The unfolding of this unlikely drama brought Matthews national attention.

It is this rumor that has heretofore introduced Matthews to fans of baseball's history. Sol White in his classic *History of Colored Baseball*, published in 1907, wrote this of Matthews:

> It is said on good authority that one of the leading players and managers of the National League is advocating the entrance of colored players in the National League with a view of signing "Matthew (sic)," the colored man, late of Harvard.[7]

Baseball historians, mining this crucial documentary source, have essentially repeated White's conjecture. Robert Peterson, in his seminal *Only the Ball was White* (1970), introduced Matthews to many, myself included, adding this information to White's claim: "(Matthews) had left Harvard that spring (1905) to play for Burlington of the Vermont League, which was not a recognized minor league."[8]

While Matthews was in Vermont in 1905, the rumor of his breakthrough surfaced in Boston newspapers. Baseball historians have long speculated that it was John McGraw, the greatest manager of that time and an acknowledged opponent of the color barrier, who was pursuing Matthews. In reality, it was Fred Tenney, then player-manager of the Boston National League nine, who was casting a longing eye at Harvard's great shortstop. Matthews, of course, was not signed; it would be another forty years before a black man was signed to a professional contract by a white major league team.

So the Jackie Robinson reference applies to Matthews' extraordinary athletic skills, his attack on baseball's "color line," his demonstrated strength and perseverance, his achievement on and off the playing field, and the respect he earned in his lifetime from peers and the public. In this time of heightened awareness of the talents and heroism of black baseball pioneers, as we approach the millennium, it is especially appropriate to acknowledge William Clarence Matthews, as a forebear of Jackie Robinson in the long march to achieve equality of opportunity in the national pastime in America.

Opportunities to Help Himself

Jackie Robinson and William Clarence Matthews share the experience of being black baseball stars toiling on the white man's playing field. Filling in the above outline of Matthews' life and accomplishment reveals the extent of their shared heritage. Matthews lived in an era quite different from that of Robinson: his abortive breakthrough was in the century's first decade; Robinson's heroic achievement was at mid-century. When Matthews died, Robinson was only nine years old, living in Pasadena, learning the shifting rules and values of an American society confounded by race. Both men died prematurely in their early 50s when they still had much to offer their country.

William Clarence Matthews' early life was spent in the Deep South in the years immediately following Reconstruction. His father, William, was a tailor and "repairer" with a shop at the rear of a drug store in Selma. His mother, Elizabeth, according to documents from the period, was occupied "keeping house."[9] He had two siblings, Fannie E., thirteen years his senior, and Buddy (Walter), nine years older. By the 1890s, his father had died and he was living in Montgomery with his mother, and his sister and her family.[10] From 1893–97, Matthews attended Tuskegee Institute, only about 25 miles from Montgomery, where he trained to become a tailor, like his father, and organized the first football team, captained the baseball team, and graduated Salutatorian of his class.[11] While he was at Tuskegee in 1896, the U.S. Supreme Court gave segregation of the races legal standing in their Plessy v. Ferguson decision. Later in his life, Matthews contended that he learned from Booker T. Washington "that the best help a man can get is an opportunity to help himself."[12]

One such "opportunity" certainly was his preparation for college at Phillips Andover Academy in Massachusetts, which he attended from 1896 to 1901. He was introduced to Andover by Washington himself, who hoped that Matthews would return to teach at Tuskegee after being educated in the North.[13] Imagine the challenges he faced, a young man of no means or status, 20 years old, the only Black in his class of 97 boys, and one of two students from below the Mason-Dixon Line. Yet, here at the training ground of the scions of the Eastern elite, Matthews thrived, using sports as the medium of his acceptance, and moving beyond to genuine school leadership.

At Andover, Matthews played football, track, and baseball, again captaining the baseball team, and in general "fitted himself" for Harvard. In his last year, he excelled in football at the position of "end rush" (team record: 5–1–2), was one of very few schoolboys to compete in the open Boston Athletic Association (B.A.A.) track meet in the winter, and presided over "the best (baseball team) we have ever had."[14] His performance at the end of the 1901 season was truly heroic, as he moved from his customary shortstop position to catcher and played with a badly broken thumb. In the season's climactic game against arch-rival Exeter, before one of the largest crowds ever to witness a baseball game at Andover, he led his team to a decisive 9–2 win and earned these plaudits from the school newspaper:

> Captain Matthews behind the bat gave an exhibition of sand that would have inspired any team to win…. *The Phillipian* wishes to thank heartily Captain Matthews for all he has done for Andover in athletics, not only baseball but in football and track, and especially for his heroic devotion to the honor of his school in playing the two decisive games with a disabled thumb.[15]

He emerged at Andover as more than an athletic curiosity. In his senior year, he was one of twelve members of the Athletic Advisory Council, an Associate Editor of *The Phillipian* (the school newspaper), a member of Inquiry, a religious debate society, and vice-president of the Republican Club. In addition to being voted the "best athlete" in his class, he was also the "most versatile." At the Senior Dinner at the Young Hotel in Boston, he was one of five students chosen to offer toasts, and at Class Day, he was Class Historian. At Graduation, he was presented with a silver loving cup by his fellow students.[16]

Of the twelve players on the Phillips Andover baseball team in 1901, two others in addition to Matthews headed to Harvard, seven went off to Yale, and one attended Princeton. According to an article on Matthews in the *New York Tribune* in 1904, Matthews chose Harvard because he believed the racial climate was better there than at Yale, where there were "more Southern students."[17] A teammate from Andover who had refused to sit at the training table with Matthews had chosen Yale the year before. Matthews' athletic ability was of great appeal to Harvard. The Principal of Phillips Andover, Cecil Bancroft, recommended the young African-American to Harvard officials as "an extremely good athlete."[18]

An Example and a Moral

At this time, baseball was singular among American sports in its organization and following, a powerful force in American life. The best of intercollegiate college sports was played in the Northeast, with Harvard and Yale preeminent. These fierce rivals played before thousands of fans in their two game series at the end of the baseball season each spring. In 1902, Matthews' first season at Harvard, 140 candidates tried out for the baseball team.[19] The team's pitchers were coached that year by Denton "Cy" Young of the Boston Americans, the game's greatest pitcher, and their batters were instructed by Brooklyn's W.H. "Wee Willie" Keeler, the era's most scientific batsman, famous for his "hit where they ain't" approach.[20] Harvard's record in Matthews' four years was a combined 75 wins against only 18 losses.

In these days, before the minor leagues were organized, colleges were a fertile breeding ground for major league talent. The great Christy Mathewson came to the New York Giants in 1900 from Bucknell University and the next year, his American League counterpart, Eddie Plank, graduated from Gettysburg and joined the Philadelphia A's. In 1905, Big Ed Reulbach left the University of Vermont (after attending Notre Dame as well) and that summer won 18 games for the Chicago Nationals, including 18 and 20 inning victories — and in 1908 became the only man ever to pitch a doubleheader shutout. Colby Jack Coombs played 14 years in the major leagues with Philadelphia and Brooklyn. Even Harvard men chose baseball as a career. The captain of Matthews' 1903 Harvard team, Walter

Clarkson, played five years for the Highlanders and Cleveland from 1904 to 1908. Matthews' keystone partner, second baseman "Harvard Eddie" Grant, played in the Majors from 1905 until 1915 for four teams.

Matthews fulfilled his athletic promise at Harvard from 1901 to 1905. He was a brilliant shortstop for the Crimson nine and played football as well. On the diamond, he was sound defensively, good with the bat, and fast on the bases. He was a genuine talent, attracting attention well beyond Cambridge and the Eastern intercollegiate world. *The Sporting Life*, a national weekly covering baseball at this time, took note of his play in college, describing Matthews as "Harvard's best shortstop since the days of 'Dud' Dean."[21] *The Boston Post*, a major daily in the first decade of this century, waxed hyperbolic, anointing Matthews as "no doubt the greatest colored athlete of all time," "the best infielder Harvard ever had," and "(Harvard's) greatest big league prospect."[22]

Most notable about Matthews, according to the newspaper accounts of the day, and later accounts by his Harvard mates, was the strength of his character. In a day when baseball was a boisterous affair, with rules and authority often winked at or flouted, Matthews was celebrated for "the sedulous manner in which he kept his record clean."[23] In a two part exposé on the "College Athlete" in the June 1905 issue of *McClure's Magazine*, Henry Beach Needham singled out Matthews for special praise. Under the heading "An Example and a Moral," Needham included a long encomium from the *Boston Globe*, celebrating the "little colored chap at Harvard":

> For seven years Matthews could have earned much money by playing for semi-professional teams but this he has refused to do.
>
> …Here is a man who to maintain his amateur standing has repeatedly refused offers of $40 a week and board to play semi-pro baseball in the summer. He had the example of many contemporaneous college ballplayers who were accepting 'indirect' compensation in an underhanded way but he has kept his record clean, and his, it is sad to say, is an exceptional case.[24]

As a black man, Matthews would have had a harder time than others avoiding even the skimpy enforcement of amateur rules at the time. Throughout his years at Harvard, he had always "earned his way," taking jobs during the school year and working summers in Pullman cars and hotels and teaching in a North Cambridge's night school. His election to the prestigious Class-Day Committee, "the first colored man the seniors of the university have chosen,"[25] is evidence of the respect with which he was held at Harvard.

His life at Harvard was anything but easy. In an atmosphere of great privilege, Matthews had little. Both his parents had died by 1902 and he was left to his own resources to raise the $150 tuition and the additional $200 or so in annual expenses. His circumstances were summarized by Principal Bancroft simply: "Is very poor."[26] Matthews depended entirely upon his summer earnings for his survival and he struggled. Clearly, he was held to a different standard from his white schoolmates. Even in this liberal racial environment, his staunchest supporters regarded him as a black man first, a ball player next, and a Harvard man and individual in that order. His classmate Barrett Wendell, Jr., described Matthews as "one of the whitest men (I have) ever known."[27] It was a compliment. Andover's Vice-Principal Alfred E. Stearns averred: "(He) is one of the very few colored fellows in whom I have placed a great deal of confidence.... and I have found him unusually reliable and straightforward, something rather rare in his race."[28] Another Andover teacher, Charles H. Forbes, was only slightly less equivocal in his endorsement of Matthews to Harvard:

> W. C. Matthews represents the best there is in a negro. He is a sensible fellow of good mental make-up. He has a rare sense of the necessity to do more than mediocre work, and lays no claim to special indulgence. There is much manhood in this boy.[29]

Harvard's Best Player

In his very first game for Harvard, against the University of Maine at Boston's Soldier's Field, Matthews demonstrated his extraordinary skill: he played short, had two hits, scored two runs, and stole a base. And in the final game of that first year, against Yale, he turned in his best performance of the year, scoring the winning run before 9000 fans. The headline in the *New York Times* read:

Harvard Defeats Yale
In Deciding Game of the Championship Series
Big Crowd at Polo Grounds

Matthews, Right-Fielder for Crimson Team, Brought
in Winning Run in Ninth Inning[30]

He also played football that year at Harvard and was the subject of a feature story in the *Crimson* under the headline, "Colored Boy from Andover Playing Wonderful Football." In the piece itself, the reporter was all enthusiasm: "Harvard has a great find in Matthews.... He weighs only 144 pounds but more than makes up for that by his wonderful quickness, pertinacity, and sand."[31]

Matthews was a regular for the next three years on the Harvard nine.

His play was hardly without incident, however. In his first year, he was held out of games played in the South at Virginia and Navy. In his second year, Harvard called off their Southern trip altogether. Later that year, the Georgetown team refused to play if Harvard insisted on Matthews' presence in the line-up. The Harvard team said Matthews would play or there would be no game. Georgetown backed down, but the incident was reported in the Washington papers. The *Star* had this account:

> Sam Apperious, Georgetown's captain and catcher, was not in the contest Saturday. He declined to go into the game because the Harvard men played Matthews, the colored shortstop, who comes from the same town in Alabama from which Apperious hails. Matthews displayed the abilities of a first-class ballplayer and conducted himself in a gentlemanly manner. Notwithstanding, there were hisses every time he stepped up to bat and derisive cheers when he failed to connect with the ball. The little shortstop took no notice of these demonstrations occasioned by the prejudice of a number of spectators.[32]

In his three years as Harvard's shortstop (he injured his knee in his first year, missing over half the season), Matthews led his team in hitting each year. He batted .333 in 1903, had four homers, and stole 12 bases; the next year, he batted .343 with 3 homers and 8 steals; and in 1905, his last year, he batted .400 and stole 22 bases, playing in all 25 of Harvard's games. As Ocania Chalk says in *Black College Sport*, "had he been white, the majors would have been fighting to sign up this awesome talent."[33]

The Northern League — 1905

Of course, he's right, and this issue of race and segregation is what makes Matthews' life more compelling than just the story of a fine college player at the turn of the century. At the end of his career at Harvard, Matthews decided it was time to earn some money for his skills on the diamond and he joined the Burlington team of the "outlaw" white Northern League ("outlaw" because it was outside the authority of the National Agreement[34]). The "Southern prejudices" which infected Matthews' baseball experience at Harvard would hardly disappear in the Northern League. In fact, Sam Apperious, the Georgetown star, the white boy from Matthews' home town of Selma, would reappear as Matthews' nemesis, playing for the Montpelier-Barre team. He continued his boycott in Vermont, bringing unwanted national attention to Matthews' attempt to find a place in the national game.

So Matthews, in the spring of 1905, left the protective embrace of

Harvard and headed north to Burlington, Vermont. Vermont was perhaps an appropriate place for a black ballplayer hoping to make his mark in a white league at the turn of the century. In the Civil War, Vermont had seen more of its sons slain (on a per capita basis) than any other Northern state and was an important stop on the Underground Railroad. The University of Vermont itself had two black players on its baseball team in 1905. The first black college graduate, Alexander Lucious Twilight, graduated from Middlebury College in 1823. While Matthews would spend only that one year in Vermont, he would later help elect one of its native sons, "Silent Cal" Coolidge, to the Presidency in 1924.

In 1905, Burlington, Vermont was a lively city of about 20,000 which counted among its baseball fans "just about every man, woman, and child" in the area.[35] The Northern League, in its fifth season in 1905, was the pride and joy of Vermont sports fans. The three largest towns in Vermont were represented in the league: Burlington (The Queen City), Rutland (the Marble City) and Montpelier-Barre (the Hyphens). A fourth team from Plattsburgh, New York, just a boat ride from Burlington across Lake Champlain, rounded out the league. Fans were carried from city to city to games by special trains and across the lake to Plattsburgh on the steamer, Chateauguay, for 50 cents.

Team leaders had met throughout the winter and spring of 1905 at the elegant Van Ness House in Burlington to lay the ground rules for the season. They would play 60 games from June 24 to September 4; each team agreed to abide by the salary limit and stay until the end of the season — or risk losing their $150 deposit. In Burlington, ticket prices were established at six dollars for a season's pass, 10 cents a game for seats in the grandstand, and two bits for a seat behind home plate with a cushion. League bosses also agreed upon a double-umpiring system involving pitchers and catchers not in the game, a concept which broke down almost immediately. By the third game of the season the *Burlington Free Press* was reporting :

> The experiment of using player-umpires proved very unsatisfactory. It caused bad feeling among the players and culminated in a fistic encounter between Cosgrove and McMahon in which blood flowed freely.[36]

The league also took steps to improve behavior at games:

> The Directors of the Burlington baseball association have voted that betting at Athletic Park this year shall be forbidden. No more excited excursionists with large rolls of filthy lucre prominently displayed will be permitted to shove their tainted money in the faces of inoffensive fans. Profanity and objectionable language will also be eliminated.[37]

The Northern League was a "fast" league, combining the talents of some veteran pros (including a number of former and future major leaguers) and numerous college boys playing illegally under assumed names to protect their amateur status. Despite the good intentions of all in the preseason, the 1905 season was one of controversy from beginning to end. The rivalries were fierce and the newspapers in each city adopted the local prejudices, reporting in the colorful style of the day. The Burlington team that Matthews joined was the defending champ and the scourge of the league. Burlington invited controversy by bringing in Matthews to play short, becoming in the process probably the only league team in the country playing a black man.[38] The team was also constantly in trouble for violating the salary limit, hiring players from National Agreement nines, and influencing the umpiring in their favor. Wealthy Senator G.E. Whitney, the Burlington manager, was generally regarded as a cheater with an unlimited bankroll. When Montpelier-Barre took the league crown from Burlington in the second to last day of the season, the glee of almost everyone outside Burlington was obvious.

Matthews' arrival in Burlington was delayed by his college obligations. Throughout the spring, the Burlington team had kept the identity of their regular shortstop a secret. On June 28, however, the story broke in Boston that Matthews was headed to the Northern League and was repeated in Vermont newspapers. He missed the first five games and then appeared on July 2 in a game against Plattsburgh. He "showed up fast" in the pregame practice and "was liberally applauded" by Burlington fans. Once the game started, the very first Plattsburgh hitter "upbounded the ball" to Matthews and "he fairly ate it up."[39]

This first game proved anticlimactic, called on account of rain with the score tied 0–0. Burlington fans would have to endure an off-day before catching Matthews again in a spectacular home and home doubleheader with "deadly rival"[40] Rutland on the Fourth of July. In those games, played in a festive atmosphere before thousands of fans traveling by train the 70 miles between cities, he would live up to his billing. Playing flawlessly at short and batting third, he rapped out three hits in eight chances as Burlington won the morning game, 5–1 before losing the nightcap, 5–3.

Harvard Negro Disrupting Vermont League

As it turned out, Matthews' summer in the Northern League was anything but anti-climactic. Sam Apperious, in his second year in the league, had become a popular player for Montpelier-Barre, and immediately announced his intention to boycott games with Burlington. "Smith," a pitcher from a Southern college, left the Burlington team because of the signing of Matthews.[41] Even more controversial than Matthews, however, was his teammate "Rube" Vickers, a talented pitcher with major league experience, who played the summer under contract to both Holyoke (MA) of a National Agreement nine and Burlington, and then left at the end of the season to join Brooklyn of the National League. Matthews had his defenders outside Burlington; Vickers did not and was nicknamed "kangaroo" for his (contract) jumping and was a constant target of fans and the press. The baseball reporter for the Montpelier paper observed after a Montpelier-Barre vs. Burlington contest in July: "Vickers came in for his usual share of attention from the bleachers and grandstand and even 'Uncle Tom' Matthew (sic) was not neglected."[42]

Just a week after his first appearance in a game, Matthews found himself the subject of a piece in the national sports authority, *The Sporting Life*, which reported under the headline "Row Over Black Player": "The advent of William C. Matthews, the Negro shortstop from Harvard, into the Vermont League, threatens to disrupt that organization."[43] The Boston newspapers, having a natural interest in Matthews, the Harvard man, also showed an interest in the Matthews-Apperious controversy. The headline, over a picture of Matthews, in the *Traveler* from August 9, 1905, read "Harvard Negro Disrupting Vermont League."

The boycott by Apperious unleashed a torrent of editorial commentary in the newspapers around the state of Vermont. For the most part, Vermonters were offended by his action. The following excerpts are typical:

> There is a chap called Apperious in Vermont — came here to play ball. Hails from a state where the "best citizens" burn people alive at the stake.... Scat! Vermont has no use for him. Better wash and go South. May get there in time to help burn the next "nigger." Move! — (*Poultney Journal*, July 29, 1905)
>
> ...up here in Vermont race prejudice has few supporters. Vermonters like to see good clean ball, and they are not fussy as to the color of the player who can deliver the right quality. — (*Wilmington Times*, July 18, 1905)
>
> Apperious displays his Southern prejudices, also his long fuzzy ears, by refusing to play in the same game as the Harvard alumnus of slightly darker, if not quite so thin skin. Apperious may be honest in this contention, but his action leads to the suspicion that way down in Dixie somewhere his ancient family must have been closely allied with the typical Alabama mule. Appy, you have strayed. You have no business pasturing in Vermont. — (*St. Johnsbury Republican*, July 22, 1905)

Matthews found support in Burlington and on his own club. Manager Whitney declared: "Vermont is not a Jim Crow state.... A white man who would not play ball with (Matthews), or even eat or sleep with him, is a cad. If Matthews goes, I go."[44] Praise from the press, both for Matthews' deportment on the field and for his actual play, was frequent. Typical is this observation from the *Burlington Free Press* on July 9, 1905: "Matthews received the glad hand from the bleachers and grandstand when he first went to bat, showing that race prejudices did not blind the eyes of the spectators so they could not distinguish a good ballplayer and a gentleman."[45]

Some newspapers, mostly in the Montpelier area, defended Apperious, saying that he was only representing the values of the South. "Apperious would be false to the traditions, sentiments, and interests of southern whites if he should in any way recognize the negro as equal," a *Montpelier Argus* editorial said. "We can do it in the North. It cannot safely be done in the South. It is rank foolishness to expect every one to bend to our ideas."[46]

At the end of the 1905 season, the *Rutland Herald* interviewed Rube Vickers on the Apperious-Matthews matter. Vickers said that Apperious "was the loser as far as favor with the crowds was concerned." As for Matthews specifically, Vickers called him a "first-class player" and "a brilliant young man, one who never causes trouble with any player."[47]

On the field, Matthews play was often celebrated because he was skilled at so many aspects of the game. The quality of his all-round play was often cited as in this account of a Burlington victory over Plattsburgh in the *Rutland Herald* on July 13: "the feature play of the day was made by Matthews who got first on a hit, stole second and third and then stole home."[48] Or this from the *Burlington Free Press* report of a doubleheader split before 1500 fans in Montpelier: "Matthews hit the first ball pitched to him in the first inning over the fence and into the river and trotted around the bases for a home run."[49]

At the plate, Matthews got off to a fast start before tailing off severely near the end of the season. After 13 games, he had 16 hits in 51 at-bats for a .314 average. On August 1, he was batting .283 but by the final Labor Day game, his averaged had dipped to .248. His late-season slump may be accounted for by the crude play of his opponents — or he may have simply been worn down by constant struggle of playing as the center of attention and controversy. Near the end of the season, the *Boston Globe* reported:

> ...some few players on all of the other teams have been "laying" for Matthews, with the result being that he has been spiked several times, and finally had to be put in the outfield from shortstop so that his chances for being hurt would be lessened.[50]

Challenging the Color Line

The *Boston Traveler* broke the story on July 15, 1905 — and then it was picked up by newspapers around the country. The *Traveler* cited "a person on the inside" who indicated that it was "probable" that Matthews would be joining the Boston National League team "very soon." The Boston team was languishing only a half game from last place and its keystone work was sadly lacking. The source discussed Tenney's need for infield help, his knowledge of Matthews' "remarkable ability" demonstrated at Harvard, and opined that "William C. is just the laddybuck he needs." Then, he added, "Of course, Captain Tenney will have to consult with the magnates but there is little fear of objection on their part." That Matthews was accepted at Harvard and was a "well-educated, gentlemanly fellow" enhanced his chances for success.[51]

In the same article in the *Traveler*, Matthews was heard from, offering this powerful statement to "a Vermont newspaper man":

> I think it is an outrage that colored men are discriminated against in the big leagues. What a shame it is that black men are barred forever from participating in the national game. I should think that Americans should rise up in revolt against such a condition.
>
> Many Negroes are brilliant players and should not be shut out because their skin is black. As a Harvard man, I shall devote my life to bettering the condition of the black man, and especially to secure his admittance into organized base ball.
>
> If the magnates forget their prejudices and let me into the big leagues, I will show them that a colored boy can play better than lots of white men, and he will be orderly on the field.[52]

In August, Matthews was quoted again in the *Traveler* on the issue of baseball's integration:

> A negro is just as good as a white man and has just as much right to play ball.... This negro question on the diamond might as well be settled now as any time. If Burlington sticks to her guns as Harvard did, men of my race will soon be playing in the big leagues.[53]

A few days after Tenney's interest in Matthews was announced, the response to this rumor was addressed in the *Traveler*. "What shall we do with Matthews?" inquired the reporter. "This question is echoing and reechoing around the baseball world." This article focused at some length on the response of Southern fans to Matthews' "queer notions about the equality of the negro," and charged that Matthews was "using his immense prestige as an educated and petted Harvard man in a mission" to open up baseball to "Negroes." This *Traveler* piece went on to excerpt commentary from two national newspapers, the *Atlanta Constitution* ("the most influential baseball newspaper of the South") and the *Chicago Daily News.*

The *Constitution* was contemptuous, referring to Matthews as a "dusky athlete" and the "human chocolate drop" and made reference to his "kinky dome." It acknowledged that as a player Matthews was plenty "fast enough," "one of the stars of the league," but asserted that he would never survive in baseball outside Harvard "where a dark brown epidermis isn't any drawback." The Chicago paper took a more reasonable approach, discussing the challenges Tenney faced in gaining the consent of the other "magnates" in the league and concluded with this observation:

> There have been and are Negro players with as much ability as any white player can develop, but the prejudice against playing with them is too strong and the probabilities are that Tenney will find no way to get around the unwritten law which stands against them.[54]

The *Daily News* was right. The unwritten law, the "color line," was upheld. The magnates did not go along with Tenney's experiment, despite Matthews' worth as a baseball player and man. One such magnate, President Hart of the Chicago Cubs, revealed his position, and the "real objection," to the Boston press shortly after the Matthews' rumor was floated:

> Personally, I have no objections to a Negro playing baseball, but I do not think it is right to inflict him on others who have objections or forcing white players to sleep in the same car with him and associate as intimately as they would have to under such conditions. That is the real objection to a negro in baseball.[55]

Hart adds that the President of the National League, Harry Pulliam, would "resign in a minute" if Tenney signed Matthews: "his good Southern blood would never stand for it."[56]

Thus, Matthews, like so many great Negro players in the next four decades, came to understand the power of the racial divide in America. Matthews resembled his legatees who toiled in the Negro Leagues in the first half of this century who knew all the while that their skills and courage were sufficient to compete successfully at the highest levels of the game. Just as they proved themselves in off-season contests with the great players of the white Major Leagues, Matthews had amply proven himself against white competition in his four years at Harvard.

A Prominent Negro Member of the Bar

Unlike many of the great black players in baseball's long segregated era, however, Matthews had options outside baseball. So when the Northern

League's 1905 season ended shortly after Labor Day, Matthews chose not to hook up with another team. Instead, now 28 years old and Harvard-educated, he headed back to Boston to get on with his life.

In his fourth year at Harvard, Matthews had taken a number of courses in the law school, so it was logical that he would consider law as a career. He never went back to the South to teach at Tuskegee as Washington had hoped. He did return in 1907 to marry Penelope Belle Lloyd in Haynesworth, Alabama, a young woman he had met at Tuskegee.[57] He enrolled in the fall of 1905 in Boston University Law School and supported himself by coaching at three different high schools in Boston (Boston Latin School, Dorchester High School, and Noble and Greenough School). Matthews' Harvard file contains correspondence from this period that highlights his dire financial circumstances. He struggled, persevered, and succeeded in passing the bar in 1908 and established a practice in Boston with William H. Lewis. He continued as an athletic coach until 1913, when his legal duties precluded further involvement in the high schools.

Lewis, his partner, was a supporter of Booker T. Washington and Matthews soon became a member of the Tuskegee political machine.[58] In 1912, Washington was helpful in procuring for Matthews an appointment as a Special Assistant to the U.S. District Attorney in Boston. After the war, Matthews became a supporter of Marcus Garvey and served as his legal counsel in the United Negro Improvement Association (UNIA) from 1920 until 1923. Even while associated with Garvey, he continued to be involved with the Republican Party politics and received an appointment in the U.S. Attorney General's Office as a reward for his crucial effort on behalf of Coolidge in the 1924 election. As an Assistant U.S. Attorney General, he was posted in Washington, D.C., Lincoln, Nebraska, and San Francisco.

William Clarence Matthews died unexpectedly on April 11, 1928, on a visit to Washington from San Francisco. The cause of death was a perforated ulcer. In its obituary, the *Boston Globe* described Matthews as "one of the most prominent negro members of the bar in America."[59] The *Boston Evening Transcript* lamented the passing of a "leader of the colored race."[60] The *Pittsburgh Courier* carried an account of the funeral, indicating that over 1500 were in attendance and "scores of telegrams" were received, including one from President Coolidge and U.S. Attorney General Sargent. In the *New York Age*, the headline on Page One announced Matthews' death — and just underneath was a picture with the caption "Matty is Dead."[61]

Clearly, Matthews was a man of extraordinary achievement as well as physical skills. For all his talent, determination, and achievement, it is fair to place him in the company of the greatest white player of his era, Christy

Matthewson. Like Matthewson, William Clarence Matthews was also "Matty" to his teammates and the public: he was "the Black Matty."

It is fair also to place him in the company of Jackie Robinson, the man who finished the job that Matthews, and so many others started. Despite their generational difference, William Clarence Matthews and Jackie Robinson were brothers in the struggle to integrate baseball. When Matthews made his forceful statements on the abilities and dignity of black men in the baseball microcosm, he was speaking for Josh and Satchel and Judy and Piper and John Henry and Cool Papa and so many, many others. Their lives were given additional meaning and poignancy by the great achievement of Jackie Robinson, whose life documents the words of William Clarence Matthews, uttered in 1905: "A negro is just as good as a white man and has just as much right to play ball."

Notes

1. *Boston Globe*, January 17, 1965.
2. *Boston Globe*, November 20, 1968.
3. *Boston Globe*, January 17, 1965.
4. W.E.B. DuBois, *The Souls of Black Folk*, ed. J. Saunders Redding (New York: Fawcett, 1961), p. vii.
5. *Who's Who in Colored America*, 1927, pp. 139, 140.
6. *Pittsburgh Courier*, April 28, 1928.
7. Sol White, *The History of Colored Baseball* (1907) (Lincoln: University of Nebraska Press, 1995), p. 78.
8. Robert Peterson, *Only the Ball was White* (New York: Prentice-Hall, 1970), p. 57.
9. 1880 Census, City of Selma, Dallas County, Alabama.
10. U.S. Census, 1900, Montgomery City, Alabama.
11. *Who's Who in Colored America*, 1927.
12. *Boston Globe*, quoted by Henry Beach Needham, "The College Athlete: His Amateur Code — Its Evasion and Administration," *McClure's Magazine*, June 1905, p. 128.
13. Letter from Washington to Dean Byron Hurlbut, Matthews' File, Harvard Archives.
14. *The Phillipian*, June 22, 1901.
15. *Ibid.*
16. *Who's Who in Colored America*, 1927.
17. *New York Tribune*, undated, Andover Archives.
18. Matthews' file, Harvard Archives.
19. *Harvard Graduates Magazine*, 1901–1905.
20. After 1902, pitchers were coached by Happy Jack Chesbro of New York (AL), winner of 41 games in 1904 and a future Hall of Famer. College teams were organized quite differently in this era from later periods. They did not have a "coach" in the contemporary sense, but rather hired instructors for the preseason preparation and then during the season had a "manager," who scheduled games and undertook other logistical demands, and a student "captain" who made strategic decisions. There was little

of the specialization we know today: teams included only about a dozen players (see *Total Baseball*, essay on "College Baseball" by Cappy Gagnon).

21. *The Sporting Life*, June 17, 1905. Dudley Dean was the Harvard Captain in 1891.

22. *Boston Post*, April 11, 1928.

23. Needham, *McClure's*, June, 1905, p. 128.

24. *Ibid.*

25. *Ibid.*

26. Matthews' File, Harvard Archives.

27. *Ibid.*

28. *Ibid.*

29. *Ibid.*

30. Ocania Chalk, *Black College Sport* (New York: Dodd-Mead, 1976), p. 12.

31. *Harvard Crimson*, October 8, 1901.

32. Chalk, p. 14.

33. Chalk, p. 17.

34. The National Agreement bound teams in organized professional baseball to honor one another's contracts, thus ensuring some degree of stability.

35. *Free Press,* June 23, 1905.

36. *Free Press,* June 28, 1905.

37. *Free Press,* June 30, 1905.

38. The *Montpelier Argus* reported that Matthews was "said to be the only colored man playing league ball," July 8, 1905.

39. *Free Press*, July 3, 1905.

40. *Free Press*, August 1, 1905.

41. *Montpelier Argus*, July 8, 1905.

42. *Montpelier Argus*, July 27, 1905.

43. *The Sporting Life*, July 22, 1905.

44. *Boston Traveler*, August 9, 1905.

45. *Free Press*, July 9, 1905.

46. *Montpelier Argus,* July 25, 1905.

47. *Rutland Herald*, August 7, 1905.

48. *Rutland Herald*, June 13, 1905.

49. *Burlington Free Press,* July 11, 1905.

50. *Boston Globe*, August 15, 1905.

51. *Boston Traveler*, July 15, 1905.

52. *Ibid.*

53. *Boston Traveler,* August 9, 1905.

54. *Boston Traveler*, July 19, 1905.

55. *Boston Traveler*, July 21, 1905.

56. *Ibid.*

57. She is referred to in the *Boston Globe* column by Harold Kaese from 1968. One of the high schoolers that Matthews coached described her as a "beautiful girl (who) kept a wonderful scrapbook of him." They had no children.

58. Marcus Garvey, *Life and Lessons* (Glossary), Robert A Hill, ed., p. 408.

59. *Boston Globe*, April 10, 1928.

60. *Boston Evening Transcript*, April 11, 1928.

61. *New York Age*, April 14, 1928.

A Story in Black and White: Baseball and Racism in 1938

Chris Lamb

During a pre-game interview at Comiskey Park in Chicago on July 29, 1938, WGN radio announcer Bob Elson asked New York Yankee outfielder Jake Powell what he did during the off-season. Powell replied that he was a policeman in Dayton, Ohio, where he kept in shape, he said, by cracking "niggers" over the head with his nightstick. Before the next day's game, a delegation of blacks presented a petition to umpires demanding that Powell be banned from baseball for life. Commissioner Kenesaw Mountain Landis suspended the ballplayer for 10 days. *The Sporting News* reported that it was the first time that a major league ballplayer was suspended for a racist remark.[1]

"*L'affaire* Jake Powell," as *The Nation* referred to it, captured the hypocrisy of segregated baseball. Landis punished a ballplayer for making a racist remark, yet he and team owners had prohibited blacks from the game since the 19th century. While baseball had thus far turned a deaf ear to criticism of its color ban, it could neither dismiss nor deny the outcry over Powell's remark, made live on radio and heard by thousands of listeners. Author William Donn Rogosin suggested that not only did the incident solidify the sense of outrage against baseball's color line, it illustrated the instability of segregated baseball, where a single intemperate remark embroiled the sport in controversy.[2] Both Commissioner Landis and the New York Yankees, the best team in baseball, were forced to take action to mollify the outrage in the black community.

It's doubtful whether Landis, known derisively in the black press as

"The Great White Father" for blocking all attempts at integration, would have suspended Powell without outside pressure.[3] Furthermore, the Yankees' management, responding to the threat of a boycott of their games, met with black journalists and activists, asking what could be done to improve relations with the black community. The team also ordered Powell on an apology tour of black newspapers and black-owned bars in Harlem. And finally, *L'affaire* Powell provided a single incident to unify segregation critics in the press — black, communist and liberal — who had become increasingly impatient and vociferous in their criticism. Powell's intemperate joke left no one laughing. But it shook baseball at its seams, publicizing the existence of the color ban, putting the game's establishment on the defensive, and unifying critics who would use the remark as a metaphor for the unfairness of segregation.

Throughout the 1930s, the black press had grown increasingly frustrated over segregated baseball. Sportswriters such as Rollo Wilson and then Wendell Smith of the Pittsburgh *Courier*, Frank "Fay" Young of the Chicago *Defender*, Joe Bostic of the *People's Voice*, Dan Burley of the *Amsterdam News*, and Ed Harris of the Philadelphia *Tribune* let their readers know that segregation denied black players an opportunity to play in the major leagues and white spectators the opportunity to watch some of the best ballplayers in the country.[4]

In 1934, Rollo Wilson wrote that racism precluded the possibility of blacks playing in the white leagues.[5] Two years later, Ed Harris criticized baseball's ban on blacks as unfair, unreasonable, and unprofitable. He said that the addition of black players would weaken racial stereotypes, improve the game, and put more fans in major league ballparks.[6] In May 1938, less than three months before the Powell interview, Wendell Smith questioned why blacks should continue to patronize major league baseball games, though they were not allowed to play in games.[7]

Black newspapers would be supported in their campaign to integrate baseball by the *Daily Worker*, a Communist daily published in New York City. The newspaper espoused the beliefs and philosophies of the U.S. Communist Party, which found it propitious to champion the cause of ending segregation in baseball, as part of an overall campaign to end discrimination against blacks in all phases of American life.[8] *Daily Worker* journalists understood that ending discrimination in baseball could make a truly revolutionary change in American society.[9]

On Sunday, August 16, 1936, the *Worker* published a page-one story with a headline that said, "Fans Ask End of Jim Crow Baseball," which became the beginning of its campaign to end discrimination in baseball.[10] Over the next decade, the newspaper's sportswriters brashly challenged baseball's establishment to permit black players; condemned white owners for perpetuating the color ban; organized petition drives and distributed anti-discrimination pamphlets; publicized the exploits of Negro League stars; and let their readers know of successes in the campaign to end segregation in the national pastime.[11]

In addition, during this period, a few progressive-minded sports columnists working for mainstream dailies, such as Hugh Bradley of the New York *Post*, Jimmy Powers of the New York *Daily News*, and Westbrook Pegler of the Chicago *Daily News*, also would take up the issue. The issue had been ignored until the early 1930s, but, during that decade, sportswriters, such as Pegler, said that the exclusion of blacks made it difficult for the sport to claim to be the national pastime. He also expressed his amazement that other journalists had not criticized the color line.[12] As Jules Tygiel wrote in *Baseball's Great Experiment*, the campaign waged by the black press, the communists, and a number of other white sportswriters helped weaken the apathy that nourished segregated baseball.[13] Powell's slur united and ignited these different voices as no story did from the early 1930s until Robinson signed a contract with the Brooklyn Dodgers' organization in 1945, ending segregation in so-called organized professional baseball.[14]

In 1938, segregation was so institutionalized that mainstream America, including the press, gave little thought to such concepts as civil rights or racial equality. To most of America, civil rights was little more than a black story.[15] This included segregated baseball. Most white sportswriters working for mainstream dailies, failed to recognize, at least in print, the severity of Powell's remark, specifically, and, more broadly, the injustice of a sport prohibiting athletes based on skin color. As one white columnist, Shirley Povich of *The Washington Post*, once put it: "I'm afraid sportswriters thought like the club owners — that separate was better."[16]

To black sportswriters and the black press, the Powell story represented something bigger than a careless remark by a bigoted outfielder. The black press was "a fighting press," largely circulated outside white America.[17] It clearly understood the need for racial equality and the evil of discrimination. In 1919, a white newspaper in Somerville, Tennessee, told its readers that no black newspaper could be circulated. In 1920, the Mississippi Legislature passed a law that made it illegal for black newspapers to promote social equality. Two decades later, the Chicago *Defender* reported that its newspapers were often removed from stands and halted at the post office.[18]

Baseball, it is important to understand, was one of the first institutions in the country to accept blacks on a relatively equal basis.[19] In recent years, scholars and other writers increasingly have studied the role of journalists — particularly black sportswriters — in their reporting of the integration of baseball. Much of this research has focused on press coverage of Jackie Robinson.[20] When Montreal signed Robinson to a contract in October 1945, sportswriters working for black weeklies reported the story as historically significant, while metropolitan newspapers treated it as relatively unimportant.[21] Additional research of Robinson's first spring training with Montreal in 1946 came to the same conclusion. [22] An analysis of press coverage of Robinson's first year with Brooklyn in 1947 found instances of subtle racial bias.[23] This article notably examines the issue not in the mid-1940s, but nearly a decade before.

In another article on the press and the integration of baseball, it was suggested that Powell's slur was one of several events that led to the signing of Robinson.[24] But there has thus far been just one study of the press and the Powell incident. Historian Richard Crepeau said that the story reflected differences in press coverage between the white and the black press. But his analysis was limited in content and in context. In addition, Crepeau perpetuated a falsehood that Powell was, as the ballplayer claimed, a Dayton policeman. This inaccuracy has been repeated in subsequent references to the incident but this does not make any more true. This article corrects that and also examines how the story was reported in the ballplayer's hometown of Dayton. It also draws from a larger sample of newspapers than Crepeau did.[25]

More importantly, though, this article fills a gap in the Crepeau research, which primarily examined the story from the time Powell made his remark until he returned to the field after his suspension. But the story transcends those two weeks. It is, as it has been suggested, an influential story in the years preceding the integration of baseball. In the early years of the campaign to integrate baseball, this story put the national pastime on the defensive, brought together different sportswriters who understood the injustice of segregation, and provided foreshadowing of the effectiveness of protest in securing civil rights. Therefore, it is important to put the story within the context of the expanding field of literature on the press and the integration of baseball but also within the larger framework of segregated American society in the late 1930s.

The publicity surrounding the Powell story made it harder, though obviously not impossible, for baseball to ignore the issue of race. If the ballplayer contributed to integrating the sport, it was not the story's only irony. For instance, Powell was suspended by Landis, an adamant segregationist. In addition, in 1936, the Washington Senators traded Powell to the New York Yankees for the virulent racist Ben Chapman, of Alabama.

Finally, Powell was never a police officer in Dayton or anywhere else—though a decade later he would die as a petty criminal in a police station in Washington, D.C. This part of the story went virtually unreported. Newspapers—with the exception of two black weeklies—reported that Powell was a policeman in Dayton without making any attempt to verify it.

Alvin Jacob Powell was born in Silver Spring, Maryland, in 1908. He played three games for the Washington Senators in 1930 and then spent the next few years on several minor league teams, including the Dayton Ducks. Powell and his wife made their home in Dayton. He talked frequently with friends of wanting to become a police officer in Dayton. According to one account, he applied once but was rejected; according to another, he was offered a job but rejected it, thinking he could become a police officer when he retired from baseball. If he were a cop, he would use his nightstick on blacks, he used to joke to friends.[26] The joke, as he would later learn, was not really that funny after all.

Powell returned to the major leagues with Washington for nine games in 1934. In his first full season in 1935, he hit .312 with 98 runs-batted-in. During the 1936 season, he was traded to New York for Chapman, who had become unpopular with the team's management after making anti–Semitic and racist slurs at fans at Yankee Stadium. The Senators, for their part, wanted to unload Powell because his creditors threatened to sue the team to settle the ballplayer's debts.[27]

Powell hit .302 in 80 games after joining the Yankees, who won the American League pennant in 1936. He led the team in hitting and runs scored during the World Series—the first of four straight series championships for the Yankees, who had a lineup that included Lou Gehrig, Tony Lazzeri, Joe DiMaggio, Bill Dickey, and pitchers "Red" Ruffing and "Lefty" Gomez, all members of Baseball's Hall of Fame. Powell played in 97 of the team's 154 games in 1937 and hit .263. His playing time was reduced more during the 1938 season—especially after his "nightstick" comment. In fact, he would play little with the Yankees after that, even though he would remain with the team for two more years. In late July 1938, Powell's statistics for the season included just 30 games, 134 plate appearances, and a batting average of .254.[28]

After Powell finished batting practice on July 29, WGN broadcaster Bob Elson asked him for a dugout interview and the ballplayer obliged. As soon as Powell made his derogatory remark, the station cut off the interview. Unaware he had said anything offensive, Powell went to the locker room to change into his uniform. He did not learn his comment had caused an uproar until he returned to the field.[29] There was some question over the precise language used by Powell. The station did not tape the broadcast.

Newspapers had different interpretations of what was said, and these interpretations varied, for the most part, according to the race of the journalist reporting the story. For instance, the *New York Times* characterized the comment as "a flippant remark that was taken to be offensive" to Chicago's black population.[30] The Washington *Post* said that Powell had made an "uncomplimentary remark about a portion of the population."[31] Shirley Povich, the newspaper's sports columnist, quipped that blacks in Dayton had little to worry about if Powell "is no more effective with a police club that he is with his bat."[32] The Associated Press characterized the comments as "slighting remarks" against blacks.[33] This description was repeated in the Dayton *Daily News* in Powell's hometown.[34] Another daily in that city, the *Journal*, published nothing about the incident. The *Sporting News*, the influential national sports weekly, described the tone of the interview as "remarks considered derogatory by the colored race."[35]

By comparison, it was a page-one story to black newspapers, which included a lot more details, including reactions from the black community. The Chicago *Defender* reported that Elson asked, "How do you keep in trim during the winter months in order to keep up your batting average?" Powell then replied: "Oh, that's easy, I'm a policeman, and I beat niggers over the head with my blackjack."[36] The same language appeared in the Dayton *Forum*.[37] The New York *Age* quoted the ballplayer as saying he spent most of his time as a policeman "whipping the heads of niggers."[38] The Pittsburgh *Courier* reported that Powell's "chief hobby was 'hitting niggers over the head.'"[39]

Hundreds of people protested the comment by calling the radio station, the commissioner's office, and the Yankees' hotel in Chicago. After Elson cut off Powell, according to the Associated Press, the station broadcast at least a half-dozen apologies and pointed out that it was unable to control the remark "because of the spontaneous nature of the interview."[40] Elson also apologized.[41] Powell initially denied making the remark, telling baseball writers that he merely explained that he was a police officer during the winter and that his beat was in the black section of town.[42]

Powell did not accompany his team the next day for another game against the White Sox at Comiskey Park in the city's predominantly black part of town, possibly for fear of concerns for his safety. In the morning, the owner of the Chicago White Sox heard the protests of a delegation, including the executive secretary of the Chicago Urban League, the wife of the former owner of the Chicago American Giants in the Negro Leagues, and executives of the Chicago *Defender*, including sports editor "Fay" Young.[43]

When umpire-in-chief Harry Geisel and the other umpires came onto the field before the game, they were met by another delegation of representatives of Chicago's black community, which presented a resolution demanding that Powell apologize and be suspended from baseball for life. A formal petition would be sent to Landis, the Associated Press reported.[44] The Chicago *Tribune* mentioned the pre-game meeting at Comiskey Park while the Chicago *Daily News* did not.[45]

The baseball establishment and the mainstream press did not recognize the severity of the comment. In his official statement announcing the suspension of Powell, Landis said: "In a dugout interview before Friday's game by a sports announcer, player Jake Powell of the New York Yankees made an uncomplimentary reference to a portion of the population. Although the commissioner believes the remark was due more to carelessness than intent, player Powell is suspended for 10 days."[46] Powell's reaction was brief: "I'm suspended. That's all there is to it."[47]

The Yankees did not question the suspension but fell short of criticizing Powell. New York general manager Ed Barrow said the comments by Powell did not reflect the attitudes of the Yankee management. Barrow said that it had denounced Ben Chapman's anti–Semitic remarks when he played for the team. He added that there was nothing more the team could do about Powell. He added that he had checked with his two "colored servants," who told him they thought it was just an unfortunate mistake and could not happen again.[48] In addition, New York manager Joe McCarthy said Powell meant no harm and blamed the radio station for broadcasting the slur.[49]

The *Sporting News* agreed with McCarthy. The fault lay not with the message but with the messenger. An editorial characterized Powell's comment as "careless" and not intentional, using practically the same language as Landis. The *Sporting News* was edited by J. Taylor Spink, whom one writer called "a spokesman for white big league resistance."[50] Landis and *Sporting News* editor J. Taylor Spink were in agreement on the issue of the color ban. According to the editorial, the remedy against such remarks was restricting radio interviews.[51]

In a column, Dan Daniel reported that the controversy would lead to a ban on broadcast interviews of ballplayers. Daniel called Powell the first player in baseball to be suspended for using derogatory language, adding that he thought the controversy would quickly fade away with no impact on the ballplayer or his career. Daniel was sympathetic: "Powell could have been more careful. But he is a hustling player, aggressive, and always getting into a jam."[52] To Daniel, talking of cracking blacks over the head with a nightstick was equivalent to trying to take an extra base on a hit.

The *Sporting News*— as with most of the mainstream press — would not give the Powell story anymore attention until the ballplayer returned to the Yankees' lineup on August 16. Daily newspapers reported the suspension and a few other details about it, then let the story fade. This reflects generalizations about press coverage of black issues in the mainstream press. One was that nothing important happened in black communities. The other was that the white press was subservient to commissioner Landis and the baseball establishment.[53]

This was not the case with black sportswriters. Ed Harris of the Philadelphia *Tribune* acknowledged that the story had received little attention in the daily press by writing that it was "astonishing the ease with which our so-called 'fair' sportswriters found it convenient not to say anything about the case of that half-wit Jake Powell."[54] "Fay" Young, however, mentioned that the communist newspaper, the *Daily Worker*, Jimmy Powers of the *Daily News*, and syndicated columnist Westbrook Pegler had criticized baseball's handling of the Powell incident.[55]

Pegler, for instance, criticized Landis and the baseball establishment for enforcing a racist policy and then suspending Powell for making a racist statement. "Powell got his cue from the very men whose hired disciplinarian had benched him for an idle remark," he wrote.[56] New York *Post* columnist Hugh Bradley accused Landis and baseball of "smug hypocrisy." Baseball executives, he said, expressed their disgust and horror at Powell's uncouth comment through Landis: "Then they calmly proceed with their own economic boycott against this minority people," Bradley said.[57] Six months earlier, he had condemned baseball owners for "not permitting a minority race" to earn a living in the game.[58] The liberal weekly, the *Nation*, editorialized that baseball was quick to denounce Powell — even though no team had any blacks on their roster.[59]

Daily Worker sports editor Lester Rodney also recognized the irony of the suspension coming from Landis and called on the baseball establishment to suspend themselves.[60] He acknowledged Powell's reputation as a dirty player, noting that he had once run over Detroit first baseman Hank Greenberg, a Jew. He also pointed out the irony that Powell had been traded to the team for the "viciously anti-Semitic Ben Chapman" to ward off a boycott by outraged fans in Yankee Stadium.[61] The newspaper reported that many people wanted Powell expelled from baseball and fired from the Dayton police department.

To black weeklies, such as the Pittsburgh *Courier*, Chicago *Defender*, New York *Age*, *Amsterdam News*, Atlanta *World*, Philadelphia *Tribune*, Norfolk *Journal and Guide*, Dayton *Forum*, and the *Afro-American* chain, the Powell incident provided an opportunity to channel their collective and long-standing indignation at a single act of racism that represented the laws and customs of the country. The *Defender* reported that the black community was incensed over the remark, adding that the city's racial climate was the worst since the race riot in 1919.[62]

The black press provided a lot more on the developments of the story, including such information as the reaction of the black community; an extensive interview with New York Yankee president Ed Barrow; and Powell's apology. The *Amsterdam News* reported that thousands of names appeared on a petition to ban Powell from the game.[63] The Philadelphia *Afro-American* editorialized that Powell merely reflected the opinions of the baseball establishment.[64] The Chicago *Defender* called Powell "a skunk," "a riot breeder," "a professional bully," and "a dangerous man to trust."[65]

The contrast in coverage between white and black newspapers was apparent in Powell's hometown of Dayton, Ohio. The *Daily News* reported in a three-paragraph story on its front page that Powell had been suspended. In its sports section, it published a separate story with more details on the suspension, including the ballplayer's denial that he had made the racist remark. In addition, it said that Powell had once played for the Dayton Ducks and had been offered a job by the police department but had rejected it to play baseball.[66] The *Journal* did not mention the incident until Powell returned to the field after serving his suspension.[67]

By contrast, the story received two front-page stories on August 5 in the Dayton *Forum*, the city's black weekly. One story told its readers that Powell had said during a radio interviewer that he was policeman in Dayton, where he "beat niggers over the head with a blackjack." A sidebar quoted the city's director of public safety as saying that the ballplayer had never been an employee of the police department. "In so many words," the official "branded as lies the alleged statement made over the air of the big-mouthed, cocky professional baseball," the article added.[68]

The *Defender* also published a denial by the mayor of Dayton that Powell was a police officer. It also told its readers that Ruppert had written a letter to the Dayton police department, asking it to "overlook Mr. Powell's thoughtless blunder and give him a second chance."[69] But the Dayton police department could not have fired Powell if it wanted; he did not work as a police officer in Dayton or in any other city. Newspapers — with the exception of the *Forum* and *Defender* — made no attempt to verify whether Powell was a police officer, simply taking the word of a racist as the truth.

The black press and black community used the threat of an economic boycott to make certain they were not only heard but listened to. A Norfolk *Journal and Guide* columnist said that if the Yankees did not do something

about Powell, not only would thousands of fans stay away from their ballpark, but others might seek revenge against Powell in Dayton.[70] Ed Harris wrote that Powell's remark could cost the Yankees. "The Yankees and
the players on other teams have got a good lesson in just what decency and
a sense of non-prejudice is worth. By the hard way — the cash box," he
said.[71]

In New York City, the New York *Age* and *Amsterdam News* reported
that blacks were calling for Powell's expulsion from baseball and the number of names on a petition to ban Powell were increasing every day. The
News' sports editor sent a telegram to the Yankees' owner demanding a
stronger punishment for the ballplayer.[72] The *Age* reported that hundreds
of letters had poured into the Yankee office.[73] Blacks in Harlem protested
outside Yankee Stadium.[74] In an open letter to brewer Jacob Ruppert, the
owner of the Yankees; Old Gold cigarettes, the tobacco company that sponsored the broadcast of the interview; and the citizens of Dayton, Ohio, the
Defender demanded that Powell be banned from baseball and fired from
the Dayton police department and insisted that Ruppert and Old Gold
cigarettes apologize to black America.[75]

Whether it was the threat of a boycott, the petition drive, or something else, the Yankees ordered Powell on an apology tour of black newspapers, businesses, and bars. Powell began at the Chicago *Defender*. The
newspaper published his letter of apology. In it, he said he regretted his
slur and asked to be forgiven by those he had insulted. He probably should
have quit there; instead, he unfortunately added: "I have two members of
your race taking care of my home while myself and wife are away and I
think they are two of the finest people in the world. I do hundreds of favors
for them daily."[76]

When the Yankees returned from their road trip, Powell went from
bar to bar in Harlem apologizing to patrons. He explained that he had not
intended to hurt anyone's feelings and offered to appear at a benefit game
for a black charity.[77] Then at some point, curiously, he began denying that
he had ever made the comment attributed to him — though tens of thousands of listeners had heard it.[78] Of the dailies in New York, only the *Daily
News* mentioned of the apology tour.[79] New York *Age* sports columnist
William Clark questioned the sincerity of the apology. It added that Powell should make his apology on the radio — in the same manner as he had
made the offending remark.[80]

The New York Yankees hoped that the story would go away. When it
did not, the team realized it needed to defend itself to the black community. In an interview with an American Negro Press reporter, Barrow
pointed out that the team distributed hundreds of complimentary tickets

every year to black spectators, donated regularly to the Harlem branch of the YMCA, and hired blacks as plain clothes security officers to patrol the stands, reporting gambling and breaking up fights."[81]

In an interview with the *Amsterdam News*, Barrow and McCarthy asked what the team could do to improve relations with the black community. When they were told that they should trade or release Powell, they responded that it would be unfair to the ballplayer who had contributed to the team's success.[82] Neither the Yankees, the mainstream press, or the white community seemed to understand what all the uproar was about. Instead of releasing the ballplayer, they kept him on the team's roster but did not play him.

The Chicago *Defender*, meanwhile, continued to press for stricter punishment against Powell and the Yankees. In a front-page editorial, the *Defender* reported that blacks in Harlem had protested outside Yankee Stadium and it called on all blacks to boycott Ruppert's beer and Old Gold Cigarettes until they apologized.[83] An editorial used the Powell story as a metaphor for "fair play" in society. Within an hour after his remark, it said, hundreds of protests had poured into the newspaper's office and WGN radio from people who recognized a violation of American ideals of decency and fairness.[84] "Fay" Young told readers to continue to put pressure on Landis and the Yankees to keep Powell out of baseball.[85] The Philadelphia *Afro-American* reported that blacks were staying away from Yankee Stadium.[86] The Dayton *Forum* said that "America is beginning to take notice when the Negro protests en masse."[87]

In his column the following week, Young wrote that the upcoming Negro league East-West All-Star game in Chicago could be a turning point for black baseball. There would be white sportswriters, baseball executives, and spectators at the game. An increasing number of white journalists, such as Powers and Pegler, had begun calling for the integration of the national pastime, joining the communist newspaper, the *Daily Worker*, and black weeklies such as the Pittsburgh *Courier*, Washington *Tribune*, and the *Defender*, Young said. "Because of the constant 'rapping at the door of the major leagues by some of our talent,' and the recent uttering of one Jake Powell," he wrote, the issue of segregated baseball had been laid at the feet of club owners and the baseball establishment.

The *Defender* reported the story not just on its front page and sports pages but also on its editorial page. In one editorial, the newspaper said that Powell reflected the prejudice and disrespect of segregation. "If black players had been in baseball," it said, "the Jake Powell incident would never have occurred, for as in Congress, legislatures and city councils, where we have elected officials, the presence of our men reminds — and demands — respect."[88]

Black sportswriters gave their readers an extensive account of the Negro league's annual All-Star game in Chicago, which drew a crowd of about 50,000, including such sportswriters as Lloyd Lewis, the sports editor of the Chicago *Daily News*.[89] Young quoted Lewis as saying it was "inevitable" that blacks would one day play in the major leagues. He said that there was not any written rule prohibiting blacks but that integration would require approval by a majority of the owners, and there was not any owner right now who was willing to go on record with such a motion. "It is inevitable," Lewis said. "Just how soon no one can tell, but it is sure to come."[90]

When Powell returned to the field in Washington on August 16, fans reacted angrily, booing, cursing, and even throwing bottles at him. There were several delays during the game as, ironically, black groundskeepers came onto the field to pick up bottles thrown by black spectators at a white ballplayer, the *New York Times* reported.[91] McCarthy defended his decision to play Powell. The *Sporting News* reported that Powell would have to "face the music" for his radio remark.[92]

Powell's return received some attention in New York City dailies and other white newspapers. The New York *Sun* called Powell's return to the lineup one of the more unpleasant situations faced by any major leaguer.[93] Writing in the Washington *Post*, Shirley Povich questioned the judgment of playing Powell in a city where blacks were segregated in one section and could feed off one another's anger.[94] New York's next road game would be in Philadelphia. In the *Tribune*, Ed Harris said that fans were preparing for Powell by warming up their throwing arms.[95]

In September, several black newspapers reported that Powell was on the trading block but the team could not unload him because of his baggage.[96] The Yankees would not trade Powell until 1943, but he became, in effect, *persona non grata* after his radio interview. He would bat just 30 times in the last two months of the 1938 season and only once in the World Series. He played 31 games in 1939 and then cracked his skull running into an outfield wall during a spring training game in 1940. After three years in the minor leagues, he was traded to Washington. About halfway through the 1945 season, he was then dealt to the Phillies, where his manager was the racist Ben Chapman.

Powell's career ended after the 1945 season. A month after the end of the season, the Montreal Royals, the Brooklyn Dodgers' top minor league team, announced it had signed Jackie Robinson, ending the national pastime's ban against blacks. After Powell retired, he returned to Dayton, where he worked as a security guard. In 1947, however, he was arrested for writing $300 worth of bad checks in a Washington hotel room but never formally charged. On November 4, 1948, Washington, D.C., police arrested him and a female companion and charged them with writing bad checks. Inside the police station, Powell shot himself to death.[97]

L'affaire Powell caused a crack in the barrier that separated the two races in professional baseball. The New York *Age* editorialized that the incident was important in molding public opinion in the black press. One of its columnists said the white press would not take up the issue but the black newspapers did, forcing an apology by Powell and concessions by his team.[98] It demonstrated the ability of the black press to mobilize public opinion and organize a significant protest to challenge racial injustices, something that would become obvious to much of the country during the civil rights movement. While the integration of baseball was still years away, those journalists who wanted to end segregation became unified over a racist remark to make their case loud and clear. In doing so, they won an early victory in their campaign to erase baseball's color line.

Notes

1. *Sporting News*, 4 August 1938.
2. Donn Rogosin, *Invisible Men* (New York: Kodanshu International, 1983), p. 192.
3. William Donn Rogosin, "Black Baseball: Life in the Negro Leagues," Ph.D. dissertation, the University of Texas, Austin, Texas, 1981, p. 234.
4. Telephone interview with Sam Lacy, 17 February 1995.
5. *The Crisis*, October 1934, pp. 305–306. See Herbert Aptheker, ed., *A Documentary History of the Negro People, 1933–1938* (New York: Citadel Press, 1974), pp. 113–115.
6. Ed Harris, "Abstract Reasoning," Philadelphia *Tribune*, 6 August 1936. See James Reisler, *Black Writers/Black Baseball* (Jefferson, North Carolina: McFarland, 1994), pp. 149–151.
7. "We keep on crawling, begging, and pleading for recognition just the same. We know they don't want us, but we still keep giving them our money, keep on going to their ball games and shouting till we are blue in the face," Wendell Smith wrote. See "A Strange Tribe," Pittsburgh *Courier*, 11 May 1938. The column was reprinted in Reisler, *Black Writers/Black Baseball*, pp. 36–38.
8. The Communist Party realized the possibilities of increasing its popularity by appealing to liberal whites and blacks; its rank-and-file members, however, sincerely believed in the cause of equality of the races. See Kelly Rusinack, "Baseball on the Radical Agenda: The Daily and Sunday Worker on the Desegregation of Major League Baseball, 1933–1947" master's thesis, Clemson University, Clemson, S.C., 1995.
9. See Chris Lamb and Kelly Rusinack, "Hitting from the Left: The Daily Worker's Assault on Baseball's Color Line," unpublished paper, 1998.
10. Lester Rodney, "Fans Ask End of Jim Crow Baseball," *Sunday Worker*, 16 August 1936, p. 1.
11. Lamb and Rusinack, "Hitting from the Left," unpublished paper, 1998.
12. Richard Crepeau, *Baseball: America's Diamond Mind, 1919–1941* (Orlando: University of Central Florida, 1980), p. 169.
13. Jules Tygiel, *Baseball's Great Experiment* (New York: Oxford University Press, 1983), p. 37.

14. The Montreal Royals, the top minor league team in the Brooklyn Dodgers' organization, signed Jackie Robinson to a contract in October 1945. Robinson played the 1946 season with Montreal, before integrating the major leagues in 1947. Organized professional baseball referred to the major and minor leagues, which had an organized schedule of games from April until October. The black leagues — or Negro leagues as they were called — played a less formal schedule.

15. Taylor Branch, *Parting the Waters: America in the King Years, 1954–1963* (New York: Simon and Schuster, 1988), p. 13).

16. Telephone interview with Shirley Povich, 8 July 1996.

17. Arnold Rose, *The Negro in America* (New York: Harper and Row, 1948), p. 289.

18. Roland Wolseley, *The Black Press, U.S.A.* (Ames, Iowa: Iowa State University, 1971), p. 53.

19. The integration of baseball came years before other landmark events in civil rights, such as the U.S. Supreme Court's decision in Brown v. Board of Education, the March on Washington in 1963, and the Civil Rights Act of 1964. See Tygiel, *Baseball's Great Experiment*, pp. 9, 99.

20. See Bill L. Weaver, "The Black Press and the Assault on Professional Baseball's 'Color Line,' October, 1945–April 1947," *Phylon*, 40 (Winter 1979): 303–317; William Simons, "Jackie Robinson and the American Mind: Journalistic Perceptions of the Reintegration of Baseball," *Journal of Sport History*, 12 (Spring 1985): 39–64; William Kelley, "Jackie Robinson and the Press," *Journalism Quarterly* 53 (Spring 1976): 137–139; Patrick Washburn, "New York Newspapers and Robinson's First Season," *Journalism Quarterly*, 58 (Winter 1981): 640–644; David K. Wiggins, "Wendell Smith, The Pittsburgh Courier-Journal and the Campaign to Include Blacks in Organized Baseball," *Journal of Sport History*, 10 (Summer 1983): 5–29; Chris Lamb and Glen Bleske, "The Road to October 23, 1945: The Press and the Integration of Baseball," *Nine: A Journal of Baseball History and Social Policy Perspectives*, accepted for publication, 6 (Fall 1997): 48–68; Chris Lamb, "'I Never Want to Take Another Trip Like This One': Jackie Robinson's Journey to Integrate Baseball," *Journal of Sport History*, 24 (Summer 1997): 177–191; and Chris Lamb and Glen Bleske, "A Different Story," accepted for publication, *Journalism History* (1998).

21. Kelley, "Jackie Robinson and the Press," pp. 137–139.

22. See Lamb and Bleske, "A Different Story."

23. Washburn, "New York Newspapers and Jackie Robinson's First Season," pp. 640–644.

24. The integration of baseball happened when it did, why it did, and how it did for several reasons, including: (1) the efforts of a number of black social activists, including sportswriters; (2) the growing popularity of Negro league baseball games, which represented a source of potential revenue for white owners who felt they could increase their attendance by attracting black spectators; (3) the Jake Powell incident; (4) the death of commissioner Kenesaw Mountain Landis; (5) a series of failed attempts that made integrationists more determined; (6) political pressures that resulted in the creation of such committees as the New York City Major's Committee on the Integration of Baseball; and (7) Branch Rickey, a white baseball executive who had the clout to make it happen, and Jackie Robinson, a black ballplayer who had courage to break the color line. See Lamb and Bleske, "The Road to October 23, 1945," p. 9.

25. The newspapers in this survey included the *New York Times*, New York *Post*, New York *Daily News*, Washington *Post*, Chicago *Tribune*, Chicago *Daily News*, Dayton *Daily News*, Dayton *Journal*, Norfolk *Virginian-Pilot*, *Daily Worker*, *Herald Tribune* (Paris edition), Portsmouth (Ohio) *Times*, *The Nation*, *Sporting News*, Chicago *Defender*, New York *Age*, *Amsterdam News*, Pittsburgh *Courier*, Baltimore *Afro-American*, Philadelphia *Afro-American*, Philadelphia *Tribune*, Dayton *Forum*, and Norfolk *Journal and Guide*.

26. Dayton *Journal*, 5 November 1948.

27. *Ibid.*

28. *Sporting News*, 4 August 1938, p. 4. By comparison, his teammate Red Rolfe had played in 84 games and batted 349 times.

29. *Sporting News*, 4 August 1938.
30. *New York Times*, 30 July 1938.
31. *Washington Post*, 31 July 1938.
32. *Washington Post*, 1 August 1938.
33. New York *Herald Tribune* (Paris edition), 31 July 1938.
34. Dayton *Daily News*, 31 July 1938.
35. *Sporting News*, 4 August 1938.
36. Chicago *Defender*, 6 August 1938.
37. Dayton *Forum*, 5 August 1938.
38. New York *Age*, 6 August 1938.
39. Pittsburgh *Courier*, 6 August 1938.
40. Portsmouth (Ohio) *Times*, 31 July 1938.
41. Chicago *Defender*, 6 August 1938.
42. This Associated Press account was published throughout the country in newspapers such as the Norfolk *Virginian-Pilot*, 31 July 1938, and Portsmouth (Ohio) *Times*, 31 July 1938.
43. Chicago *Defender*, 6 August 1946
44. Norfolk *Virginian-Pilot*, 31 July 1938.
45. Chicago *Tribune*, 31 July 31 1938.
46. Chicago *Daily News*, 30 July 1938.
47. New York *Herald Tribune* (Paris edition), 31 July 1938.
48. Norfolk *Journal and Guide*, 13 August 1938.
49. Chicago *Defender*, 6 August 1938.
50. Mark Ribowski, *A Complete History of the Negro Leagues, 1884–1955* (New York: Birch Lane Publishing, 1995), 253.
51. *Sporting News*, 4 August 1938.
52. *Ibid.*
53. Crepeau, "The Jake Powell Incident," p. 36.
54. Philadelphia *Tribune*, 4 August 1938.
55. Chicago *Defender*, 13 August 1946.
56. Chicago *Daily News*, 4 August 1938.
57. New York *Post*, 4 August 1938.
58. Ira Berkow, *Red* (New York: New Times Co., 1986), p. 108.
59. *The Nation*, 6 August 1938.
60. *Daily Worker*, 13 August 1938.
61. *Daily Worker*, 2 August 1938.
62. Chicago *Defender*, 6 August 1938.
63. *Amsterdam News*, 13 August 1938.
64. Philadelphia *Afro-American*, 20 August 1938.
65. Chicago *Defender*, 6 August 1938.
66. Dayton *Daily News*, 31 July 1938.
67. Dayton *Journal*, 17 August 1938.
68. Dayton *Forum*, 5 August 1938.
69. Chicago *Defender*, 6 August 1938.
70. Norfolk *Journal and Guide*, 6 August 1938.
71. Philadelphia *Tribune*, 4 August 1938.
72. Crepeau, "Jake Powell Incident," p. 38.
73. New York *Age*, 13 August 1938.
74. Chicago *Defender*, 6 August 1938.
75. *Ibid.* "(Black) fans are wondering why Jake Ruppert, owner of the New York Yankees, who hires Powell, will continue to let him play when Mr. Ruppert enjoys the patronage of thousands of black citizens in his Yankee Stadium and sells his beer all over Harlem to black people, making thousands of dollars from this race. Old Gold cigarettes that sponsored Powell's talk also enjoys lucrative business from the black race, but so far has been

entirely mum on an apology. Black people have learned how to 'fight fire with fire' and will expect all sources in any way connected with Powell and his slur to see that he is banned from baseball and kept where he will not have the opportunity to exhibit his ignorance," the letter said.

76. Chicago *Defender*, 20 August 1938.

77. New York *Age*, 20 August 1938.

78. Pittsburgh *Courier*, 20 August 1938.

79. Crepeau, "Jake Powell Incident," p. 40.

80. New York *Age*, 20 August 1938.

81. Dayton *Forum*, 12 August 1938.

82. New York *Age*, 1 October 1938.

83. Chicago *Defender*, 20 August 1938.

84. Chicago *Defender*, 13 August 1938.

85. Chicago *Defender*, 6 August 1938.

86. Philadelphia *Afro-American*, 3 September 1938.

87. Dayton *Forum*, 12 August 1938.

88. Chicago *Defender*, 20 August 1938.

89. The annual East-West game drew crowds of 50,000 in the mid–1930s and 1940s. But, more importantly, it gave black stars the opportunity to display their skills in front of white spectators and sportswriters. On August 7, 1941, Ed Harris wrote in the Philadelphia *Tribune*: "You read about the 50,000 persons who saw the East-West game and the thousands who were turned away from the classic, and you get to wondering what the magnates of the American and National Leagues thought about when they read the figures." See Reisler, *Black Writers/Black Baseball*, pp. 158–159. Author William Donn Rogosin called the annual East-West All-Star game "the single most important black sports event in America" in the 1930s and 1940s. Many of the games attracted crowds of 50,000. See Rogosin, *Invisible Men*, p. 25. Mark Ribowsky also devotes a lot of attention to the importance of the All-Star game in generating a lot of interest in integrating the national pastime. See Ribowsky, *A Complete History of the Negro Leagues, 1884–1955*.

90. Chicago *Defender*, 27 August 1938.

91. *New York Times*, 17 August 1938.

92. *Sporting News*, 25 August 1938.

93. Crepeau, "Jake Powell Incident," p. 42.

94. *Washington Post*, 17 August 1938.

95. Philadelphia *Tribune*, 25 August 1938.

96. Crepeau, "Jake Powell Incident," p. 44.

97. Dayton *Daily News*, 6 November 1948.

98. New York *Age*, 1 October 1938. See Crepeau, "Jake Powell Incident," p. 44.

Something to Cheer About: The Negro Leagues at the Dawn of Integration

James E. Overmyer

In 1998, fifty years after they left town, the Newark Eagles were inducted into the New Jersey Sports Hall of Fame. The timing was important — the old Negro leagues, in which the Eagles were an outstanding entry, are riding high on a flood tide of nostalgia these days, like a ghost ship still under sail even though it was sent to the scrapyards years ago.

There are more fans now who know about the old black stars like Josh Gibson and Cool Papa Bell than could have told you anything significant about their careers after they had stopped playing a half century ago. Like Joe Dimaggio, Ted Williams and Ebbets Field, the Negro leagues represent a less complicated, seemingly better time during a period when modern baseball's image is often on the ropes.

But, all these years removed from the reality, it's easy to miss the point that to be a person of color in America until well after World War II was to live a life within rigorously circumscribed boundaries. The Negro leaguers themselves were as hemmed in as anyone by segregation. But they played the same game on the field as their white major league counterparts, and while watching them an African-American man, or a boy, could dream big league dreams.

The good Negro teams and the African-American communities in which they played often forged a more profound connection than that made by their white counterparts. The Negro league teams simultaneously represented for their fans a shared reality of discrimination, but also something a great deal better. They stood for the aspirations, acted out in the open before thousands of onlookers, of what black Americans could do if given a chance. When two Negro league teams competed, the playing field was as level symbolically as it was topographically, and the players' achievements were fairly won and memorable.

For a dozen years beginning at the end of the Great Depression and ending after World War II, Newark, New Jersey, was a city whose white and black communities loved their baseball teams. But Newark was also a place in which to look for that special extra link between Negro fans and their squad.

The city was doubly blessed with baseball then. Its Ruppert Stadium was home to the Newark Bears, arguably the best minor league team in white organized baseball, and the Newark Eagles, one of the dominant, and one year the predominant, East Coast Negro league team.

The Bears, a top New York Yankee farm team, won seven pennants and a Little World Series crown while finishing in the International League's first division all 15 times between 1932 and 1946. Among Bears alumni who made it to the major leagues were Joe Gordon, Charlie Keller, Dixie Walker, Red Rolfe, Tommy Holmes and Hall of Famer Yogi Berra. The Eagles were perennial high finishers in the Negro National League, as well as 1946 Negro World Series champs. When the color line dropped they sent Larry Doby, Monte Irvin and Don Newcombe to the majors, and Irvin, Doby, Ray Dandridge, Leon Day and Willie Wells have been picked for the Hall.

Beginning in 1920, the best black baseball teams in America formed their own leagues and competed among themselves in a parallel version of what the white establishment called "Organized Baseball." The original Negro National League opened play in 1920. The Great Depression almost finished off organized black baseball in 1932, but the National League, to which the Newark Eagles would shortly belong, was reconstituted in 1933 and a companion Negro American League opened up in 1937.

These leagues provided the only opportunities for black baseball players, both African-Americans and Latin Americans leaving their own countries' leagues for the higher competition in the United States. Negro league teams were also the only chance for the black entrepreneurs who would be team owners.

As to Newark, 50 and 60 years ago it was a thriving industrial center, an ethnic polyglot with a sizable African-American population. But although Newark, and all of New Jersey for that matter, was integrated by law, it was still a divided city. Even if conducted civilly, de facto segregation was the rule.

Newark's 45,000 African-Americans made up more than 10 percent of the city's population in the 1940 census, but they constituted its poorest racial and ethnic group. Black population in the city and in New Jersey as a whole had grown phenomenally during World War I, fueled in great part by migration from the South. The lure was jobs, as Northern New Jersey saw its already large industrial capacity mushroom in response to the demands of equipping the American Expeditionary Force for combat in Europe in 1918.

Despite the availability of work during and after the war, and although Newark was a far cry from the super-segregated South, there was no mistaking it for a land of equality, either. Of about 20,500 adult blacks in Newark who had jobs in 1930, well over a third were employed as domestics or in other types of personal service. While there were slightly more than that number working in manufacturing or mechanical industries, that total masked a truer reality — while black males held almost 10 percent of those types of jobs in the city, they represented a full third of the common laborers.[1]

Thus, set up for a fall by the white economic structure, the black population of Newark saw its fortunes plummet farther than most groups when the Depression pulled the rug out from under everyone. Those who had been categorized, fairly or not, as being the least likely to succeed were, of course, among the first let go and the ones left jobless the longest when businesses shrank. In the early 1930s, when the Depression was deepest, blacks represented one third of all relief cases in the city, although they made up only one twelfth of Newark's population.[2]

The New Jersey *Herald-News*, one of the black weeklies published in Newark, claimed in 1939 that the status of its race in that city could be summed up thusly: "Newark, with the largest colored population in the State, has the lowest average income, the less percentage employed in governmental work, and has no physicians or nursing students in its public-supported hospital, the largest percentage of houses unfit for habitation and is shockingly deprived of representation on policy-fixing boards."[3]

To be fair, Newark had no exceptional record of either violence or flagrant official discrimination against its African-American citizens. Still, public swimming pools were completely closed to blacks until 1932, and thereafter open to them only during certain hours when whites were not present. And, the city's municipal hospital was closed to black patients, as was its medical staff to African-American doctors and nurses.

Blacks who lived in the Newark area in those days recall the subtleties of segregation, such as having to sit in the balcony or in the very back of a movie theater, and being served out of a paper cup instead of a glass when going into a white-run bar. Monte Irvin, one of the Newark Eagles' best players, grew up in the adjacent community of Orange. He recalls being in a group of black youngsters denied service in a restaurant right around the corner from Orange High School, from which they had graduated that very evening.[4]

The discrimination was by no means a figment of blacks' imaginations. John Cunningham, who worked for the Newark *Evening News*, the city's major daily paper, recalls that one day he was working as a desk man, taking the details of a classic human interest story over the telephone from another reporter: "A child had been left in a church, had been there two or three days. I turned to the managing editor and said, 'There's a good story coming in on a kid abandoned in a church.'

"He said, 'Black or white?'

"I said, 'Black.'

"He said, 'Forget it.'"[5]

But to stress just this version of black life in Newark in the 1930s and 1940s is to do a great disservice to the time and place and to the people who lived there, for they also recall a good side to being an African-American in the city. Although Irvin remembers the area's segregation, his primary recollection of Newark is that it was "just a wonderful city. A lot of the big stores were there and it was very clean and it was just first rate." For a youngster, "a good outing was to just get on a bus and go to Newark and do some shopping, or to go to Newark to the theater or for some amusement or go down to see a baseball game at Ruppert Stadium."[6]

The black community's social structure was tied together by its churches, a number of adult social clubs and, for the youngsters, the black YMCA on Court Street. As Connie Woodruff, a Newark native who later became a journalist, remembered it, "if I was going to a dance and it wasn't at the Y, my mother wouldn't let me go. The perception was that they were God fearing, nice people running the Y, so your kids could go there and be safe."[7]

Black entertainment thrived in the city. The big black bands of Jimmie Lunceford, Earl "Fatha" Hines, Cab Calloway, Lionel Hampton, Fletcher Henderson and Count Basie all played Newark in those days, as did Ella Fitzgerald and Fats Waller.

Blacks in Newark, while always up against reminders of their separateness, could also see much evidence of the potential of their togetherness. When the Baltimore *Afro-American* newspaper established a New Jersey edition in Newark in 1941 the city had three black weeklies. They all energetically mined the two mother lodes of black news — what blacks were being denied by whites and what they were accomplishing in terms of "firsts" in American society.

This was the town to which Abraham and Effa Manley brought their baseball business in 1936. Abe Manley, who apparently amassed a comfortable sum running an illegal but highly popular numbers business in Camden, N.J., had founded the Eagles in Brooklyn in 1935. After suffering through an unprofitable season there, the Manleys bought the similarly struggling Newark Dodgers franchise, merging the two clubs to create a new Newark entry in the Negro National League.

The Manleys were an outwardly mismatched couple who nevertheless combined to create one of the best run teams in Negro league baseball. Abe, an affable, stocky, dark-skinned man, seemed happiest in two not-so-different roles. One was riding in the front seat of the team bus with his team (and it was *his* team — he had personally scouted many of the players). The other was relaxing over beer and poker at Dan's Tavern on Wickliffe Street in Newark when the squad returned home.

Effa was extremely light-skinned. In her old age she revealed herself to be a Caucasian who had been brought up in the African-American community in her native Philadelphia, then had decided to live with the race for the rest of her life. She did not make that fact known in her Newark days (it would have been a most unsettling revelation then), and aspired to membership in the highest levels of Newark black society. She was attractive and consistently well dressed, but outspoken and fiery-tempered, which probably worked to deny her the total acceptance in the upper crust she craved to join. Nonetheless, she paid her societal dues, energetically raising funds for the NAACP, the Urban League and other African-American institutions in the Newark area.

Abe and Effa separately embodied the two spheres in which Negro league baseball was important. Their ability to combine the two, the fielding of a competitive team and the making of the team into a community institution, has made the Eagles memorable to this day to African-Americans who lived in Newark before and during World War II.

The players Abe put on the field provided quality sports entertainment. The Eagles were unable until 1946 to finish in front of the East's best black team, the Homestead Grays of Pittsburgh. But in the 11 seasons prior to that year the National League, sometimes playing split seasons, produced 16 sets of standings. Newark finished in second place seven times and third three others, about the best second-best team in the East.

Although the Eagles played many non-league games against New Jersey and New York City white semi-professional teams, and although Effa Manley tried hard to interest Newark's white population in attending Eagle games, the team's real audience was the black fans in its home city and in the cities of its league opponents. While most of them might not have been inclined to buck the existing segregationist attitudes of the 1930s and 1940s, they were personally aware they were not members of an inferior race.

Following logically from that awareness, they knew the skills of the best black ballplayers were not inferior to those of major leaguers, even if the Negro leaguers were denied an opportunity to play alongside them. Effa knew this, just as she knew that it was lack of opportunity, not ability, which afflicted the entire Negro population. She was determined to make her team a community asset, no less so than the teams which existed in the parallel world of white baseball. In the world of Newark baseball, that meant keeping up with the Bears.

The annual frenzy of the Bears' fans began just before Opening Day, when the team arrived by train from Spring training in Florida. According to Jerry Izenberg, the Newark *Star-Ledger* sports columnist who grew up with both the Bears and Eagles, "the Bears would come to Penn Station [in Newark], and be put into open cars. The high school bands would be there, sometimes more than one. The boosters would be there. They would march through the city to Ruppert Stadium, unpack, and work out. Often there would be 5,000 fans in the stands on a work day, watching them work out."

How important was Opening Day itself? Izenberg dryly observes, "The mayor of Newark, if he chose not to be reelected, could ignore the Bears' home opener."[8]

Negro league baseball aimed to model its baseball structure on the white major leagues as a way to claim legitimacy. But Effa Manley also insisted on emulating white teams even in purely symbolic ways. According to Izenberg, she strove to elevate the Eagles to the point "where the white mayor of Newark was always at their opener, too, and always sat in Effa Manley's box."[9] This was nothing new for her. She had also gotten Fiorello La Guardia, the mayor of New York, to show up at the Brooklyn Eagles' home opener in Ebbets Field in 1935.

Money for baseball tickets might seem to have been scarce in the Negro community, given its economic disadvantages. But the Eagles, with both player recruitment and public relations done energetically and astutely by the Manleys, appear to have outdrawn the extremely successful Bears by nearly two to one within their respective racial groups. Attendance figures from the 1930s enable a rough calculation to be made — the wildly popular Bears' annual attendance of a little more than 200,000 from 1932 through 1938 represented about 1 of every 3.5 white residents in Newark and adjacent communities, while the 32,646 the Eagles drew to Ruppert Stadium in 1939, by comparison, was 1 of every 2 African-Americans in those communities.[10]

This was so because the Negro leaguers offered a dimension of anticipation to Eagle fans beyond that experienced by the whites who flocked to see the Bears. A Bears fan might see in one of these Yankee farmhands his wished-for baseball self, in the bright future if he were a son, or in the fading past if he were a father. But the perceptive African-American saw something else. The poet and writer Amiri Baraka, an Eagle regular as a teenager, saw it. He said that popular entertainment was full of comically subservient black stereotypes, but the meaning of the Negro leagues was that "it made us know that the Mantans and Stepin Fetchits were clowns,... (but) we knew, and we knew, that they wasn't us. We was NOT clowns and the Newark Eagles laid that out clear for anyone to see!"[11]

By 1939, when a reported 10,000 people showed up for opening day against the Philadelphia Stars, Newark's African-Americans had become great fans of the Eagles. So popular was the team in Newark that Max Manning, one of its star players, later invoked baseball's gold standard in describing the town and team relationship: "The Eagles were to Newark what the Dodgers were to Brooklyn."[12]

By 1937, Abe Manley was beginning to find the star players he had been looking for, and the Eagles were playing consistently winning baseball. As the team on the field grew stronger, so did the relationship between the club and the community which supported it, until it far transcended the previous peripatetic history of Newark and black baseball that had existed before the Eagles came. As Abe's continuous quest for the best players and managers he could hire built the team on the field, Effa carried out her equally important role of establishing the complementary relationship in which black Newark helped the Eagles, and the Eagles helped black Newark.

She made sure that the team had an image of upholding the African-American community's best standards, to the extent that even if they had only won now and then, the Eagles might still have had a place as fundraisers and publicizers of charities and helping organizations.

Effa, a member of the National Association for the Advancement of Colored People since she had helped the Citizens League for Fair Play picket department stores over job equality in Harlem in 1934, used game days to raise funds for the organization. For example, on opening day in 1946, young women volunteers with NAACP banners draped from their shoulders canvassed 8,500 fans there for the Eagles game with the Philadelphia Stars.

Other owners did this, too, but Effa's NAACP fund-raising tactics were different. They were quite reminiscent of her previous role as forthright negotiator who shocked white department store officials in Harlem by equating young black girls turning to prostitution with the denial of the stores' retail jobs. At one point she ran a "Stop Lynching" campaign at Ruppert, selling NAACP-sponsored buttons with that hard hitting slogan for a dollar apiece (and getting a newspaper publicity photo taken while selling one to the Newark mayor).[13]

The Eagles worked especially hard for the institutions that promoted the welfare of Northern New Jersey blacks.

With African-Americans effectively barred from Newark's medical professions, a black hospital, the Booker T. Washington Community Hospital, was established in the city. On Aug. 20, 1940, the Eagles played the first of periodic benefit games to raise money towards new medical equipment. "This hospital is the only one in the State offering an opportunity for colored physicians and nurses to get hospital training," Effa's advance publicity noted. "This is a civic responsibility no one should shirk and everyone should be proud to meet."[14]

The team played several games to benefit black Elks lodges, a major part of African-American urban social life, and also honored special achievements by individuals. John Borican was a black track star from nearby Bridgeton, N.J., who had held six world records and had won several national track titles before tragically dying of pernicious anemia in 1942 at age 29. But while still at the height of his career, on August 31, 1941, he was guest of honor at "John Borican Day" at the stadium. The Manleys staged one of the Negro leagues' most attractive types of events, a "four-team doubleheader." Instead of the home team and a visiting squad playing each other twice, two different teams played in each game, thus exposing black baseball fans to twice as many of the well known players that they hungered to see.

There were added attractions in the form of "track and field" events for the players, including a 100-yard dash competition. The winning player would race Borican. The field managers of the four teams, perhaps in recognition of their burdens of command, were to compete in a wheelbarrow race.[15]

The Eagles, once well established as an authentic sports fixture in New Jersey, were also in demand for fundraising outside the Newark area. In 1939 Edward White of the Urban League in New York City wrote Effa seeking the team for a benefit game at Yankee Stadium. Despite the existence of black teams in New York, White wrote, "we want your team as the home team because we believe it to be the most substantial organization in this section ... also because we believe you are personally interested in the work of the Urban League."[16]

Perhaps the most interesting tie Effa forged between her team and the black community was with its youths. The Eagles had a regular "Knothole

Gang" organization, which derived its name from the old-time kid base-ball fan's trick of watching games for free through the holes in the pine board fences surrounding early ballparks. As run by the Eagles, it (of course) copied the practice of the white Newark Bears, allowing youngsters actual free admission to games.

"If I had a dime to ride the bus to Ruppert Stadium and back, I went," recalls Melvin Sanders of Montclair, a Newark youngster at the time; "if we didn't have a nickel, we used to ride on the back of the buses to get there, and jump off if we saw a policeman." Effa also organized an Eagle-spon-sored youth team, the Newark Cubs, on which Sanders played until he was 14 years old, in 1942. "She was one of the few blacks who had a little money, and she put some back into the community," he said; "kids were robbin' and stealin', they didn't have enough to do." Sanders remembers the Cubs as "an arm of the Eagles — we were proud to be a part of the organization."

She and Abe bought uniforms and equipment for the team, while the players had to provide their own shoes and baseball gloves. They played other youth teams, and eventually became the only black squad in a Newark league. There were two aspects of the Manleys' involvement with the Cubs that perfectly mirrored their roles in adult baseball. According to Sanders, they were personally involved, often attending the Cubs' games, where "she was out front, while he was supportive, and took a back seat."[17]

The other point was Effa's concern for doing things in a businesslike fashion with the public impact of the players' actions always in mind. These were enduring characteristics of her involvement with the Eagles and Negro league baseball in general. Each Cub had to sign a receipt for his uniform, which came "complete with belt, socks and cap." Furthermore, the boys had to acknowledge that:

"I promise to keep care of the suit, wash it when it gets dirty, or when the Coach tells me to, and bring it back to Mrs. Manley clean for safe keep-ing at the end of the season, or when I am asked for it. I promise to con-duct myself in a sportsmanlike manner at all times on the ball field, and to keep in good physical condition by doing any exercise the Coach demands. I will be punctual for ball games, and will try in every way to set a high standard for boys my age."[18]

The best way to appreciate the Eagles, as Melvin Sanders points out, was to go see them play at Ruppert Stadium. Negro league club owners almost never had access to the financial capital needed to build their own ball parks, and finding a first-class place to call home was often a prob-lem. In Newark, playing at Ruppert meant that the best black players, the Negro leaguers, were showcased in the ballpark of a top flight white pro-fessional team, giving appropriate, even if rented, status to the black game.

Ruppert Stadium sat in the midst of an industrial area near the Passaic River called the "Ironbound," so called because of the railroad tracks that defined its boundaries. The European blue collar immigrants who lived there gave the neighborhood a flavor quite different from the black sections of town. Amiri Baraka says that to go to an Eagles game there, on almost foreign soil, emphasized the special quality of the experience: "But coming down through that would heighten my sense because I could dig I would soon be standing in that line to get in, with my old man. But lines of all black people! Dressed up like they would for going to the game, in those bright lost summers. The Newark Eagles would have your heart there on the field.... [These were] legitimate black heroes. And we were intimate with them in a way and they were extensions of all of us, there, in a way that the Yankees and Dodgers and what not could never be!"[19]

Attending Eagle games at Ruppert, especially the Sunday afternoon doubleheaders against other black teams, was as much a social as a sporting occasion. Connie Woodruff, who went to Eagle games with her father, then later wrote feature stories about the team when she became a newspaperwoman, remembers Sundays at the stadium as "a combination of two things, an opportunity for all the women to show off their Sunday finery, and also the once a week family affair.

"People used to come to the games with big baskets of chicken, potato salad, all the things you would have on a picnic. The women would come with flowery dresses, it reminded me of the English going to Ascot. The flowery dresses, the big hats, the hair done just right. I'm sure all those women didn't understand baseball, but it was the thrill of being there, being seen, seeing who they could see. The men who escorted them were dressed to the nines, and these women would stroll in on their arms. Who was with whom was the talk of the next week."[20]

The relationship between the Eagles and their audience was best demonstrated by Opening Day, each season's rite of renewal. Effa, who handled the program, invited local and state dignitaries, who, of course, were usually white. But beginning with the opening ceremonies, which usually featured a black school band, sometimes professional entertainers from Harlem night spots and always an American flag color guard, the Attucks Guard from Newark's black American Legion post, the first game pageantry was almost entirely by and for the black community.

Opening day ceremonies frequently celebrated African-American aspirations for equality. As the country began beefing up its armed forces in 1940 to be prepared for the onset of war, the black press hotly debated two questions about Negroes and the military. One was whether or not black servicemen would actually be allowed to fight for their country, as opposed to being Navy kitchen help or Army ditch diggers. The other was whether their invariably segregated units would be led by black officers. There was plenty of reason to wonder about that, since the Army itself reported in 1941 that of 88,000 regular, reserve and National Guard officers, only 259 were black, and only six of them were regular Army men.[21]

A result of black leaders' pressure on Washington was the mobilization of the all-black, black-led 372nd Infantry Regiment at Fort Dix, New Jersey. Effa's subsequent response to the formation of the 372nd was to invite the entire regiment, 2,500 strong, to attend opening day in 1941, and to have Mayor Meyer C. Ellenstein declare an official "372nd Day." In 1943 Effa extended an invitation to the black members of the Free French forces at Fort Dix, organized to help retake their invaded country. Her invitation also included a handwritten postscript to Lieutenant Beauregard, the unit commander, allowing that if there was sufficient room, the white members would also be welcome.[22]

The celebrity picked to throw out the ceremonial first ball from the grandstands was very often emblematic of black progress, particularly in sports. In 1941 Lt. Col. Alexander Stephens of the 372nd had the honors, but in other years the track star Borican and boxers Henry Armstrong and Beau Jack officiated.

The young men who were the Eagles were greatly admired in the essentially small town world of Newark's African-American neighborhoods. James "Red" Moore, a first baseman for the team in 1936 and 1937, recalls that "when I was there, fans would recognize us more or less as celebrities." James Walker, a pitcher before World War II, says that "to be an Eagle meant you could do no wrong."[23]

Francis Matthews, another first baseman who came along in 1938 after Moore left, recalls with a little embarrassment a particular show of fan support he might have wanted to have done without during a "Ladies' Night" promotion: "I fielded a sharply hit ball, and tried to make a double play by throwing it to my right as I was running. But, I threw it over the shortstop's head at second, into left field. It was the first time in my career I got booed. As I was running back to the dugout, Mrs. Smith (who was the madam of a local house of prostitution, at the game with several of her girls), stood up and shouted 'Don't worry, baby, we're all with you.'"[24]

The fans' connection with the Eagles could continue after the end of a home game at Ruppert when the team and its closest followers repaired to the unofficial club headquarters, the Grand Hotel. The Grand was a two-story hotel at West Market and Wickliffe streets. Although it was not very large, it was one of the few commercial lodging places for blacks in Newark. Several of the players boarded there during the season, and the bar and dining room on the first floor is etched in the memories of Eagle players.

To them, the Grand was a haven, providing the kind of relaxation that comes from completely belonging. To the fans, the hotel presented an opportunity to join the ballplayers' special circle, and translate their stardom into whatever gave meaning to the followers. Women looking to make a connection with an unattached ballplayer would sit on one side of the crowded dining room and try to get the attention of players they had seen at the ball park. If they didn't know a player's name, they would have him paged by his uniform number.[25]

Baraka remembers his father taking him to the Grand as a teenager after Eagles' games, where "the ball players and the slick people could meet. Everybody super-clean and highlifin', glasses jinkling with ice, black people's eyes sparklin and showin their teeth in the hippest way possible.... The movies I dearly dug but you never got to go behind the screen and shake hands with the heroes. But at the Grand Hotel you could."[26]

In every dedicated baseball fan there lurks that desire to shake hands with the heroes, and vicariously share in their heroism. This is why there are baseball fan clubs. But in the case of the Negro leagues, the connection between the black game and the fans ran deeper, down to strata that underlay what it meant to be black, shut out of white society but with one's own exciting people and places. For Benjamin Hawkins Jr., seeing the Eagles was a way to let off the head of steam built up during long days of the hard work that simply surviving required of African-Americans in the 1930s. "It was like an outlet, you know, see, because a lot of times [black fans] lost interest in the National and American League, because there wasn't any blacks playing in it ... so all the attention was centered on [the Eagles]."[27]

Before he became one of the fans' idols himself, Monte Irvin as a youth growing up in nearby Orange thought that the meaning of black baseball to black working men was that it was "an inspiration for the waiters, the janitors, the maintenance guys. [They would say] 'well, goddamn it, maybe there's some hope,' in other words it gave the black people something to cheer about."[28]

The strong pull Negro league baseball exerted on African-American fans was especially noticeable during World War II when the financial fortunes of the black teams improved dramatically. Rare was the Negro league team which couldn't make money, possibly for the only time in its existence. The industrial buildup required to enter the war dwarfed that of World War I, and an enormous wave of black migration to the North occurred again to fill the new manufacturing jobs. To illustrate the new levels of migration and employment in Newark, the number of black jobs more than tripled, from a little less than 8,000 in 1940 to 27,000 by 1945.[29]

With gasoline rationing and long work hours restricting how far people could travel for entertainment, the predictions of longtime Negro league observer John Clark came true. He had written in March 1943 that the teams "should have an unprecedented year financially" since "the majority will play in boom towns where people spend freely and like sports after a hard day of work in a defense plant."[30]

The unique opportunities created for the Negro leagues by the changing demographics of wartime actually put black franchises on a relatively more profitable footing than their white counterparts, the only time this ever occurred while the two sides of professional baseball co-existed. The white major league clubs had fought their way out of the Depression by 1939, showing their best profits in 10 years, when the uncertainties of wartime operations reversed this trend. In 1942 and 1943, the white big league teams, as a group, actually lost money, an average of 2.2 percent of gross receipts.[31]

The war made profits for both Negro league owners and players (Satchel Paige, at a reputed $40,000, was probably the highest paid professional baseball player in 1944), and gave them all something to brag about. Black baseball saw itself firmly established in the wartime scheme of things, as evidenced by the cover illustration of the 1945 "Negro Baseball Pictorial Year Book." Posed in tandem were Homestead Gray's starting pitcher Elmer "Spoon" Carter, about to hurl a baseball, dwarfed in the background by a black infantryman about to lob a hand grenade.

Ironically, the infantryman, depicted in dominating dimensions to acknowledge how baseball only complemented the war effort, turned out to have more enduring meaning for the Negro leagues than Spoon Carter and all of his teammates on one of the Negro leagues' most dominant teams. The seeds of the civil rights successes which began in the late 1940s were sown during the war, for once blacks had risked and lost their lives for the United States, it would become increasingly difficult to deny them equality. It's important to remember that before he was Nation League Rookie of the Year, Jackie Robinson

In 1951 Walter White, the NA   ued 15
major areas in which blacks had att   ribed
the breaking of the color line in pro   e sign
of change to most Americans." He   rvin,
Larry Doby and the other new black   ment
to baseball: "few persons thought of   only
as good ball players."[32]

An athlete's advancement toward potential stardom is one of the most purely merit-based progressions known in America. It doesn't help to know someone powerful, or to be someone's son-in-law. As of the late 1940s, race was at last no longer a qualifier, either. But when baseball gave African-Americans something to really cheer about, it simultaneously set in motion the demise of the Negro leagues.

This was as true in Newark as anywhere. Eagle attendance dropped by more than two thirds between 1946 and 1948, from about 120,000 to 35,000, as Newark's black fans left behind the Negro leaguers, the symbols of what ought to be in their own lives, in favor of the new black big leaguers, who were actually delivering the bright new promise of integration. The Manleys sold the Eagles after the 1948 season, and the new owners moved the team to Houston. The Negro National League itself died that cold December. The Eagles and the other remaining clubs were consolidated in the Negro American League, which soldiered on until 1960, although it was of little consequence after the mid–1950s.

By the way, this time at least the Eagle set the pace for the Bears. After the 1949 season the Yankees pulled out of Newark and the Bears, sold to the Chicago Cubs, opened the next year in Springfield, Massachusetts. Television, particularly the growth of televised major league baseball, coupled with the changing demographics in Northern New Jersey that made it a more comfortable trip for white fans to go across the George Washington Bridge and see the Yankees and Giants, did in the Bears.

The Eagles and the Negro leagues, though, were quite simply killed off by integration before any other societal factors could affect them. And they were by no means the only segment of African-American popular culture to fall victim. The once-thriving black weekly newspapers, for decades leading voices trumpeting the accomplishments of black Americans and demanding their inclusion in general society, also tumbled as mainstream papers began to cover their black communities, often with black reporters and editors. For example, the Pittsburgh *Courier*, long the most read black paper in the Eastern United States, declined from a record circulation of more than 357,212 in May 1947 to about 100,000 by 1960.[33]

The Negro league owners, with their investments and in some cases their livelihoods slipping away before their eyes, tried to cross the color line along with their players. There were a series of meetings in 1946 with baseball Commissioner Albert "Happy" Chandler and other white officials, in which the Negro leagues sought status as recognized minor leagues. But there were powerful, self-interested forces working against a true white-black merger. A draft of a major league planning document in 1946, later edited to make it less incendiary, originally maintained that big league organizations made substantial sums from renting major and minor league parks (such as the Yankees' Ruppert Stadium) to Negro league teams, and that total integration would wipe out that income source.[34]

In the end, the Negro league teams were never actually denied membership — Organized Baseball just never quite got around to ruling on their requests, and then it was too late.

The thriving of the Negro leagues in their heyday represented proof of what the black man could do, even if he had to create his own opportunities in a world circumscribed by segregation. Then, when baseball was desegregated, there could have been no early crop of black big league stars without their having learned their competitive skills in the Negro leagues. Even before there was hope of integration, as it turned out, black baseball was establishing the performance standards which made it possible for Robinson, Doby, Irvin and the others to step right into the limelight.

That's the positive meaning of the Negro leagues. The other lesson is that, for inclusion to be truly successful, it must go all the way to the top. The Negro league owners, who provided the continuity to their half of baseball, and whose ranks contained several competent baseball business people, yearned to join the mainstream, too. But to a man (and woman, in Effa Manley's case), they were not welcomed by white ownership, their bids to at least join the minor leagues were ignored, and their teams withered away.

As a result, things have not turned out as well as integrationists might have hoped. Black players have been successful, and on their merits, too. But on the management level, major league baseball has struggled to break the 20 percent level in front office minority employment, and still is noticeably lacking in top management representation. Largely because the original group of owners and field managers who would have "seeded" Organized Baseball with black talent in the late 1940s were frozen out, blacks now neither figuratively nor literally "own" a share of professional baseball commensurate with their overall level of participation.

Once, they did. John "Buck" O'Neil, the Kansas City Monarch who has become a spokesman for the Negro leagues, recalls making it to the big cities as a ballplayer: "I saw so many things in the social world, and it was totally, more or less, a black world, because ... we kind of owned that world. We really did. But once we started with integration, I think it took a little something from us, as far as owning things."[35]

Notes

1. Jackson, Kenneth T., and Barbara B. Jackson, "The Black Experience in Newark, the Growth of the Ghetto, 1870–1970," in *New Jersey Since 1860: New Findings and Interpretations*,

ed. William C. Wright (Trenton: New Jersey Historical Commission, 1972), p. 45; Price, Clement A., "The Beleaguered City As Promised Land: Blacks in Newark, 1917–1947," in *Urban New Jersey Since 1870*, ed. William C. Wright (Trenton: New Jersey Historical Commission, 1975), p. 27.

2. Jackson and Jackson, "The Black Experience," p. 46; Cunningham, John T., *Newark* (Newark: New Jersey Historical Society, 1966), p. 282.

3. New Jersey *Herald-News*, March 11, 1939.

4. Interviews with Eddie Wilkerson and Monte Irvin, by Dr. Lawrence D. Hogan and Thomas C. Guy, Jr.

5. Interview with John T. Cunningham, by author.

6. Interview with Monte Irvin, by author.

7. Interview with Connie Woodruff, by author.

8. Interview with Jerry Izenberg, by author.

9. *Ibid.*

10. *Newark Eagle* files, 1939; Sixteenth Census of the United States, *Characteristics of the Population*, 2nd Series, New Jersey, 1942; Linthurst, Randolph, *Newark Bears* (Trenton, NJ, self published, 1978), p. 5.

11. Baraka, Amiri, *The Autobiography of Leroi Jones* (New York: Fruendlich, 1984), p. 36.

12. Interview with Maxwell Manning, by author.

13. Rogosin, William Donn, *Invisible Men: Life in the Negro Baseball Leagues* (New York: Athenaeum, 1987), p. 94; interview with Effa Manley by William Donn Rogosin.

14. *Newark Eagle* files, 1940.

15. *Newark Eagle* files, 1941.

16. *Newark Eagle* files, 1939.

17. Interview with Melvin Sanders, by author.

18. *Newark Eagle* files, 1941.

19. Baraka, *Autobiography*, p. 34.

20. Woodruff interview.

21. Pittsburgh *Courier*, July 12, 1941.

22. *Newark Eagle* files, 1943.

23. Interviews with James Moore and James Walker, by author.

24. Interview with Francis Matthews, by author.

25. *Ibid.*

26. Baraka, *Autobiography*, p. 35.

27. Interview with Benjamin Hawkins, Jr., by Dr. Lawrence D. Hogan and Thomas C. Guy, Jr.

28. Irvin interview by author.

29. Jackson and Jackson, "The Black Experience," p. 50; Pittsburgh *Courier*, August 25, 1945.

30. Pittsburgh *Courier*, March 6, 1943.

31. Voigt, David Quentin, *American Baseball*, Vol. 2 (Norman, OK: University of Oklahoma Press, 1970), p. 269.

32. White, Walter, "Time for a Progress Report," *Saturday Review of Literature*, Sept. 22, 1951.

33. Hogan, Lawrence D., *A Black National News Service: the Associated Negro Press and Claude Barnett, 1919–1945* (Cranbury, NJ: Associated University Presses, 1984), pp. 235–237.

34. "Report for Submission to National and American Leagues on 27 August, 1946," in Albert B. "Happy" Chandler papers, University of Kentucky, pp. 19–20.

35. Interview with John "Buck" O'Neil, by Dr. Lawrence D. Hogan and Thomas C. Guy, Jr.

References

INTERVIEWS

Amiri Baraka, by Dr. Lawrence D. Hogan and Thomas C. Guy, Jr.
John T. Cunningham, by author
Benjamin Hawkins, Jr., by Dr. Lawrence D. Hogan and Thomas C. Guy, Jr.
Monte Irvin, by author and by Dr. Lawrence D. Hogan and Thomas C. Guy, Jr.
Jerry Izenberg, by author
Effa Manley, by William Donn Rogosin
Maxwell Manning, by author
Francis Matthews, by author
James "Red" Moore, by author
John "Buck" O'Neil, by Dr. Lawrence D. Hogan and Thomas C. Guy, Jr.
Melvin Sanders, by author
James Walker, by author
Eddie Wilkerson, by Dr. Lawrence D. Hogan and Thomas C. Guy, Jr.
Connie Woodruff, by author.

BOOKS

Baraka, Amiri. *The Autobiography of Leroi Jones.* New York: Fruendlich Books, 1984.
Cunningham, John T. *Newark.* Newark: New Jersey Historical Society, 1966.
Hogan, Lawrence D. *A Black National News Service: The Associated Negro Press and Claude Barnett, 1919–1945.* Cranbury, NJ: Associated University Presses, 1984.
Jackson, Kenneth T. and Barbara B., "The Black Experience in Newark, the Growth of the Ghetto, 1870–1970," *New Jersey Since 1860: New Findings and Interpretations,* ed. William C. Wright. Trenton: New Jersey Historical Commission, 1972.
Linthurst, Randolph. *Newark Bears.* Trenton: Self-published, 1978.
Price, Clement A. "The Beleaguered City As Promised Land: Blacks in Newark, 1917–1947," *Urban New Jersey Since 1870,* ed. William C. Wright. Trenton: New Jersey Historical Commission, 1975.
Rogosin, William Donn. *Invisible Men: Life in the Negro Baseball Leagues.* New York: Athenaeum, 1987.
Voigt, David Quentin. *American Baseball,* Vol. 2. Norman, OK: University of Oklahoma Press, 1970.

ARTICLES

White, Walter, "Time for a Progress Report," *Saturday Review of Literature,* Sept. 22, 1951.

NEWSPAPERS

New Jersey *Herald-News.*
Pittsburgh *Courier.*
Public Records and Archives
Albert B. "Happy" Chandler papers. University of Kentucky Library, Lexington, KY.
Newark Eagles files. Newark Public Library, New Jersey Collection. Newark, NJ.
Sixteenth Census of the United States. *Characteristics of the Population,* 2nd Series, New Jersey, 1942.

Jackie Robinson and the American Zeitgeist

William Simons

"Jackie Robinson and the American Zeitgeist" is intellectual history from the vantage point of baseball. By examining journalistic commentary concerning the October 23, 1945, announcement that Jackie Robinson had signed a contract to play with the Montreal Royals, a minor league affiliate of the Brooklyn Dodgers, this paper analyzes American perceptions of race at the opening of the post-war era. Utilizing content analysis of contemporary print media — metropolitan newspapers, sporting publications, and magazines, "Jackie Robinson and the American Zeitgeist" explores the extensive public discussion about race, consensus, conflict, democracy, and national character generated by baseball's "great experiment."[1]

Robinson's Organized Baseball debut followed a war that had encouraged Americans to define themselves by a liberalism not found in Nazi Germany. In *An American Dilemma: The Negro Problem and Modern Democracy*, published almost simultaneously with the signing of Robinson, sociologist Gunnar Myrdal argues that most Americans believe in a shared creed. This American Creed, contends Myrdal, endorses the "ideals of the essential dignity of the individual human being, of the fundamental equality of all men, and of certain inalienable rights to freedom, justice, and a fair opportunity."[2] "Jackie Robinson and the American Zeitgeist" will seek to demonstrate that the tenets of Myrdal's American Creed significantly shaped press coverage of the reintegration of baseball.

Emphasis on the chronological context of Robinson's signing in the immediate aftermath of World War II is essential. World War II was a "turning point" in the struggle for civil rights.[3] Although wartime progress against racism was circumscribed, the conflict created some significant opportunities for blacks.[4] The Fair Employment Practices Commission, for example, enlarged the black presence in war industries.[5] By introducing the United States "to conspicuously racist enemies and ... (dramatizing) the gap between democratic ideals and racism at home," World War II prompted Americans "to reexamine their racial attitudes."[6] For many Americans, World War II made suspect the racist arguments formerly employed by baseball segregationists.[7]

The conventional wisdom holds that baseball mirrors American values, and scholarship suggests that in some eras it has.[8] At the time of Robinson's signing, however, the media often asserted that baseball's conservative racial practices lagged behind practices already prevailing in America. Black journalists frequently termed baseball inferior to certain sports in living up to America's egalitarian beliefs. Although pugilism involved "brutal body contact," the *St. Louis Argus* argued that integrated boxing matches outside the South proceed "in grand style."[9] The *Pittsburgh Courier* also noted prior "achievements of colored men and women ... in various branches of sports."[10] A third black newspaper, the *Amsterdam News,* quoted Douglas Hertz, a promoter of inter-racial games: "It is extremely gratifying to see at this late date organized baseball has finally seen the light." And the black press reported a comment by a member of New York City's Mayor Fiorello La Guardia's Committee on Unity, which suggested that baseball was tardy in conforming to practices long accepted by other sports: "There is every reason to hope that this will lead to a constructive solution by which organized baseball will be brought in line with those other sports in which Negroes have for a long time been participants."[11]

Not only did it appear negligent in comparison with other sports, baseball, asserted pundits, failed to keep pace with racial practices prevalent on a macrocosmic level. As "the nation moves toward a postwar lessening of discrimination," chided the *Brooklyn Eagle*, "the national game of Americans ... cannot forever lag behind."[12] A letter to the editor of the *Detroit News* argued, "Colored artists and performers in all other fields have proved that the absence of a colored player in the major leagues of baseball is nothing more than the absence of the true American spirit in the greatest of American sports."[13] Aside from athletics, American blacks had already made notable contributions "in drama, opera, music, the stage," and other endeavors.[14] Beyond harboring reactionary attitudes, baseball, implied the press, practiced hypocrisy and irrationality in the enforcement of the color barrier. Writers frequently noted the participation of numbers of blacks in Organized Baseball before the establishment of the unofficial color line in the late nineteenth century.[15] Contemporary journalists also commented extensively on integrated play during post-season barnstorming, often featuring exhibition games that matched the ageless Satchell Paige against white stars.[16] When "baseball club owners are perfectly willing to take the money of Negro fans at the gate," editorialized the *St. Louis Post-Dispatch*, while excluding Negroes from the playing field, the failure of "the Great American Game" to live up to its name became most evident.[17] Moreover, pundits claimed that a few twentieth-century blacks had entered Organized Baseball under the guise of an Indian or Cuban identity.[18] Negro newspapers and, indeed, most of the general circulation press assumed blacks had earned the right to compete in the National Pastime without concealing their identities. "We want Jackie to meet the test as a Negro," asserted a black journalist, "not as a sun-tanned white man or Eskimo."[19] World War II, claimed the press, rendered arguments based on racial inequality un-American. Columnist Dink Carroll believed the war demonstrated that baseball segregation derived from Southern exceptionalism, a violation of American democracy:

> ...Many Americans have criticized baseball for drawing the color line, and have argued that it couldn't truly be called America's national game because of this discrimination ... hostility to colored players didn't originate with the club owners or with the leagues, but with the players themselves. A good many of the players are Southerners ... part of the Japanese propaganda in the Pacific was to point out that colored people were discriminated against in the United States. Many Americans had to ask themselves should they not courageously back up their fighting men — of all races, creeds and color — by eradicating the color line at home?[20]

Indeed, asked the *Boston Daily Globe*, did "the masters of baseball" forget that America's mortal enemy, Nazi Germany, had domiciled the "boastful headquarters of the 'master race' theory?"[21] Journalists frequently quoted the tribute by Hector Racine, president of the Montreal Royals, to black efforts during World War II: "Negroes fought alongside whites and shared the foxhole dangers, and they should get a fair trial in baseball."[22] A *Pittsburgh Courier* respondent employed similar rhetoric: "Those who were good enough to fight by the side of the whites are plenty good enough to play by the side of whites!"[23] Ironically baseball, which during World War II was frequently employed as a patriotic icon, at conflict's end came to appear as a transgressor of American values.

So pervasive was the liberal consensus that even opponents of baseball integration generally exhibited careful avoidance of public statements that violated egalitarian principles. Rather than attacking integration directly, opponents typically utilized more circuitous stratagems. Critics sought to avoid the stigma of illiberalism. One tactic of obstructionists was to raise doubts about Robinson's baseball abilities. Ignoring Robinson's fine record in the Negro American League and employing sophistry to explain the failure of his own team to sign "Jackie" after having granted him a try-out, Eddie Collins, general manager of the Boston Red Sox, told the press, "Very few players can step off a sandlot or college diamond into a major league berth...."[24] A United Press release implied that Robinson's baseball skills might not measure up to his proficiency in other sports by juxtaposing football, basketball, and track achievements with a former coach's observation that "Jackie didn't try too hard at baseball...."[25] Terming Robinson's background in other sports a liability, Bob Feller, star pitcher for the Cleveland Indians, authored perhaps the most widely quoted expression of doubt about Robinson's baseball potential:

> He's a typical football player — they're all alike.... He is fast as blazes and a great athlete, but that doesn't make him a ball player.... Honestly, I can't see any chance at all for Robinson. And I'll say this — if he were a white man I doubt if they'd even consider him as big league material.[26]

Like others who questioned Robinson's future in baseball, Feller eschewed overt racism despite his belief that no contemporary black player possessed major league skills: "When you say things like that, somebody usually accuses you of racial discrimination ... but ... I'm not prejudiced in the least."[27] And an editorial in "the baseball bible," *The Sporting News*, pontificated, "Robinson, at 26, is reported to possess baseball abilities which, were he white, would make him eligible for a trial with, let us say, the Brooklyn Dodgers' Class B farm at Newport News, if he were six years younger ... the waters of the International League will flood far over his head."[28]

Silence, however, constituted the most common public image of non-support. Journalists frequently perceived those who refused to comment "cool" toward integration.[29] The *St. Louis Post-Dispatch*, believed, for example, that those who spoke "with extreme caution" left "the impression that they were pulling their punches."[30] Since reform could succeed only by eliciting a positive response from the public, reticence implicitly provided support for the existing arrangements that excluded blacks from Organized Baseball. With sophistry Bill Klem, Chief of Staff for the National League's umpires, justified his "no comment" by arguing, reported the United Press, "That's the proper stand for an umpire."[31] Connie Mack, dean of major league managers, told the *Philadelphia Inquirer*, "I am not familiar with the move. I don't know Robinson and wouldn't care to comment."[32] A *Sporting News* editorial regarded those who "refused to comment" more diplomatic and effective than those openly "blasting the hiring of a Negro."[33] One could thus impede integration without appearing to challenge the liberal consensus.

Critics of the Robinson signing often tried desperately to portray themselves as opponents of discrimination and thus the true proponents of American values. A number of newspaper articles reflected the viewpoint of individuals concerned that Robinson's entry into Organized Baseball would undermine the Negro leagues; this line of argument purported that the Negro leagues provided important opportunities for black entrepreneurs and athletes. Tom Baird, white co-owner of the Kansas City Monarchs, the Negro baseball team for which Robinson played during 1945, protested the "steal" of Robinson by Rickey.[34] Angry that Rickey had not reimbursed the Monarchs for Robinson, the Kansas City co-owner feared, "If the wholesale robbery of Negro players from our league continues we may as well quit baseball."[35] A *Washington Post* editorial agreed: "A general competition among major and minor league owners for the best Negro players would certainly wreck the Negro leagues and with them the not inconsiderable capital investment of Negro entrepreneurs."[36]

Some prominent figures from Organized Baseball also expressed concern that the signing of Robinson would prove detrimental to Negro baseball. According to the *Brooklyn Eagle*, Larry MacPhail, president of the New York Yankees,

> took the view that signing Negroes at the present time would do the cause of Negro baseball more harm than good. He pointed out that Negro baseball is now a $2,000,000 business and Negro clubs pay salaries ranging up to $16,000 a year.
> He pointed out that comparatively few good young Negro players were being developed. He feared that if Organized Baseball raided the Negro League and took their good young players, the Negro Leagues would fold, the investments of the club owners would be lost and a lot of professional Negro ball players would lose their jobs.[37]

Journalists frequently quoted the caveats of Clark Griffith, 75-year-old owner of the Washington Senators.[38] Condemning Rickey's signing of Robinson, Griffith denounced those who "steal" from the Negro leagues and "act like outlaws": "In no walk of life can one person take another's property unless he pays for it."[39] Griffith exhorted, "We have no right to destroy" the Negro leagues.[40] Griffith's dissatisfaction with the Robinson signing culminated in a long letter of counsel and praise for Negro baseball that the *New York Age*, a black newspaper, printed in its entirety. Part of the letter read:

> Your two (Negro) leagues have established a splendid reputation and now have the support and respect of the colored people all over this

country as well as the decent white people. They have not pirated against organized baseball nor have they stolen anything from them and organized baseball has no moral right to take anything from them without their consent.

Anything that is worth while is worth fighting for so you folks should leave not a stone unturned to protect the existence of your two established Negro leagues. Don't let anybody tear it down.[41]

Nevertheless, the press generally represented the attempt to link concern with the survival of Negro baseball with misgivings about the Robinson signing as a cynical distortion of American values. Negro newspapers, in particular, reflected a disdain for obstructionists who clothed themselves in the rhetoric of racial justice. Both the metropolitan and Afro-American press noted that some blacks connected with Negro baseball, such as Effa Manley, co-owner of the Newark Eagles, felt Rickey was wrong to sign Robinson without compensating his former team. The media agreed, however, with near unanimity that black America viewed integration as a more important goal than the economic prosperity of Negro baseball. Earl Brown, a columnist for the *Amsterdam News,* pointed out the illogic of owners of Negro baseball teams posing as apostles of opportunity for black athletes: "Most Negro ball clubs are owned by enterprising white men who pay a few star exhibitionists, such as Satchel Paige and Josh Gibson, good salaries, but who pay the average player starvation wages."[42] The *St. Louis Star Times* pointedly noted "that Baird is white, not a Negro." And the *Chicago Daily News* said of Baird's original statement, "The attitude of the Kansas City Monarchs in the Negro National League ... for whom Robinson played last year ... is not commendable. They should be enough interested in what Robinson may accomplish in the majors ... both for himself and his race ... to let him go without any monetary furor about it."[43]

The Negro press argued that obstructionists were disingenuous about their motives. Attributing Griffith's support for Negro baseball to his rapacity, the National Negro Press Association stressed that rentals of Griffith Stadium to the Homestead Grays, a black team, constituted a significant source of revenue.

The Old Fox, as Griff is known in organized baseball, is a shrewd business man.

It's his business acumen that causes him to compliment the National Negro League by saying it is well established and organized baseball shouldn't raid it by taking their players....

But Griff is no liberal by any means. Not until colored baseball made the turnstiles click in figures comparable to those of the Nationals did he allow colored clubs to play white clubs in Griffith Stadium.[44]

The *Amsterdam News* denounced the "unholy, reactionary, anti–Negro setup led by Clark Griffith 'for attempting' to beat Rickey's attempts to Americanize baseball and allow all qualified to do so to participants [sic]."[45] In addition many general circulation newspapers, such as the *St. Louis Globe-Democrat*, found Griffith's piety hypocritical given his disregard for the stability of Latin American baseball: "Certainly Clark Griffith of the Senators should have little to say about that. He's been raiding Cuban, Mexican and even South American leagues for playing talent for years and up to now we've heard little about his buying the players' contracts."[46] Likewise, several newspapers, including the *The Washington Post,* published Larry MacPhail's admission that self-interest influenced his position on the Robinson signing: "President Larry MacPhail of the Yankees admits that park rentals to colored teams at Yankee Stadium, Newark and Kansas City produce $100,000 in revenue for the Yankee chain annually."[47]

Negative images of the black leagues abounded in the Negro and general circulation press, but they possessed an almost visceral intensity in Afro-American newspapers. These criticisms extended beyond disappointment over black baseball's reaction to the Robinson signing. Noting the diffuse organizational structure of the Negro leagues, including an absence of binding player contracts, and the dominance of white promoters and entrepreneurs, numerous articles quoted Branch Rickey, "There is no Negro league as such as far as I am concerned. Negro baseball is in the zone of a racket...."[48] One of the most scathing indictments of Negro baseball appeared in the *Amsterdam News*:

> Mr. Rickey said one thing about Negro baseball with which I emphatically and enthusiastically concur: it is a racket. At least it was when I used to play on Negro teams and recent checks with sports writers (Negro) and players (also Negro) corroborated Mr. Rickey's and my statements.... There is little or no discipline among the ⌐¹   e league had no constitution, by-laws or wor⌐   r which to go ... and the league ⌐ ascending from the mogul's st⌐

But misgivings about Negro baseb   ˙mis-
management and corruption.

Discrimination, contemporary   ˙om
the American values but rather from   the
mid–1940s regarded integration as a ⌐   he
distinctions that radicals of a latter gei   ⌐-
ration and segregation were perceived   ⌐k
newspapers. Since the Negro press terme   , undemocratic,
and anti-American, images of Negro bast   ⌐noted an accommodation

to an unjust situation. Thus, a *Pittsburgh Courier* editorial condemned the "foolish protest" of those who felt protecting the sanctity of contractual agreements in the Negro leagues more important than advancing the cause of integration:

> For many years colored organizations and institutions have fought against jim crowism in major league baseball, and now that a small victory has been won with the selection of one colored player, it is annoying to have a wrench thrown into the machinery.
>
> Let us not at this juncture play the part of a crab in a barrel of crabs. Instead of trying to hamper those who have made a step forward, let us help them as much as we can.[50]

The assault against segregation, voluntary or involuntary, by several Afro-American publications included proposals to admit white players into black baseball and for the Negro leagues to become part of Organized Baseball.[51] A letter to the editor of the *Chicago Defender* reflects the disdain the black press typically directed at those who attempted to elevate "voluntary segregation" into a positive good:

> There are occasions when segregation is practical, due to the existing laws and traditions that are next to impossible to contest openly. A Negro youth in a southern community wishing to attend a college and his funds are limited, naturally should take advantage of the nearest institution until time warrants his condition as to improve upon this condition.
>
> But this is not enough. It is up to every Negro to aid himself and his entire group. If it's freedom from discrimination that we desire, then we should cast away all types of discrimination from our programs....
>
> The protest of the Negro baseballers is as selfish as any plantation owner of slavery-bound men in the days prior to the Civil War. Their own interest is above that of their nation. This is an appeal to all Negroes to avoid this, for their freedom means freedom to all men, and courage to men of other lands. Segregate yourselves and others will do no better.[52]

The general circulation press also overwhelmingly rejected, albeit with less vigor, attempts to portray black separation as compatible with American values. The *Boston Herald*, for example, related integration to "equal opportunity."[53]

Racism remained a national phenomena during the mid–1940s. Race riots in New York City and Detroit documented the intensity of group conflict. A shared consensus supporting the American Creed, brought to its zenith by World War II, made it difficult for Americans to acknowledge that their values deviated significantly from their behavior. A means was needed to recognize conflict without challenging the belief in consensus.

An emphasis on Southern exceptionalism became the means by which many Americans of the mid–1940s reconciled consensus and conflict. Racism and discrimination obviously existed, but they were typically termed Southern, rather than American, phenomena. Newspapers did acknowledge obstacles, actual and potential, that were not exclusively Southern — "icy stares and a boatload of caustic remarks," restrictive hotels in the North, "snobs and discrimination in cities where the Dodgers play other National League teams," "no little prejudice from a few members of his team," "insults," "racial strife in the grand stand," and a "terrible riding from the bench jockeys."[54] But references to racism outside the South were muted. Obviously the black press demonstrated a greater awareness of Northern racism. Yet even commentary in the black press on Northern racism lacked a certain precision. American racism during the Robinson controversy thus appeared an attribute primarily distinctive to the South; its people and its institutions, tarnished by segregation law and practice, deviated from the national consensus. Journalistic concern with Southern exceptionalism took on great importance due to the perception that the region significantly shaped baseball's ambiance, thus threatening the game's position as the National Pastime.

Despite the occasional use of code language, context left little doubt that phrases like "some parts of the United States where racial prejudice is rampant" meant the South.[55] "Although fans in Northern cities will be extremely friendly," the *Boston Herald* believed that "the Southern player and the Southern fan are in the wrong," ready to create "a most harrowing situation."[56] Journalists examining racism wrote of "the Southern attitude," "the Southern interests," "those in the South," and "the baseball constituency which hails from the South."[57] While not objecting to Robinson playing on integrated teams in the North, the sports editor of the Spartansburg (S.C.) *Herald Journal* warned, "Segregation in the South will continue to be an unalterable rule...." The Northern pattern of "Negroes and whites mix(ing) in practically every undertaking" was rejected by the Jackson (TN) *Sun:* "Here in the South we believe in the segregation of Negro and whites. This rule applies to baseball teams as well as to every other sport activity."[58] The press reported that both Branch Rickey, Jr., head of the Dodger farm system, and his father felt that most criticism of their actions would come from the South.[59]

As portrayed by the media, the South appeared a region apart. Judge William G. Bramham of Durham, the president of the National Association of minor leagues, received greater press visibility than any other advocate of separation to comment on the Robinson signing. Bramham, however, attempted to synthesize Southern exceptionalism and American values. Bramham presented himself as committed to justice for all people, both black and white. After Bramham noted with undisguised disappointment that the rules of the National Association provided him with no basis for disqualifying Robinson's contract, he claimed that segregation provided the most beneficent context for the advancement of blacks:

> It is my opinion that if the Negro is left alone and aided by his unselfish friends of the white race, he will work out his own salvation in all lines of endeavor.
> The Negro is making rapid strides in baseball, as well as other lines of endeavor. They have their own form of player contracts and, as I understand it, their organizations are well officered and are financially successful. Why should we raid their ranks, grab a player and put him, his baseball association and his race in a position that will inevitably prove harmful?[60]

Utilizing Reconstruction imagery to demonstrate that Southern paternalists understood blacks better than Northern liberals, Bramham told the press: "It is those of the carpet-bagger stripe of the white race under the guise of helping, but in truth using the Negro for their own selfish interests, who retard the race."[61] Writing for *The Sporting News*, Jack Horner of the *Durham Morning Herald* praised Bramham:

> Bramham has been an outstanding fighter for the Negro cause during his 40-odd years of residence in Durham. Bramham helped the Negroes form their own separate fire department. He has been influential in assisting the Negro to better his conditions in many other ways.[62]

Outside of the South, however, the press generally viewed Bramham as spokesman for a regional code that defied the national consensus.

The press made clear that not all Southerners camouflaged their racism in the paternalism and self-righteousness employed by Bramham. Unlike Bramham some Southern whites quoted by the press did not leaven their advocacy of racial separation with the assumption that such an arrangement would produce equality.[63] Fred (Dixie) Walker, a popular Brooklyn Dodger outfielder, for example, proclaimed that he most definitely did not want Robinson for a teammate: "As long as he isn't with the Dodgers, I'm not worried."[64] Likewise, Spud Davis, catcher-coach for the Pittsburgh Pirates, responded, "So long as the Pittsburgh Club hasn't signed a Negro there's no need for me to worry now."[65] George Digby was more emphatic: "I think it's the worst thing that can happen to organized baseball. I think a lot of Southern boys will refuse to compete with Negroes in baseball.[66]

Many newspapers published a prediction by Branch Rickey, Jr., which some mistakenly attributed to his father, that white Southerners might refuse to play for the Dodgers: " If they come from certain sections in the South, they may steer away from a team with colored players."[67] The younger Rickey then added, "But, they'll be back in baseball after a year or two in the cotton mill."[68] Significantly those journalistic acknowledgments of Southern resentment over the younger Rickey's remarks derived from his implication of a lack of resolve, not to his assumptions about regional racism. The *St. Louis Globe-Democrat*, for example, described the reaction of Southern athletes to young Rickey's statement from an interesting vantage point: "if the subject had been left untouched especially the sneering part about the cotton mills, the boys probably would have taken it even if they didn't like it."[69] Likewise, a *Sporting News* article argued "ball players resented the comment, since the majority of Southern boys in baseball came off the farms."[70]

Due to "strict race segregation laws" in Daytona Beach, Florida, site of the Dodger organization's pre-season training camp, "the possibility was considered," reported the United Press, "that the team may have its new recruit train somewhere north of the Mason-Dixon line...."[71] Journalists left little doubt that the South would enforce its "segregation rules," and that a black athlete would receive no exemption.[72] In Daytona Beach, commented *La Presse* (Montreal), "Robinson will not be permitted to live in the hotel as the other players of the Montreal club because of a special law. The city has also special lines of buses for men of color and for the white race."[73] A myriad of articles quoted the Daytona Beach city manager's concept of "a very good situation between the races here": "we never have had mixed teams."[74] With consistency media images cast the people, customs, and laws of the South as a threat to baseball integration.

Baseball, implied the media, had long violated the nation's egalitarian values due to the influence of the South. Often described as the national game, baseball, at this particular juncture, appeared in danger of becoming the Southern game. Just as the press exaggerated the South's role in promoting racism in the nation at large so it also facilely attributed baseball's conservatism to the Southern influence. Given that none of the 16 major league franchises were located further South than St. Louis, the press emphasis on Southern exceptionalism takes on an insistent tone. But farm team nurseries for the big leagues, asserted the *St. Louis Post-Dispatch*, frequently "operate below the Mason-Dixon line."[75] And with the war over and travel restrictions lifted the South would once again provide spring training sites for major league teams. Moreover, despite the Northeast and Midwest domiciles of major league franchises, "many big leaguers," emphasized numerous articles, "are from Southern areas."[76] Various estimates of the number of major league "players born below the Mason-Dixon line" appeared in the press, ranging from "approximately 27 percent," a fairly accurate count, to "a guess ... (of) 50 percent," a highly exaggerated figure.[77] The press could thus attribute baseball's conservatism to a regional aberration without questioning the national commitment to liberal values. Scribes found college football, track, boxing, and army athletics less restrictive than baseball. A *Detroit News* editorial stated, "More than most sports, organized baseball clings to ... color line."[78] And a *Boston Daily Globe* editorial employed sarcasm: "In other fields of sport, news percolated around long ago that Grant had taken Richmond. Baseball has hitherto displayed hesitation about crediting that somewhat ancient news."[79]

Despite a predilection for identifying racism with Southern exceptionalism, Americans tended to believe, that in time the South would conform to national standards. Certain media images offered hope that, despite deeply entrenched prejudice, the Robinson episode would eventually help move the South into the mainstream of American life. Some Northern journalists suggested that segments of the Southern press questioned the South's racial protocols. The *New York Age* generalized, "Sports writers by and large, North and South, have given Robinson good press."[80] The United Press also indicated, "With few exceptions ... Sports writers both north and south of the Mason Dixon line agreed that it was eminently fair that a Negro should have a chance to play in organized baseball...."[81] A few Afro-American and sporting publications even featured compilations of Southern press opinion. Representative of the Southern press comment most favorable to Robinson were assessments similar to the following — "if Jackie Robinson hits homers and plays a whale of a game ... the fans will lose sight of his color"; "If he is qualified, then give him an opportunity"; "A star is a star no matter what his race"; and "It all makes far keener competition and most definitely will raise the standard of major league baseball...."[82] Acknowledging that some Southern journalists adopted a progressive stance on the race issue, however, did not fundamentally alter the media's perception of the region's dissent from national values. Nevertheless, paralleling the younger Rickey's "they'll be back" prognosis, several pundits hoped that a transformation of Southern values would follow the initial period of turbulence. For instance, an editorial in the black *Michigan Chronicle*, declared, " It is our guess, like that of the Dodger management, that the southern white boys who may be shocked will recover in due time. A good stiff democratic shock in the right place might do them a lot of good."[83]

Several black and general circulation newspapers contended that Robinson had, and thus could again, help Southerners to recognize the incompatibility of their regional code with national values. Jackie Reemes,

Amsterdam News reporter, wrote: "I can recall Robinson's basketball days at U.C.L.A. There were several southern white boys on the team with Robinson who handled any opposing players who unduly roughed up colored members of U.C.L.A. If those lads, three of them from the heart of Texas, learned to overcome their prejudices others can and will learn the same lesson."[84] Southern exceptionalism thus obstructed the liberal consensus, but time and effort, suggested the press, would render justice triumphant over regional conservatism. Not surprisingly, given the association drawn between baseball and Southern exceptionalism, the press frequently depicted the redemption of the National Pastime emanating from forces external to the game. Many images of Rickey as an emancipator appeared, and more than one pundit discovered Lincolnesque qualities in Rickey. Some journalists called the Dodger president a "hero," a "savior," "courageous," "meritorious," "liberal," "sincere," "just," "democratic," "idealistic," "righteous," and "strong hearted."[85] Other images, however, leavened praise for Rickey's altruism and morality. Both the black and general circulation press frequently suggested that Rickey was not the prime mover behind the game's belated experiment in integration. Many articles contained Rickey's denials that he had yielded to outside forces. "No pressure groups had anything to do with it...." Rickey told the Associated Press.[86] Yet, a wire service article reported his admission that macrocosmic considerations made integration an inevitability: "racial equality in all sports must be an eventual fact...."[87] Employing contradictory logic, Rickey steadfastly portrayed himself immune to influence emanating from outside Organized Baseball while acknowledging, "some of these owners who declared that they're not going to hire Negro players are going to run into difficulty.... This is a movement that cannot be stopped by anyone."[88] Referring to antidiscrimination legislation, the Dodger owner confessed to *The Sporting News*, "The time is nearing fast when every professional baseball club operating in the state of New York will have to hire Negro players."[89] Thus, Rickey portrayed himself as a free agent while depicting societal pressures foreclosing traditional options to his fellow owners. Rickey's claims of exemption from external considerations, however, did not emerge as the dominant media perception of events. A plethora of articles served to undermine the inclination to view Rickey as a disinterested moralist. According to the Associated Press, for example, Rickey himself admitted, "I have never meant to be a crusader, and I hope I won't be regarded as one."[90] Typically journalists implied that forces outside of baseball were prodding the game to reflect the national consensus.

Although the normative media approach to this episode recognized the salutary influence of pressures external to baseball on the game, a minority response articulated misgivings about the impact of such outside forces. Ed Danforth, sports editor of the *Atlanta Journal*, warned, "The only menace to peace between the races is the carpet-bagger white press and agitators in the Negro press who capitalize on racial issues to exploit themselves."[91] Writing for *The Sporting News*, Joe Williams recalled memories of having witnessed "the Negro ... cruelly victimized by pressure groups, social frauds and political demagogues."[92] Likewise, a *Cleveland Press* sportswriter denigrated "high-geared groups (who) tried to force their way into the major leagues...."[93] Much more common in both the black and general circulation press, however, was the belief that outside influences had a positive impact on the National Pastime.

Journalists claimed "the long-sought opening wedge into the big leagues"[94] represents the first success scored by all the organizations and individuals who have been clamoring for big league baseball to end its ... discrimination against colored ball players."[95] Dave Egan, sportswriter for the *Boston Daily Record*, believed "major league moguls" would not truly accept integration "until public opinion forces them to accept the basic principles of such an old and conservative document as the Constitution of the United States of America."[96] Some general circulation newspapers, including the *Philadelphia Record*, congratulated themselves for prompting Rickey's decision. More frequently, however, the white press attributed the integration of baseball to "all the recent laws and rulings aimed at an end of racial discrimination." The *Baltimore Morning Sun*, for example, noted "that the legislatures of many states had passed bills in recent years aimed at eliminating racial prejudice."[97] The *New York Post* acknowledged that the "anti-discrimination Ives-Quinn law, written into the New York State statutes this summer, increased the demands of those organizations, who now had the law on their side."[98] And some articles in general circulation journals commented on efforts by Negroes themselves to create opportunities for blacks in Organized Baseball.

For their part, black newspapers thanked white allies for their assistance. The *Amsterdam News*, for example, "spotlighted the liberal viewpoint of Gov. Thomas E. Dewey of New York, whose insistence that a State Fair Employment Practice Commission be established, formed the opening wedge by which Negroes are being integrated into all avenues of employment, including professional sports."[99] Similarly, the *Boston Guardian* praised the "Boston *Daily Record* ace sports columnist, Dave (The Colonel) Egan ... (who) led the fight in the daily newspapers...."[100] To a much greater extent than the general circulation press, however, the black press emphasized that the efforts of Negroes themselves played a pivotal role in forcing baseball to acknowledge its delinquency. Negro newspapers

pointed to black civil rights organizations, bl~~¹~~   ion, and black
standard bearers who contribut~~ed~~   of Negroes for
the white major leagues to   ."¹⁰¹

The Negro press tend   e behind the
signing of Robinson. Sam L   *Afro-Amer-*
ican, remarked, "I have had   impaign to
break down the major league   *on Chron-*
icle writer claimed, "This colu   nany seasons at the illogical viewpoint"   tegration
of Organized Baseball."¹⁰³ The   fforts ...
of colored writers."¹⁰⁴ Readers o   ...ded that
"Dr. C.B. Powell, editor of the *A*   .. was a member of the
... commission against discrim   ... which drafted the Ives-Quinn
Bill...."¹⁰⁵ Don Le Leighbur wrote in the *Philadelphia Tribune*, "I have been
in the forefront of the fight for years against these reactionaries in organized baseball to relax color bans...."¹⁰⁶ The *Pittsburgh Courier* reminded
readers of "its intensive campaign to smash the color barriers in organized
major league baseball...."¹⁰⁷ Although Negro pundits differed about the
importance of their own individual contributions to the campaign against
discrimination, they agreed that the collective efforts of the black press
had a decisive influence on the signing of Robinson. A number of articles
employed Robinson's tribute to the black press for confirmation:¹⁰⁸ "I cannot thank the Negro press too much ... for the wonderful things they have
said and done in my behalf and in behalf of the hundreds of other Negro
ballplayers down through the years."¹⁰⁹ Indeed, a *Baltimore Afro-Ameri-*
can headline exclaimed, "It's a press victory...." Recent scholarship suggests that the black press did indeed make vital contributions to the long
campaign to eradicate segregation from Organized Baseball.¹¹⁰ The historian David Wiggins, for example, has documented the nearly twelve year
publicity campaign waged by the *Pittsburgh Courier* against Jim Crow practices in the National Pastime.¹¹¹ As believers in the liberal consensus, black
journalists congratulated themselves for forcing Organized Baseball to
yield to national values.

American values synthesized self-interest and mortality. Baseball integration, implied the press, would promote utilitarian benefits for both
blacks and whites. By signing Robinson, suggested scribes, Rickey had chosen to transform blacks into an opportunity for the Dodgers specifically
and for Organized Baseball in general. Both the black and general circulation press gave much attention to the benefits they believed Rickey would
soon derive. The *New York Times* depicted Rickey primarily motivated by
a desire "to win baseball games."¹¹² Black players constituted a potentially

rich reservoir of untapped talent for a man anxious to "win the pennant for Brooklyn."[113] In the *New York Age*, "Buster" Miller wrote, "he (Rickey) was in the market for a shortstop and went and bought what he thought was the best he could get for his money. Don't we all, whether its shortstops, shoes or sealing wax, cabbages or kings?"[114] Other newspapers, including the *Philadelphia Record*, reinforced the perception that integration would prove "profitable" to Organized Baseball.[115] Alluding to the growing presence of blacks in the urban North, several articles viewed the Robinson signing as a ploy to attract black fans: "If Negro players were included in the lineups of the major league teams, many new fans undoubtedly would be recruited from the large colored populations of cities like New York and Chicago."[116]

Perhaps the most representative media image germane to the Robinson signing derived from a widely quoted remark by Frank Shaughnessy, president of the International League. Shaughnessy endorsed racial integration "as long as any fellow's the right type and can make good and can get along with other players .[117] A *Sporting News* article, considering the various opinions expressed, declared, "Shaughnessy ... seemed to strike the most intelligent note."[118] Numerous articles echoed Shaughnessy's assumption that Organized Baseball would give the "right type" of black a fair trial. With few exceptions the media employed phraseology, such as "right type of fellow," "right man," "right boy," "a credit to the race," "no better candidate," "ideal candidate," and "ideal Negro," that portrayed Robinson as a good choice to reintegrate baseball."[119] The Robinson portrayed by the media was "the right type" because rather than challenge the liberal consensus he appeared to apotheosize it.

Athletic skills alone were not sufficient to win Robinson "the right type" designation. Nevertheless, both the general circulation and black press gave extensive and glowing attention to Robinson's accomplishments while a collegiate football, track, basketball, and baseball star and to his stellar performance for the Kansas City Monarchs, a Negro American League team.[120] Yet Rickey and much of the press knew that there were better and more experienced baseball players in Negro baseball than Robinson.[121] The Robinson described by the press in the aftermath of his signing was not the man the press would depict in latter years. Recognizing that "the right type" of black would encounter fewer difficulties, the Dodger president and the Negro athlete became collaborators.[122] Robinson's intelligence, poise, courage, and athletic ability were assets, but his independence and his anger, actually more radical in its intensity than its content, might have made him appear a critic of American values if not muted. As part of Rickey's stratagem for ameliorating opposition to the integration of Organized Baseball, Robinson, for a time, agreed to assume the personae of "the right type" of Negro.[123]

At times misinformation or omissions served to reinforce positive images of "Jackie's" personal history. Many articles referred to the migration of Robinson's family "when he was a year old" from Cairo, Georgia, to Pasadena, California.[124] Yet articles that appeared in print during 1945 failed to acknowledge one of the major reason's for the migration: Robinson's father had deserted the family.[125] The *Philadelphia Record*, for example, printed Robinson's fallacious account of the past: "I've never known my father. He died when I was a baby."[126] Miscegenation, like familial instability, might pose image difficulties for an individual seeking identification with the values integral to the national consensus. But the press clearly implied nocturnal adventures, interracial or otherwise, obviously held little appeal for a man who planned to soon marry a woman he had known since his college days.[127] The *Philadelphia Evening Bulletin* went as far as to explicitly identify Robinson's fiancee as "a Negro."[128]

The building of a usable history extended to Robinson's education. Copious references to Robinson's association with the University of California at Los Angeles appeared in the press.[129] Repeated use of phrases such as "college bred," "an educated man," and "was educated" juxtaposed with references to "UCLA" implied Robinson graduated college.[130] Very few articles admitted that Robinson did not receive a degree, and even these extremely atypical accounts generally invented compelling excuses for Robinson's withdrawal from UCLA. The *Sporting News*, for example, gave the false impression that "he was a senior at University of California in Los Angeles" when he patriotically "enlisted" in the army.[131] Long after Robinson signed his first Organized Baseball career he candidly described his decision to quit college: "After two years at UCLA I decided to leave. I was convinced that no amount of education would help a black man get a job."[132] In 1945, such an admission by a black might have appeared as disillusionment with American values.

Likewise, journalistic ellipses and inaccuracies distorted Robinson's military record. Numerous articles noted that Robinson was a "former army lieutenant."[133] Yet sportswriters omitted the most significant aspect of Robinson's army career; he faced court-martial, "charged with willful disobedience and disrespect."[134] The episode evolved from Robinson's refusal to submit to racial discrimination on a bus at Camp Hood, and he was ultimately acquitted.[135] Acknowledging that baseball violated the liberal consensus was legitimate; the "right type" of black did not, however, suggest that national values were unjust. A number of journalists also attributed "31 months overseas" service to Robinson although he remained stateside during the war.[136] The media Robinson was defender, not critic, of the American creed.

"The right type" imagery enveloped every aspect of Robinson's personality and character. Almost uniformly the media portrayed Robinson's devotion to values sanctioned by the national consensus — patriotism, patience, self-denial, and hard work. Black newspapers often appeared even more eager than the general circulation press to identify Robinson with these values. According to the Pittsburgh *Courier*, Robinson coupled gratitude toward Rickey with appreciation of country: "when I think of this opportunity, I'm very glad that I'm an American, because with all its so-called faults, it's the only place in the world where a young man can get such a chance — a chance to make a success out of life on his ability."[137] Images of Robinson's "confidence," "self-assurance," "intelligent" manner, and determination to strive for his "best" appeared within a journalistic context that frequently alluded to the athlete's "level-headed," "shy," "well-behaved," "quiet," "modest," "responsible," and "sincere" demeanor.[138] Devoid of bravado, Robinson, as portrayed by the media, was "a high type of fellow" and "a high-class citizen."[139] His "good habits" and a "good character" encompassed abstinence from "drink or smoke."[140] Restraint and caution figured prominently among the traits newspapers attributed to this "fine type of young man."[141] The image of Robinson as deferential and soft-spoken that the press projected in 1945 differed markedly from the athlete's true self. Rickey and Robinson were thus successful in encouraging the press to view the athlete as "the right type" of black, one who sought to affirm, not challenge, American values. For the liberal consensus would reciprocate by demanding equality of opportunity for Robinson. In contrast the "bad nigger" imagery — carnality, miscegenation, bravado, iconoclasm, flamboyance, hostility toward whites, assertiveness, and irresponsibility — once embodied by boxer Jack Johnson, evoked fear from white Americans. Joe Louis, the current heavyweight champion, had already demonstrated the press' willingness to identify "the right type" of black with the liberal consensus.[142]

The American press displayed little sense of irony that a foreign country would host the integration of the National Pastime. Some elements of the Canadian press did engage in self-congratulatory comparisons between the two nations, and the Pittsburgh *Courier* was also impressed by the benevolence of "French Canadian fans."[143] Nevertheless, typically American newspapers, including the black press, implicitly portrayed Montreal's ambiance as an extension of the racial practices normative north of the Mason-Dixon line. Newspapers perceived Rickey's assignment of Robinson to the Montreal Royals as an attempt to minimize Southern interference with integration of baseball. Both Afro-American and general circulation journals noted that, aside from the Daytona Beach training camp and a franchise in the border city of Baltimore, the Montreal Royals would avoid areas influenced by Southern mores.[144] In addition to Montreal and Baltimore, the International League included Jersey City, Newark, Toronto, Rochester, and Syracuse. Due to the nature of "International League membership," host cities other than Baltimore, reported the United Press, "were expected to show no unusual interest" in a black athlete.[145] Outside the South "the right type" of black, indicated journalists, could expect the fair trial dictated by national ideology.

While journalistic opinion overwhelmingly favored granting "the right type" of black "the chance ... to make the big league grade,"[146] neither the general circulation nor Afro-American press suggested that a Negro athlete should receive special consideration. The *St. Louis Argus* counseled blacks to remember that they shared in Robinson's testing and warned "Tan" fans of "Jackie's" against "loud provocative remarks" that would "stir race hatred."[147] The liberal consensus encouraged those who espoused equal opportunity for Robinson to often neglect the obvious: historical deprivation and endemic racism necessitated positive intervention on Robinson's behalf to create conditions amenable to equal opportunity. Endorsements for such positive intervention extended no further than supporting Rickey's pledge to take "adequate steps" against players in the Dodger organization who "openly worked against Robinson."[148] Without hesitation, however, Rickey indicated that Robinson would not remain in Montreal "if he doesn't make good...."[149] The press did not seek absolute assurances that major league rosters would include black players. Media images reflected no significant pleas for guarantees in regard to outcome. Essentially the burden rested with Robinson to "go as far as he can."[150] A headline in the *Syracuse Herald-Journal*, for example, proclaimed, "Player Must Prove Worth on Diamond."[151] Although Arthur Siegel, *Boston Traveler* sportswriter, called the signing of Robinson "very nice," Siegel asked, "Is he (Robinson) of fast enough caliber to make the International League team?"[152] "Whether Jackie Robinson is or is not a good ballplayer," stated the *Saturday Review of Literature*, "is the only question at issue."[153] Robinson himself, suggested scribes, felt his fate should hinge only on his abilities.[154]

Nor did the black press ask any more for Robinson than a trial decided "solely on his baseball merits."[155] "Can Jackie Make The Grade?" questioned a *Detroit Tribune* article: "Branch Rickey may have opened the gates ... but it is up to Jackie himself to prove whether he can stay inside the field."[156] The "End Jim Crow in Baseball Committee," stated the *Amsterdam*

News, felt only a "competent Negro player who is qualified" should "play in the major leagues."[157] Likewise, the Pittsburgh *Courier* shared Rickey's aspiration that the Robinson's episode could become "just a matter of giving another young man a chance."[158] Unlike racial spokesmen of a latter generation the contemporary black press's interpretation of opportunity did not include quotas or affirmative action. All Negroes wanted, indicated the *Michigan Chronicle,* was acceptance "on the basis of merit."[159]

The prevailing consensus largely checked the impulse to portray baseball segregation as a microcosm of American society. Instead the press generally depicted the Robinson signing as a stratagem for redeeming the National Pastime. Relatively few media images suggested that the signing of Robinson was a disproportionately modest response to combat a problem as central to the social structure as racism. Even that media commentary most derisive of baseball's conservatism generally avoided placing such phenomena within a context that implied the game merely reflected national life. Dave Egan, for example, of the Boston *Daily Record,* charged, "generations of Jackie Robinsons now dead and gone must have smiled indulgently, when Christy Matthewson was called the greatest pitcher of all time, when they felt, all along the black Matthewson, Joe Mendez, was entitled to the place reserved for whites alone in the Hall of Fame."[160] Likewise, the Cleveland *Plain Dealer* believed, incorrectly as it turned out, that time had run out for the great Satchel Paige.[161] As *The Washington Post* noted, if Rickey truly regarded talent as the only germane criteria for evaluating an athlete, baseball integration might have occurred years ago.[162] These general circulation newspapers, however, reminded readers that baseball had arrived too late for many great Negro athletes without characterizing national life off the diamond as suffused with racism.

Criticism of baseball's recalcitrance was more apparent in the black press than in the general circulation press. Although accolades for Rickey appeared in the Pittsburgh *Courier,* this same newspaper carried lawyer Louis Nizer's statement "that what the Montreal Royals did in signing Jackie Robinson should have been done many years ago."[163] Earl Brown, a black columnist, expressed bitterness over "the fact that Jackie Robinson, a young Negro who is intellectually, culturally and physically superior to most white baseball players, has signed a contract to play in a minor league has caused a national sensation."[164] Similarly, the *Amsterdam News* printed the caveat of a civil rights group that "this is only the beginning...."[165] Writing for the *Michigan Chronicle,* Horace White strongly argued that tokenism of the sort employed by Rickey exploited blacks:

> The minority groups usually succumb to these controls of the majority group. One way of succumbing to the controls of the majority is

to bite for every sap that the majority group hands out. The assigning
of a Negro to a berth in organized baseball is an example of what is
meant here. The Negro population has been lead to believe that
Negroes have gained something by the very fact that the young man
has been assigned to play with the Brooklyn Dodgers. Still, nothing has
been gained. [166]

Even within the black press, however, White's tone was unusual.
White clearly believed that the mere signing of a single black to an Organized Baseball contract failed to address a problem with dimensions broad
as that of American racism. The extent of his resentment was atypical. In
the black press strong disapproval of baseball's illiberalism almost always
avoided suggesting a general disillusionment with American values.

The liberal consensus evident in press commentary on the signing of
Robinson closely resembles the mid–1940s American Creed described by
Gunnar Myrdal. Despite regional, class, and racial distinctions, Myrdal
reported "that most Americans have most valuations in common." This
shared Creed, stated Myrdal, is for "liberty, equality, justice, and fair
opportunity for everybody." Myrdal argued that the prevalence of group
and individual strife did not vitiate the consensus supporting the American Creed. Indeed, he perceived the need to reconcile belief with practice
the nation's central dilemma. And no issue, Myrdal asserted, more vividly
illuminated those contradictions than the status of the American Negro.
World War II made domestic dissent from the tenets of the American Creed
most difficult. "In fighting fascism and Nazism," wrote Myrdal, "America
had to stand before the whole world in favor of racial tolerance and cooperation and of racial equality." Even racists found it difficult to publicly
disavow the Creed. Despite discrimination, blacks, argued Myrdal,
endorsed the values of the American Creed: "Negroes show, by taking that
position, that they have not lost their belief that ultimately the American
Creed will come out on top." Northerners, contended Myrdal, exaggerated
the South's contributions to contemporary racism. Perhaps even more
significant, Americans, he reported, seriously minimized the extent of
racial conflict in the North.[167]

Examination of press reaction to the Robinson signing suggests that
Americans had little awareness of the extent and severity of racism in the
nation's social fabric. The media fallaciously depicted prejudice as largely
a regional problem. Race riots, housing discrimination, limited employment opportunities, and economic disparities make clear that the liberal
consensus described a belief system rather than empirical phenomena.[168]
Most Americans, however, mistook their values for both a system of belief
and a method of operation while, in fact, it constituted only the former.

By emphasizing unity, consensus, commonality, and agreement, the liberal consensus obscured conflict. Analysis of the mid–1940s media attests to the pervasiveness of shared values. A people highly cognizant of their similarities found it difficult to acknowledge their differences. It was possible to acknowledge isolated defiance of the consensus, as with Southern exceptionalism, but to acknowledge a sociological divergence from that belief system endemic to national life would throw into question the essence of the consensus, the belief that it could compel compliance from Americans. Furthermore, World War II encouraged Americans to view the United States in terms of characteristics antithetical to the racism and illiberalism of Nazi Germany. The crusade against Hitler nurtured a sense of national exaltation that acted as a deterrent against acknowledging the severity of America's domestic problems. Thus, in the mid–1940s a consensus about values flourished despite the existence of significant social conflict. Racism, a major contradiction to the consensus, could thus appear a manifestation of an atavistic region's refusal to conform to the consensus rather than as a criticism of the American way of life itself. Americans could then keep "to liberalism as a national creed, even if not as its actual way of life."[169]

In retrospect it is apparent that the signing of Robinson was primarily a symbolic breakthrough. Over the next decade integration in America proceeded slowly even within the context of baseball. Five years after the signing of Robinson, only a dozen blacks had played in the big leagues, and until late July 1959, fourteen years after the announced reintegration of baseball, the Boston Red Sox excluded Negroes from their lineup. No black managed in the major leagues until 1975. Indeed, in the 1990s blacks remain grossly under represented at the coaching, managerial, executive, and entrepreneurial levels of baseball. "Stacking," the practice of concentrating black athletes at certain positions, still continues.[170] More significantly, the emphasis on symbolism obscured the irony that as the Dodgers accepted racial integration, de facto segregation increased in Brooklyn and in many other Northern cities in the years following the signing of Robinson. The emphasis on symbolism detracted from attention to racism outside the South, contributing to the "invisible man" phenomena of the 1950s.

Extensive analysis of the contemporary print media reveals a nearly universal belief in the American Creed on both sides of the color line. As Myrdal recognized, blacks, as well as whites, tended to believe in the promise of the Creed: "The American Negroes know that they are a subordinated group experiencing more than anybody else in the nation the consequence of the fact that the Creed is not lived up to in America. Yet their faith in the Creed is not simply a means of pleading their unfulfilled rights. They, like the whites, are under the spell of the great national suggestion. With one part of themselves they actually believe, as do the whites, that the Creed is ruling America."[171] Black and white journalists generally shared similar assumptions about the benevolence of the American Creed. Excerpts from two letters, one written to a black newspaper and the other to a general circulation journal reflect this common perspective. The Chicago *Defender* correspondent wrote, "the placement of a Negro in major league baseball is very encouraging. At last America's favorite pastime has accepted the democratic principle that accompanies the American ideal."[172] An epistle to the *Baltimore Morning Sun* articulated the same sentiment, "The recent signing of a Negro player by a major league baseball club was a definite step toward the attainment of that American way of life chartered by our forebears."[173] Unlike militants of the late 1960s social critics of the mid–1940s reflected an ideological consensus; injustice, they believed, deviated from, rather than expressed, American values. Thus, "the right type" of black could redeem Organized Baseball from Southern practices and allow the game to once again truly embody American values. Sportswriters were wrong, however. To deal with racism effectively, Americans had to acknowledge it as more than a regional malady. "The Negro problem," wrote Myrdal, "is an integral part of ... the larger American civilization. It cannot be treated in isolation."[174]

The ideological consensus suggested by media reaction to the Robinson signing obviously did not signify social consensus. Juxtaposing the near unanimity of the liberal response to the Robinson signing with race riots, housing and employment discrimination, the confinement of Japanese-Americans to concentration camps, and other contemporary phenomena indicates consensus about values amid social conflict. Media reactions to the signing of Robinson criticized the particular, the South and Organized Baseball, while exalting the universal, the American Creed. External conflict stimulated internal cohesion, and World War II created a need to define America in terms diametrically opposed to those embodied by Nazi Germany.

Jackie Robinson's courage challenged the nation to live up to the American Creed. An ESPN documentary reveals that "plans to boycott Robinson if he stepped on the field ... suggest a virtual conspiracy."[175] Robinson's wife Rachel recalls "deliberate efforts to physically hurt him, "abusive language," "vicious baiting," and death threats.[176] Yet, despite enduring the furnace of racism, Robinson still struggled to create an America shaped by the Creed. As Roger Kahn recounts,

He does not want society to burn. Burn America and you burn the achievements of Jackie Robinson. After ruinous, anarchic blaze, who will remember the brave, fatherless boyhood, the fight for an inch of Army justice, the courage in baseball, the leadership and the triumph of a free man who walked with swift and certain strides.[177]

Jackie Robinson facilitated progress, significant albeit incomplete, against racism both in baseball and the larger society. Jules Tygiel observes that "the elements that contributed to the desegregation of baseball — direct confrontation and personal courage, economic pressures and moral persuasion by the mass media — have been recreated in many other areas of American life."[178] Future progress, however, is impeded by the partial eclipse of the American Creed.

In the years directly following World War II, the American Creed possessed a power that it no longer fully retains. Today the politically correct shrilly deride the Creed as an amalgam of hypocrisy and oppression. White and blacks have expressed such different attitudes toward the Rodney King and O.J. Simpson trials as to question whether they any longer share a common creed. Christopher Darden, an African-American attorney and a prosecutor in the Simpson criminal trial, asserts of contemporary American values: "for many people, black and white ... justice is in the eye of the beholder. Justice is defined by race."[179] Jackie Robinson reminds us of a time when the American Creed was a vital force for social justice. "And," concludes Tygiel, "if the vision of an integrated and equal society, free from racism and discrimination, which impelled Rickey and Robinson to launch their 'great experiment,' remains unfulfilled, their efforts have brought it closer to reality."[180]

Notes

1. An earlier version of this study appeared as William Simons, "Jackie Robinson and the American Mind: Journalistic Perceptions of the Reintegration of Baseball," *Journal of Sport History*, 12 (Spring 1985): 39–64.

2. Gunnar Myrdal with Richard Sterner and Arnold Rose, *An American Dilemma: The Negro Problem and Modern Democracy* (New York: Harper & Brothers Publishers, 1944), 4.

3. Doris Kearns Goodwin, *No Ordinary Time: Franklin & Eleanor Roosevelt: The Home Front in World War II* (New York: Simon & Schuster, 1994), 627.

4. Goodwin, *No Ordinary Time*, 626.

5. William L. O'Neill, *A Democracy at War: America's Fight at Home & Abroad in World War II* (New York: The Free Press, 1993), 430.

6. G. Edward White, *Creating the National Pastime: Baseball Transforms Itself, 1903–1953* (Princeton: Princeton University Press, 1996), 147–148.

7. *Boston Herald*, Oct. 24, 1945, 24; *Detroit Tribune*, Nov. 3, 1945, 11; *New York World Telegram*, Oct. 25, 1945, 30.

8. Steven Riess, *Touching Base: Professional Baseball and American Culture in the Progressive Era* (Westport Conn.: Greenwood Press, 1980), 7; Richard Goldstein, *Spartan Seasons: How Baseball Survived the Second World War* (New York: 1980), 33.

9. *St. Louis Argus*, Nov. 3, 1945, 17.

10. *Pittsburgh Courier*, Nov. 3, 1945, 13.

11. *Amsterdam News* (New York), Nov. 3, 1945.

12. Editorial, *Brooklyn Eagle*, Oct. 25, 1945, 12.

13. Letter to the Editor, *Detroit News*, Oct. 30, 1945, 14.

14. *Pittsburgh Courier*, Nov. 3, 1945, 13.

15. *The Sporting News*, Nov. 1, 1945, 6; *Philadelphia Record*, Oct. 25, 1945, 18.

16. *New York World Telegram*, Oct. 25, 1945, 30; *Washington Daily News*, Oct. 25, 1945, 34; *Cleveland Plain Dealer*, Oct. 26, 1945, 19.

17. Editorial, *St. Louis Post-Dispatch*, Oct. 25, 1945, 26.

18. *New York World Telegram*, Oct. 25, 1945, 30; *Washington Daily News*, Oct. 25, 1945, 38; *Washington Evening Star*, Oct. 25, 1945, 16.

19. *New York Daily Mirror*, Oct. 25, 1945, 26.

20. *Montreal Gazette,* Oct. 24, 1945, 14.

21. *Boston Daily Globe*, Oct. 25, 1945, 14.

22. *Cleveland Press*, Oct. 24, 1945, 16; *La Presse* (Montreal), Oct. 27, 1945, 36; *Washington Daily News*, Oct. 24, 1945, 40.

23. *Pittsburgh Courier*, Nov. 3, 1945, 12.

24. *Boston Daily Globe*, Oct. 24, 1945, 17.

25. *Philadelphia Inquirer*, Oct. 15, 1945, 24.

26. *Baltimore Afro-American*, Nov. 10, 1945, 18; *Chicago Daily News*, Oct. 31, 1945, 29; *Washington Post*, Oct. 25, 1945, 22.

27. *Syracuse Herald Journal*, Oct. 27, 1945, 6.

28. *The Sporting News*, Nov. 1, 1945, 12.

29. *Baltimore Afro-American*, Nov. 3, 1945, 23; *Pittsburgh Courier*, Dec. 1, 1945, 12.

30. *St. Louis Post-Dispatch*, Oct. 28, 1945, 1B.

31. *Detroit News*, Oct. 25, 1945, 46.

32. *Philadelphia Inquirer*, Oct. 24, 1945, 28.

33. *The Sporting News*, Nov. 1, 1945, 12.

34. *Cleveland Press*, Oct. 24, 1945, 16.

35. *Washington Daily News*, Oct. 24, 1945, 40.

36. *Washington Post*, Oct. 27, 1945, 10.

37. *Brooklyn Eagle*, Oct. 24, 1945, 17.

38. *Detroit News*, Oct. 25, 1945, 46; *New York Herald Tribune*, Oct. 25, 1945, 26; *New York Times*, Oct. 24, 1945, 17.

39. *Boston Daily Globe*, Oct. 25, 1945, 8; *Montreal Gazette*, Oct. 25, 1945, 16; *Philadelphia Inquirer*, Oct. 25, 1945, 24.

40. *Chicago Daily Tribune*, Oct. 25, 1945, 29; *Cleveland Plain Dealer*, Oct. 25, 1945, 16.

41. *New York Age*, Nov. 17, 1945, 75.

42. *Amsterdam News* (New York), Nov. 3, 1945, 12.

43. *Chicago Daily News*, Oct. 25, 1945, 33.

44. *Amsterdam News* (New York), Nov. 10, 1945, 10.

45. *Amsterdam News* (New York), Nov. 17, 1945, 24.

46. *St. Louis Globe Democrat*, Oct. 25, 1945, 36.

47. *Washington Post*, Oct. 27, 1945, 18; *New York World Telegram*, Oct. 25, 1945, 30; *New York Sun*, Oct. 25, 1945, 29.

48. *Chicago Defender*, Nov. 3, 1945, 9; *Philadelphia Record*, Oct. 25, 1945, 18; *Syracuse Post-Standard*, Oct. 24, 1945, 10.

49. *Amsterdam News* (New York), Nov. 3, 1945, 12.

50. *Pittsburgh Courier*, Nov. 24, 1945, 6.

51. *Philadelphia Tribune*, Dec. 29, 1945, 9; *St. Louis Argus*, Nov. 2, 1945, 17; *Amsterdam News* (New York), Nov. 3, 1945, 14.

52. Letter to Editor, *Chicago Defender*, Nov. 10, 1945, 14.

53. *Boston Herald*, Oct. 24, 1945, 24.

54. *Baltimore Afro-American*, Nov. 10, 1945, 18; *Boston Daily Globe*, Oct. 24, 1945, 22; *Boston Guardian*, Nov. 3, 1945, 4; Editorial, *Detroit Tribune*, Nov. 3, 1945, 6; *Amsterdam News* (New York), Nov. 10, 1945, 13; *Brooklyn Eagle*, Oct. 31, 1945, 17.

55. *Chicago Herald American*, Oct. 26, 1945, 29; *New York Times*, Oct. 25, 1945, 16.

56. *Boston Herald*, October 24, 1945, 24.

57. *Pittsburgh Courier*, Nov. 3, 1945, 1; *The Sporting News*, Nov. 1, 1945, 12; *Chicago Daily News*, Oct. 24, 1945, 26.

58. *Chicago Defender*, Nov. 3, 1945, 7.

59. *Baltimore Morning Sun*, Oct. 24, 1945, 1; *Chicago Daily News*, Oct. 26, 1945, 33.

60. *The Sporting News*, Nov. 1, 1945, 4.

61. *Baltimore Morning Sun*, Oct. 26, 1945, 20; *Chicago Herald American*, Oct. 25, 1945, 22; *Cincinnati Enquirer*, Oct. 26, 1945, 12.

62. *The Sporting News*, Nov. 1, 1945, 4.

63. *Baltimore Afro-American*, Nov. 10, 1945, 18; Editorial, *Chicago Defender*, Nov. 10, 1945, 14; *Detroit Tribune*, Nov. 3, 1945, 6.

64. *Boston Chronicle*, Nov. 3, 1945, 7; *New York Herald Tribune*, Oct. 25, 1945, 26; *Philadelphia Record*, Oct. 25, 1945, 18.

65. *Boston Traveler*, Oct. 24, 1945, 21; *Pittsburgh Post-Gazette*, Oct. 25, 1945, 14; *Washington Daily News*, Oct. 25, 1945, 38; *Washington Times Herald*, Oct. 25, 1945, 38.

66. *New York Daily Mirror*, Oct. 25, 1945, 34; *New York World Telegram*, Oct. 24, 1945, 40.

67. *Chicago Daily News*, Oct. 25, 1945, 33; *Cleveland Press*, Oct. 24, 1945, 16; Editorial, *Washington Post*, Oct. 27, 1945, 10; *Boston Chronicle*, Nov. 3, 1945, 7.

68. *New York Age*, Nov. 3, 1945, 6; *Philadelphia Tribune*, Oct. 27, 1945, 1; *Brooklyn Eagle*, Oct. 25, 1945, 17.

69. *St. Louis Globe Democrat*, Oct. 25, 1945, 3C.

70. *The Sporting News*, Nov. 1, 1945, 4.

71. *Boston Traveler*, Oct. 24, 1945, 21.

72. *Detroit News*, Oct. 25, 1945, 45; *Pittsburgh Post-Gazette*, Oct. 25, 1945, 14; *St. Louis Star Times*, Oct. 24, 1945, 21.

73. *La Presse* (Montreal), Oct. 25, 1945, 21. Quoted material from *La Presse*, a French-language newspaper, appears in English translation thanks to Richard Schadt, Professor of History, State University of New York, College at Oneonta.

74. *New York Daily Mirror*, Oct. 25, 1945, 34; Chicago *Defender*, Nov. 3, 1945, 9; *New York World Telegram*, Oct. 24, 1945, 40.

75. *St. Louis Post-Dispatch*, Oct 25, 1945, 6C.

76. *St. Louis Post-Dispatch*, Oct. 28, 1945, 1B; *Boston Daily Globe*, Oct. 24, 1945, 22.

77. *The Sporting News*, Nov. 1, 1945, 6; *The Sporting News*, Nov. 29, 1945, 6; *New York World Telegram*, Oct. 25, 1945, 30.

78. Editorial, *Detroit News*, Oct. 26, 1945, 22.

79. *Boston Daily Globe*, Oct. 25, 1945, 14.

80. *New York Age*, Nov. 3, 1945, 6.

81. *Cleveland Press*, Oct. 25, 1945, 26; *Detroit News*, Oct. 25, 1945, 45; *Syracuse Herald Journal*, Oct. 25, 1945, 38.

82. *The Sporting News*, Nov. 1, 1945, 5; *Chicago Defender*, Nov. 3, 1945, 1.

83. *Michigan Chronicle*, Nov. 3, 1935, 6.

84. *Amsterdam News* (New York), Nov. 3, 1945, 20.

85. *Boston Chronicle*, Oct. 27, 1945; *Boston Chronicle*, Nov. 3, 1945, 7; *Boston Chronicle*, Nov. 10, 1945, 7; *Boston Herald*, Oct. 26, 1945, 26; *Chicago Defender*, Nov. 3, 1945, 7; *Detroit Tribune*, Nov. 24, 1945, 11; *Amsterdam News* (New York), Oct. 27, 1945, 1; *Amsterdam News* (New York), Nov. 3, 1945, 1, 17, and 25; *Amsterdam News* (New York), Nov. 17, 1945, 24; *New York Herald Tribune*, Oct. 26, 1945, 26; *New York Times*, Oct. 25, 1945, 16; *Philadelphia Evening Bulletin*, Oct. 26, 1945, 30; *Pittsburgh Courier*, Nov. 3, 1945, 1 and 4; *St. Louis Argus*, Nov. 2, 1945, 17.

86. *Baltimore Morning Sun*, Oct. 25, 1945, 20; *Philadelphia Inquirer*, Oct. 25, 1945, 24; *Philadelphia Evening Bulletin*, Oct. 25, 1945, 30.

87. *Philadelphia Inquirer*, Oct. 24, 1945, 29.

88. *Pittsburgh Courier*, Nov. 3, 1945, 1.

89. *The Sporting News*, Nov. 1, 1945, 4.

90. *Baltimore Morning Sun*, Oct. 24, 1945, 15.

91. *Chicago Defender*, Nov. 3, 1945, 1.

92. *The Sporting News*, Nov. 1, 1945, 12.

93. *Cleveland Press*, Oct. 25, 1945, 26.

94. *Detroit News*, Oct. 24, 1945, 21.

95. *New York Post*, Oct. 24, 1945, 68.

96. *Boston Daily Record*, Oct. 25, 1945, 36.

97. *Baltimore Morning Sun*, Oct. 24, 1945, 1.

98. *New York Post*, Oct. 24, 1945, 68.

99. *Amsterdam News* (New York), Oct. 27, 1945, 1.

100. *Boston Guardian*, Oct. 27, 1945, 1.

101. *New York Age*, Nov. 10, 1945, 11.

102. *Baltimore Afro-American*, Nov. 10, 1945, 18.

103. *Boston Chronicle*, Nov. 3, 1945, 7.

104. *Boston Guardian*, Oct 27, 1945, 1.

105. *Amsterdam News* (New York), Oct. 27, 1945, 1.

106. *Philadelphia Tribune*, Dec. 29, 1945, 9.

107. *Pittsburgh Courier*, Nov. 3, 1945, 12.

108. *Baltimore Afro-American*, Nov. 3, 1945, 23; *Pittsburgh Courier*, Nov. 10, 1945, 1.

109. *Pittsburgh Courier*, Nov. 3, 1945, 12.

110. *Baltimore Afro-American*, Nov. 3, 1945, 1.

111. Wiggins, "Wendell Smith, the *Pittsburgh Courier Journal* and the Campaign to Include Blacks in Organized Baseball," 5-29.

112. *New York Times*, Oct. 25, 1945, 17.

113. *New York Post*, Oct. 25, 1945, 53.

114. *New York Age*, Nov. 10, 1945, 11.

115. *Philadelphia Record*, Oct. 24, 1945, 22.

116. *Pittsburgh Courier*, Nov. 3, 1945, 12.

117. *Christian Science Monitor* (Boston), Oct. 27, 1945, 14; *Detroit News*, Oct. 24, 1945, 21; *New York Sun*, Oct. 24, 1945, 36.

118. *The Sporting News*, Nov. 1, 1945, 12.

119. *Syracuse Herald Journal*, Oct. 27, 1945, 6; *Boston Daily Record*, Oct. 24, 1945, 29;

New York Herald Tribune, Oct. 25, 1945, 26; *Brooklyn Eagle*, Oct. 26, 1945, 15; Editorial, *Detroit News*, Oct. 26, 1945, 22.

120. *New York Times*, Oct. 24, 1945, 17; *Chicago Daily News*, Oct. 25, 1945, 33; *Pittsburgh Sun Telegraph*, Oct. 24, 1945, 20; *St. Louis Argus*, Oct. 26, 1945, 1.

121. Tygiel, *Baseball's Great Experiment*, 50.

122. Ibid., 67.

123. Robert Peterson, *Only the Ball Was White* (Englewood Cliffs, N.J.: Prentice-Hall, 1970), 189–190; Arthur Mann, *Branch Rickey: American in Action* (Boston: Houghton Mifflin Co., 1957), 218.

124. *Michigan Chronicle* (Detroit), Oct. 27, 1945, 1; *New York Daily Mirror* Oct. 24, 1945, 14; *Philadelphia Evening Bulletin*, Oct. 24, 1945, 20.

125. *The Sporting News*, March 20, 1971, 30.

126. *Philadelphia Record*, Oct. 28, 1945, 23.

127. *Baltimore Afro-American*, Nov. 3, 1945, 1; *Detroit Tribune*, Nov. 17, 1945, 11; *Michigan Chronicle*, Nov. 10, 1945, 6.

128. *Philadelphia Evening Bulletin*, Oct. 26, 1945, 36.

129. *Washington Times Herald*, Oct. 24, 1945, 22; *Washington Daily News*, Oct. 25, 1945, 30; *New York Sun*, Oct. 26, 1945, 34; *Detroit Times*, Oct. 25, 1945, 18C.

130. *Detroit Free Press*, Oct. 27, 1945, 6; *Baltimore Afro-American*, Nov. 10, 1945, p. 18; *New York Times*, Oct. 25, 1945, 16.

131. *The Sporting News*, Nov. 1, 1945, 5.

132. Jackie Robinson and Alfred Ducket, *I Never Had It Made* (New York: G. P. Putnam's Sons, 1972), 23.

133. "A Negro on the Farm," *Newsweek* 26 (Nov 5, 1945), 95; "Jackie Robinson," *Life* 19 (Nov. 26, 1945), 133; *Washington Daily News*, Oct. 24, 1945, 40.

134. Jackie Robinson and Charles Dexter, *Baseball Has Done It* (Philadelphia: J. B. Lippincott, 1964), 37.

135. Jules Tygiel, "The Court-Martial of Jackie Robinson," *American Heritage* 35 (Aug./Sept. 1984), 34–39.

136. *Philadelphia Evening Bulletin*, Oct. 24, 1945, 20; *Philadelphia Tribune*, Dec. 1, 1945, 13.

137. *Pittsburgh Courier*, Nov. 3, 1945, 12.

138. *Baltimore Afro-American*, Nov. 3. 1945, 1; *Chicago Herald American*, Oct. 24, 1945, 26; *St. Louis Post-Dispatch*, Oct. 24, 1945, 6C; *La Presse* (Montreal), Oct. 30, 1945, p. 16; *New York Age*, Nov. 3, 1945, 6; *Amsterdam News* (New York), Oct. 27, 1945, 5; *Brooklyn Eagle*, Nov. 3, 1945, 6; *Philadelphia Evening Bulletin*, Oct. 24, 1945, 20; *Pittsburgh Courier*, Nov. 3, 1945, 12; *The Sporting News*, Nov. 1, 1945, 5.

139. *Pittsburgh Courier*, Nov. 3, 1945, 1; *Brooklyn Eagle*, Oct. 26, 1945, 15.

140. *Brooklyn Eagle*, Oct. 25, 1945, 17; *New York Post*, Oct. 25, 1945, 53; *Detroit Tribune*, Nov. 17, 1945, 11; *The Sporting News*, Nov. 11, 1945, 6.

141. *Montreal Gazette*, Oct. 24, 1945, 14; *Pittsburgh Courier*, Nov. 3, 1945, 1.

142. Al-Tony Gilmore, *Bad Nigger: The National Impact of Jack Robinson* (New York: Kennikat Press, 1975); Dominic Capeci and Martha Wilkerson, "Multifarious Hero: Joe Louis, American Society and Race Relations During World Crisis, 1935–1945," *Journal of Sport History*, 10 (Winter 1983), 5.

143. *La Presse* (Montreal), Oct. 25, 1945, 20; *Montreal Gazette*, Oct. 25, 1945, 16; *The Sporting News*, Nov. 1, 1945, 6; *Pittsburgh Courier*, Nov. 10, 1945, 11.

144. *La Presse* (Montreal), Oct. 24, 1945, 18.

145. *Detroit News*, Oct. 25, 1945, 45; *Syracuse Herald Journal*, Oct. 25, 1945, 38.

146. *Pittsburgh Post-Gazette*, Oct. 25, 1945, 6.

147. *St. Louis Argus*, Nov. 2, 1945, 17.

148. *Detroit News*, Oct. 25, 1945, 45; *New York Herald Tribune*, Oct. 25, 1945, 26; *Brooklyn Eagle*, Oct. 24, 1945, 17.

149. *Brooklyn Eagle*, Oct. 25, 1945, 17; *New York Herald Tribune*, Oct. 25, 1945, 26: *Boston Daily Globe*, Oct. 24, 1945, 22.

150. *Washington Evening Star*, Oct. 20, 1945, 12.

151. *Syracuse Herald Journal,* Oct. 25, 1945, 38.

152. *Boston Traveler*, Oct. 24, 1945, 20.

153. J. T. Winterich, "Playing Ball," *Saturday Review of Literature* 28 (Nov. 24, 1945), 12.

154. *Chicago Herald American*, Oct. 26, 1945, 12.

155. *Detroit Tribune*, Nov. 3, 1945, 11.

156. *Detroit Tribune*, Nov. 17, 1945, 11.

157. *Amsterdam News* (New York), Nov. 3, 1945, 14.

158. *Pittsburgh Courier*, Nov. 3, 1945, 1.

159. *Michigan Chronicle*, Nov. 3, 1945, 6.

160. *Boston Daily Record*, Oct. 25, 1945, 36.

161. *Cleveland Plain Dealer*, Oct. 26, 1945, 19.

162. *Washington Post*, Oct. 27, 1945, 18.

163. *Pittsburgh Courier*, Nov. 10, 1945, 11.

164. *Amsterdam News* (New York), Nov. 3, 1945, 12.

165. *Amsterdam News* (New York), Nov. 3, 1945, 14.

166. *Michigan Chronicle*, Nov. 3, 1945, 6.

167. Myrdal, *An American Dilemma*, xlviii, 600, 799, and 1004.

168. John Hope Franklin, *From Slavery to Freedom: A History of Negro Americans*, 5th ed. (New York: Alfred A. Knopf, 1980), 442–444.

169. Myrdal, *An American Dilemma*, 12.

170. Merl Kleinknecht, "Integration of Baseball After World War II," *Baseball Research Journal* 12 (1983), 104–105; Benjamin G. Rader, *Baseball: A History of America's Game* (Urbana and Chicago: University of Illinois Press, 1992), 153.

171. Myrdal, *An American Dilemma*, 4.

172. Letter to the Editor, *Chicago Defender*, Nov. 10, 1945, 14.

173. Letter to the Editor, *Baltimore Morning Sun*, Oct. 28, 1945, 12.

174. Myrdal, *An American Dilemma*, liii.

175. *New York Times*, February 28, 1997, B9; "Breaking the Line: The Legacy of Jackie Robinson," ESPN, February 28, 1997.

176. Rachel Robinson with Lee Daniels, forward by Roger Wilkins, *Jackie Robinson: An Intimate Portrait* (New York: Harry N. Abrams, 1996), 72–75.

177. Roger Kahn, *The Boys of Summer* (New York: Harper & Row, 1971), 402.

178. Jules Tygiel, *Baseball's Great Experiment: Jackie Robinson and His Legacy* (New York: Oxford University Press, 1983), 344.

179. Christopher Darden, "Justice Is in the Color of the Beholder," *Time*, 149 (Feb. 17, 1997), 38.

180. Tygiel, *Baseball's Great Experiment*, 344.

Part 2

ROBINSON AND SOCIAL CHANGE

Working in the Shadows of Rickey and Robinson: Bill Veeck, Larry Doby and the Advancement of Black Players in Baseball

Peggy Beck

"All the players were standing by their lockers as Boudreau [Manager Lou Boudreau] introduced me. But two refused to shake my hand" (Sudyk, n.p.). Larry Doby's experiences just after signing a major league baseball contract differed from those of Jackie Robinson. The team owner Doby worked for, Bill Veeck, also differed from Branch Rickey, the owner of Jackie Robinson's team, the Brooklyn Dodgers. Although Rickey and Robinson deservedly receive most of the credit for breaking the color line in traditional professional baseball, Veeck wasn't too far behind. In fact, it could be argued that Veeck worked on the integration of baseball ahead of Branch Rickey. Veeck did not offer the first contract to a black player, though. Even though Doby's signing was four months after Robinson's, Veeck was the first owner to consider integrating his team. Succumbing to pressure from the Commissioner and other owners, Veeck gave up his plan and waited for the game of baseball to move at its own pace.

Veeck's reputation as a master promoter encouraged history to overlook his contributions to the advancement of black players in baseball. The title of Veeck's own book, *The Hustler's Handbook*, didn't help history in remembering or recording his contributions to integration of the game of baseball. Without much acclaim from fans, players or the media, Bill Veeck quietly made several important contributions to the game.

First, Veeck signed Larry Doby, Satchel Paige, and Luke Easter to professional contracts during his tenure as team owner (from 1946 through 1949). These signings made the Cleveland Indians the most integrated team in baseball during that era.

Second, Veeck *purchased* contracts on Doby, Paige and Easter from the Negro League teams. By doing so, he offered the teams something in return for the talents of their players. Most Negro League players were signed to professional baseball contracts without consideration (money) offered to Negro League team owners.

Third, Veeck hired the first black public relations man in baseball (Lou Jones) to help ease Doby's transition into the League.

Fourth, Veeck moved the Indians Spring Training camp from Florida to Arizona in 1947 because Jim Crow laws controlled seating in many Grapefruit League cities. Segregation ruled.

At the announcement of Satchel Paige's induction into the National Baseball Hall of Fame in 1971, Robert Lipsyte said that "the integration of baseball was a great deal more public and spectacular than the integration of almost any other aspect of American life, and so baseball has been made to feel particularly defensive about its segregated years" (n.p.). Bill Veeck's actions as the owner of the Cleveland Indians showed that he had nothing to be defensive about; he just saw a wrong that needed to be made right.

A 1996 feature article in *The National Review* makes this point very clearly. Steve Sailer notes in his article titled "Competition v. Discrimination: How Jackie Robinson Desegregated America" that "...most American League teams also lagged at integrating. The main exception was the Cleveland Indians.... As the AL's most integrated team, from 1948 to 1956 the Tribe would average 94 wins, peaking with a 111–43 record in 1954, the best anywhere since 1906" (p. 5).

The Signings of Doby, Paige, and Easter

Branch Rickey and Jackie Robinson and the phenomenal attention that followed them overshadowed the work of Bill Veeck with Larry Doby, Satchel Paige and Luke Easter. Veeck had a reputation as a master of promotion and hucksterism. Unfortunately, that reputation led some of baseball's leaders to doubt the sincerity of his work in integration. Even Lou Boudreau, the Indians' manager when Larry Doby signed his contract, had some skepticism regarding Doby's signing: "Knowing Veeck, and knowing his penchant for promotion, I immediately wondered if signing a black player was another publicity stunt. He assured me it wasn't"(Boudreau, n.p.). J.G. Taylor Spink, the editor of *The Sporting News*, accused Veeck of the same thing when he signed Satchel Paige in 1948. Paige was believed to be 42 years old at the time, but he didn't disclose his age. Veeck's decision to sign Paige to a contract turned out to be a good one, as Paige helped the Cleveland Indians win the 1948 World Series.

Veeck's concern and desire to sign black players can be documented long before 1946 and signings of Larry Doby and Jackie Robinson. In 1943, a full three years before Robinson's signing, Veeck intended to purchase the Philadelphia Phillies and stock the team with good players from the Negro League teams. Although the Phillies were struggling both on the field and off at the time, and the new plan would have helped their financial condition considerably, Judge Kenesaw Mountain Landis put enough pressure on Veeck that he backed out of the deal to buy the Phillies (Schneider 327). He later regretted backing out, but Robinson's signing signaled a perfect opportunity for Veeck to bring in a player from the Negro Leagues.

After purchasing the Indians in 1946, Veeck began the process of finding and signing a black player. On the heels of the Robinson signing, Veeck hired Bill Killefer, a good friend of his, to scout the Negro Leagues for black players to sign. In addition to Killefer, he also consulted with Wendell Smith (the sportswriter of the Pittsburgh *Courier*, a leading black newspaper) and Abe Saperstein (the promoter of the Harlem Globetrotters). One change in Veeck's thinking between Philadelphia and Cleveland revolved around the number of black players he wished to sign. In Philadelphia, his plans were to sign a few of them, while in Cleveland he chose to sign one, because "...despite the glowing credentials I have given myself, I felt that I had to be in a position to extricate the club fairly easily in case we ran into too many problems" (Hodermarsky 21).

Even after signing Doby, Veeck's fellow owners didn't always support his efforts. In a *Cleveland Press* article entitled "Doby Signing Wins Magnates Approval," Larry MacPhail's "approval" of the Doby signing consisted of "no comment" (p. 18). When Veeck signed Satchel Paige, Franklin Lewis noted in his *Cleveland Press* column that "Veeck dared precedent with his signing of Larry Doby [in 1946] and [now he feels] the chill in the glances of many fellow owners about this [the signing of Satchel Paige]" (1951, n.p.).

In the Preface of *Pride Against Prejudice — The Larry Doby Story*, Thomas Moore highlights the difference between Doby and Robinson and their entrances into Major League Baseball:

> Foremost, of course, is that Robinson was first. He played in New York, not Cleveland. He became a spokesperson for a large segment of black America, while Doby remained publicly silent. He played on a team immortalized as "The Boys of Summer," not the mortal Indians. He was enshrined in the Hall of Fame, while Doby was not. And in a society where most people cannot name the most recent, or perhaps the current vice-president of the United States, we relegate number two to an often undeserved obscurity (ix).

Veeck worked with the editors of the *Call and Post* (Cleveland's black newspaper), the mayors of primarily black suburban cities and other city leaders in Cleveland to help make the transition easier for Doby: "I spoke to the Negro leaders of the city and told them I was going to hold them responsible for policing their own people in case of trouble." Veeck later said "There was nothing for them to be responsible for, of course. We never had one fight in Cleveland in which a Negro was involved" (Hodermarsky 21).

Opinions varied as to how difficult the journey would be for Larry Doby. Cleveland Jackson, sports writer for *The Call and Post*, noted "Out there on the playing field, Doby will probably run into fewer rough, antagonistic encounters than any other player in the league" (Jackson, 1947, p. 9-B). The fact that Larry Doby was a sentimental favorite of the black fans and readers of *The Call and Post* is not disputed. But the difficulty of Doby's battle showed to those who knew him, and especially to the team owner, Bill Veeck.

Bill Veeck had one goal in mind when he signed Larry Doby — winning the pennant for the city of Cleveland. *Call and Post* writer Cleveland Jackson said "the Cleveland Indians chief has not only demonstrated that he will leave no stone unturned in his all-out effort to bring a championship team to Cleveland, but he also fulfilled his promise to Cleveland that he would give any likely prospect a chance regardless of race, color, or creed" (1947, p. 9-B).

Veeck states in his biography *Veeck — As in Wreck*, that he was closer to Doby than any other player he ever knew. Veeck also felt that the strain of being the first black player in the American League had an effect on Larry. He writes that "...It was a very real and bitter and gnawing battle for Larry all the way. With all that, his inner turmoil was such a constant drain on him that he was never able to realize his full potential" (Hodermarsky 24).

Although Doby had fewer struggles than Robinson, he still had problems. There were racial slurs from fans and opponents. Bob Sudyk writes in a *Cleveland Press* article on November 29, 1973 that "a third baseman once spat right in his face [after he hit a triple]" (p. E1). Franklin Lewis of the *Cleveland Press* wrote about an embarrassing incident that occurred during Doby's farewell ceremonies in Newark: "In the middle of farewell ceremonies for L. Doby in Newark last Friday, the public address system announcer inserted a blurb for an anti-lynch meeting scheduled within a few days" (n.p.).

Marsh Samuel, the publicity director of the Cleveland Indians when Larry Doby was signed, told a revealing story at a recent interview. During a "barnstorming" exhibition game stop in Arkansas, Doby couldn't stay in the team hotel, so he lived with a host family. He didn't appear for the game until well into the fourth inning. When Boudreau (the manager) asked what took him so long, he told Lou, "I couldn't get a ride to the ballpark."

Branch Rickey played a peculiar role in Bill Veeck's signing of Larry Doby. Rickey had a scout looking at Doby as a possible player for the Dodgers. After Rickey signed Robinson, "...there were not enough seats at Ebbets Field for those wanting to buy tickets" (Pratkanis and Turner 268). So Rickey told the scout to "let him go over to the other league. It will help the movement" (ibid). Rickey's confessed regret was all Bill Veeck needed to hear. Veeck was dealing with financial struggles in Cleveland. His club needed the attendance to help pay the bills. Bill Veeck was the last of the non-millionaire owners in baseball and he had financial struggles with the Indians (Pratkanis and Turner 269).

There is one similarity in the stories of Robinson and Doby — both had one good friend on the team. As Pee Wee Reese became a good friend and teammate of Jackie Robinson, so Joe Gordon became a good friend and teammate to Larry Doby. An unfortunate incident occurred the first day Doby went to play first base, and that incident forged the friendship between Joe Gordon and Larry Doby. Used as a pinch-hitter and then going into the game to play first base on July 5, 1947, Doby found himself without a first baseman's mitt (he was a natural second baseman). No one on the team would lend Doby a first baseman's mitt, least of all the player he had just replaced (Samuel 1997). Joe Gordon found one in his locker and lent it to Doby. When Gordon was introduced to Doby the day before, Doby said "he grabbed my hand and squeezed it hard in welcome. Gordon was great to me. He usually warmed up before the game with Boudreau, but from that day on, it was with me" (Sudyk E1). Gordon also sat next to the reserved Doby on the bench and the two would talk baseball.

Dan Dodson, a New York University sociologist gave some advice to Branch Rickey, when he signed Jackie Robinson. The same advice also applied to Bill Veeck and his signing of Larry Doby:

> Don't worry about the attitudes of people who are asked to accept new members. When relationships are predicated on the basis of goals other than integration — in the Dodger [Indian] case, winning the pennant — the people involved would adjust appropriately (43).

The coverage of Larry Doby's arrival and career with the Cleveland Indians by the *Call and Post* (the highly-recognized black newspaper in Cleveland) often included commentary about the plight of black players in baseball. In a particularly pointed article, Cleveland Jackson said:

> News that he [Doby] would be able to stay with the team in every city except Chicago and St. Louis brought many cries of surprise from multitudes of Negro baseball fans who for many years have listened to the chest thumping of braggadocio sepia Chicagoans who have boasted about the hospitality of the Windy City. St. Louis, of course, was expected to follow their chosen path (9B).

The editorial page of the *Call and Post* carried this paragraph of support on July 12, 1947:

> Clevelanders have already demonstrated their ability to attend and enjoy sporting events where a mixed cast provides the thrills — to attend and enjoy mixed boxing, professional football and basketball with the easy aplomb of the real sportsman. Let us continue this exemplary behavior at all games in Cleveland Stadium.

In the same edition of the *Call and Post*, a poem appeared that best expressed the wishes of the readership for Larry Doby. Another interesting comment from Cleveland Jackson appeared in the same paper: "Intentional or not, it was noted that many of the Negro churches dismissed their congregations earlier than usual. Entire congregations came directly from church to the ballpark..." (n.p.).

Legendary sportswriter James E. (Jimmy) Doyle whose column was carried in the *Cleveland Plain Dealer*, made two comments concerning the Doby signing, both complimentary about the city of Cleveland and the Cleveland Indians organization. On July 8, he wrote: "Cleveland's man in the street is the right sort of American, as was evidenced right solidly once more by his response to the question: "How does the signing of Larry Doby by the Indians strike you? Said the man in the street: Can he hit? ...That's all that counts." (p. 14). On July 5, the day after his signing, Doyle had this to say: "As Dodger Jackie Robinson might remark to Indian Larry Doby [who played first base in his first field appearance]: Who said colored baseball players would never get to first base in the major leagues?" (p. 12).

By 1951, the city of Cleveland had shown its true colors, weathered the storm of controversy about black players in baseball, and given deserved credit to Larry Doby. Doby was named "Man of the Year" in 1950 and he proved himself on the field, holding many mid–season records. He lead the Indians in hits, home runs, doubles, and runs scored.

One of Doby's favorite memories in baseball revolves around a picture in which Doby and Steve Gromek are shown celebrating on October 9, 1948 as the Indians won the fourth game of the 1948 World Series. Gromek, the winning pitcher, had limited the Boston Braves to just one run in nine innings. Doby hit a 2-run home run, which won the game for the Indians, 2–1. This is one of the first pictures of two men, black and white, celebrating together. It was carried by papers nationwide and has become one of Doby's fondest memories. In his biography, Doby says: "The picture was more rewarding and happy for me than actually hitting that home run. It was such a scuffle for me ... until that picture. The picture finally showed a moment of a man showing his feelings for me ... I think enlightenment can come from such a picture" (p. 4).

The signing of Satchel Paige, coming only one year after Doby's signing (July 7, 1948), created a different type of stir for Bill Veeck. In mid-summer of 1948, Bill Veeck knew that his team had a chance to win the pennant. Even though he risked the disdain from other owners, "he chucked all feeling about other owners" (Lewis) and signed Paige. J.G. Taylor Spink (Editor of *The Sporting News*) wrote about Paige in his editorial when he said: "To bring in a pitching 'rookie' of Paige's age casts a reflection on the entire scheme of operations in the major leagues. To sign a hurler of Paige's age is to demean the standards of baseball in the big circuits" (Schneider 211). In the same editorial, Spink said of Veeck "if Paige were white, he would not have drawn a second thought from Veeck." Bill Veeck would never let an opportunity pass him by, so after Paige pitched a three-hit shutout against Chicago, Veeck sent a telegram to Spink which said "Paige pitching. No runs. Three hits. He definitely is in line for the *Sporting News* 'Rookie of the Year' Award" (Schneider 211). Eventually, Spink wrote a retraction.

Bill Veeck knew he would get the last laugh on Mr. Spink. Paige's try-out with the Indians is best described by Manager Lou Boudreau in his book *Covering All the Bases*:

> He [Satchel Paige] handed me a folded up handkerchief, told me to put it on the plate wherever I liked. First, I put it on the inside corner. He wound up and threw ten pitches — and nine of them were right over the handkerchief. He told me to move the handkerchief to the other side of the plate, and he threw ten more pitches the same as before. Seven or eight of them were right over the handkerchief, and the ones that weren't, didn't miss by much (Boudreau 112–113).

Satchel Paige drew one of the largest crowds in Cleveland Indians history as 72,434 people watched him pitch in his first start for the Indians, which he won 5 to 3. He also drew the largest night crowd (regular season game) in Cleveland Indians history, when 78,342 people watched him blank the Chicago White Sox 1 to 0 (Daley, n.p.). Paige's ability to draw fans to the ballpark was not lost on Mr. Veeck.

Satchel Paige had a reputation for being a "character," which he promptly proved to everyone in Cleveland. Marsh Samuel, the Indians' publicity director when Paige was signed, passed along this story regarding Paige at a photo layout for *Life Magazine*. The photographer from the magazine snapped many pictures of him in uniform, with a baseball, and throwing pitches from the mound. Paige also played the guitar, and the photographer asked him to pose for a picture with his guitar. Paige dryly said "That will be ten dollars" (1997). Paige drove Boudreau crazy, as he would often miss trains or take a plane by himself rather than travel with the team. Stories abound about Satchel Paige and his dry sense of humor. One of the famous examples of Paige's wit is his advice on "How to Keep Young."

One fact about Paige is difficult to fathom: he made close to $40,000 per year while barnstorming outside of traditional professional baseball. Paige took a $25,000 a year pay cut to pitch for the Indians(Daley). Paige signed his last professional players contract at the age of 42. At the conclusion of that contract, he had played long enough to receive a pension from Major League Baseball and to be eligible for selection to the National Baseball Hall of Fame.

The next black player signed by Veeck during his tenure as team owner was Luke Easter. He was called "the black Babe Ruth" during his days in the Negro Leagues from 1946 through 1948. In 1949, Veeck purchased his contract from the Homestead Grays and the Indians traded Mickey Vernon back to the Washington Senators to make room for Easter at first base. By the time Luke Easter arrived in Cleveland, most of the concerns over black players in baseball had evaporated. His contributions to the Indians included the longest home run in Cleveland Stadium history (477 feet). He built an outstanding record of involvement in public service and community relations for the Indians. Easter's signing gave Veeck the most integrated team in baseball, but Easter was also the last Negro League player purchased by Bill Veeck before he sold the Indians in November of 1949.

Bill Veeck Purchases the Contracts of Negro League Players

One radical difference between Bill Veeck and Branch Rickey exists in the approach that each took toward the Negro Leagues. While Branch

Rickey contracted with Negro League players without regard to their contract status in the Negro Leagues, Bill Veeck paid the Negro League teams for the talents of Larry Doby, Satchel Paige and Luke Easter. "Developing a pool of talent for integrating the white leagues" was one of the stated objectives of the Negro National League, according to Pratkanis and Turner (p. 262).

Veeck spent a total of $30,000 paying Negro League teams for the right to contract with their players, and even more if you consider the additional deals that he included. For the rights to Larry Doby, Veeck paid $10,000 to Effa Manley, the wife of Newark Eagles owner Abe Manley (Schneider 140). The deal for Satchel Paige cost Veeck and the Indians more than that. The Kansas City Monarchs received $15,000 for selling the rights to Satchel Paige to the Indians. In addition, Paige received $25,000 ($10,000 for his signature and $5,000 per month for July, August, and September) and Abe Saperstein (who brought Satchel to Veeck's attention) received $15,000 (Lustig n.p.). On the other hand, Veeck purchased the rights to Luke Easter for a mere $5,000.00 (Schneider, 1996, p. 144).

Veeck's deals with the Negro Leagues are significant, because they showed some effort by traditional professional baseball to "pay back" the Negro Leagues for the developmental role they played in the lives of players. Also, it enabled the Negro Leagues to continue to exist and give other players opportunities. In many ways, the leagues acted as a "farm system" for black players in the early years and teams deserved some consideration for their work. This caused considerable financial difficulties in the Negro Leagues as the best black players were scouted and signed away into traditional professional baseball, leaving the Negro League teams without their star attractions. In response to that crisis, Cleveland Jackson wrote in his column for the *Call and Post* on July 26, 1947, that the Negro League teams needed to "establish definite ties and working agreements with Major League organizations so as to maintain a steady flow of promising young players into their ranks" (p. 9B).

The Hiring of Lou Jones

Lou Jones holds the title as the first black public relations person in baseball. He was hired, in the words of Bill Veeck, "to prepare the black segment of Cleveland for the arrival of a black ball player, unnamed" (Moore 39). Veeck hired him to perform two specific jobs: to be helpful to Larry Doby and to assist in publicity. Jones lasted only one year in the role. According to those who worked with him, he wasn't particularly effective performing in either capacity. As Jones' immediate supervisor, Samuel said that he was "…too militant, he tried to take on the league and tried to have rules revised. He would make demands of the Commissioner's Office" (1997).

Jones had a prominent role in the early days Doby spent with the Indians, being dispatched to pick up Doby in New Jersey and travel with him to Chicago where he signed his contract and became a traveling companion during the first few hectic months. Jones' role was to protect Doby from autograph seekers and well-wishers as well as those intent upon harming him. Jones once said of Doby "I don't think we'll ever have to worry about his getting in bad by talking too much or saying the wrong thing. He doesn't speak a half dozen words an hour" (Gibbons 17A).

Larry Doby's own reminiscences speak loudly of the relationship between the two. The presence or absence of Jones made "no difference" to Doby: "Even when he was supposed to be with me, he wasn't" (Moore 68). By mid-February, Jones had been dismissed "…in part for not fulfilling Veeck's expectations of him as Doby's traveling companion" (Moore 68). Veeck's action left Doby without a roommate and baseball without a black man in a front office position. It remained that way for years.

Spring Training Moves to Tucson

Prior to 1947, the Cleveland Indians trained in Florida as members of the "Grapefruit League." During the 1946 spring training campaign, Bill Veeck noticed something when his team went to Ocala, Florida (the spring training home of the Milwaukee Brewers): "Our clubhouse was way out in left field, and the Jim Crow section was between the clubhouse and the edge of the stands" (Hodermarsky 23). Veeck confessed to being rather "naive" about segregation, and after seeing the segregated stands, he chose to move the team in preparation for his plans to sign a black player. Veeck's naiveté about segregation was also mentioned by Marsh Samuel in an interview, when he said: "Bill never thought about it [segregation]. He grew up in a small town where everyone was accepted" (1997). From 1947 until 1994, the Cleveland Indians Spring Training headquarters remained in Tucson, Arizona.

In his biography *Veeck — As in Wreck*, Veeck says: "In those days, it wasn't really publicized that much, as I suppose many Northern soldiers who took back seats in buses found out" (Hodermarsky 23).

Summary and Conclusion

Bill Veeck, as owner of the Cleveland Indians, broke the color barrier in the American League. Over three years, he created the most integrated team in baseball, purchased the contracts of three good black players from the Negro Leagues, integrated the Indians front office, and moved the team's spring training site to a more conducive place for the integrated team he built. Veeck also predicted history when he said "within ten years, Negro players will be in regular service with big league teams, for there are many colored players with sufficient capabilities to make the majors" (UPI n.p.).

Marsh Samuel remembers Veeck as "...unique. People liked him so much, and liked what he did, that criticism was infrequent" (1997).

Larry Doby felt that the biggest injustice shown to black players was the view that the former Negro Leaguers were "pathetic figures of history." He reflected on the issue this way:

> We had our good times (said Doby). The Negro League players were dedicated athletes playing a game they loved. There was laughter and songs in the bus, new people, fans in every town. When you come down to it, all the major leagues offered was more: more money, more bars, more women, more friends, more opportunities (Lipsyte n.p.).

Epilogue

Larry Doby, Satchel Paige and Bill Veeck have been elected to the National Baseball Hall of Fame. Luke Easter, murdered while cashing checks for co-workers at a factory in Cleveland, has a baseball park named after him in Cleveland. Cleveland Indians Manager Ken Aspromonte hired Larry Doby to coach the 1974 season. Prior to coaching in Cleveland, he held a front office position as a troubleshooter with the Montreal Expos. Unfortunately for Doby, Cleveland's front office wasn't happy with Aspromonte's performance and Frank Robinson had expressed interest in moving into a player-manager role somewhere. The Indians signed Robinson. Doby also wished to manage and he found himself in competition for the manager's position with a marquee player (Robinson) that the Indians had just obtained. In an article in the *New York Times*, Red Smith quoted Doby: "I want to manage ... If some other black guy got it before me I'd be a little hurt, but not [if it is] Frank Robinson" (Smith n.p.). When the Indians hired Robinson on October 3, 1974, Doby was quoted as saying "But I am happy that baseball is now showing it's not prejudiced [by naming its first black manager]" (Schneider, 1974).

Works Cited

Boudreau, Lou, with Russell Schneider. *Lou Boudreau: Covering All the Bases*. Champaign, IL: Sagamore Publishing, 1993.

Cleveland Indians. *Barrier Breakers: Cleveland's Significant Firsts*. 1994.

Cobbledick, Gordon. "Doby Shows He Has Strong Arm." *Cleveland Plain Dealer* 6 July 1947: p. 16A.

Daley, Arthur. "Sports of the Times: Satch Bows Out." *New York Times* 19 February 1950: n.p.

Darvas. "Larry Doby." Published in the *Cleveland Plain Dealer*, Cleveland, OH.

"Dr. Chas. Wesley Makes A Wise Decision." Editorial. *Call and Post* 12 July 1947: 1B.

Doyle, James E. "The Sports Trail: The Times Do Change." *Cleveland Plain Dealer* 5 July 1947: p. 12.

_____. "The Sports Trail: Man in the Street All Right." *Cleveland Plain Dealer* 8 July 1947: p. 14.

Gergen, Joe. "Robinson Honor Is a Double Play." *New York Newsday* 27 February 1997: A87.

Gibbons, Frank. "Indians Sign Negro Star." *Cleveland Press* 3 July 1947: p. 1+.

Hodermarsky, Mark (Ed.). *The Cleveland Sports Legacy Since 1945*. Cleveland: Cleveland Landmarks Press, 1991.

"Indians Sign Negro Player." Editorial. *Cleveland Press* 3 July 1947: p. 6.

Jackson, Cleveland. "Bill Veeck, Lou Boudreau Pursue Promising Policy With Larry Doby: Rookie May Figure in Title Drive." 19 July 1947: p. 8B.

_____. "Headline Action." *Call and Post* 2 August 1947: p. 9B.

_____. "Headline Action." *Call and Post* 19 July 1947: p. 9B.

_____. "Headline Action." *Call and Post* 26 July 1947: p. 9B.

_____. "Believe Newark Star Headed for Indians." *Call and Post* 5 July 1947: p. 1.

"Larry Doby." *Major League Baseball*. Online. 20 March 1997.

Lipsyte, Robert. "Sports of The Times: A Little Rusted Up." *New York Times* 11 February 1971: n.p.

Lewis, Franklin. "Never Thought He'd See Paige Back in Majors." *Cleveland Press* n.d.: n.p.

Loeb, Charles H. "Editorial in Rhyme: To Larry Doby." *Call and Post* 12 July 1947: p. 1B.

Lustig, Dennis. "Whatever Happened to ... Satchel Paige?" *Cleveland Plain Dealer* 15 February 1974: n.p.

Moore, Joseph Thomas. *Pride Against Prejudice: The Biography of Larry Doby*. Westport: Praeger, 1987.

Pratkanis, Anthony R., and Marlene E. Turner. "The Year Cool Papa Bell Lost the Batting Title — Mr. Branch Rickey and Mr. Jackie Robinson's Plea for Affirmative Action." *Nine* (1993): 260–276.

_____. "Nine Principles of Successful Affirmative Action: Mr. Branch Rickey, Mr. Jackie Robinson, and the Integration of Baseball." *Nine* (1993): 36-61.

Ruscoe, Michael. *Baseball: A Treasury of Art and Literature*. New York: Macmillan, 1993.

Sailer, Steve. "Competition v. Discrimination: How Jackie Robinson Desegregated America." *National Review* feature. Online. 8 April 1996.

Schneider, Russell. *The Cleveland Indians Encyclopedia*. Philadelphia: Temple University Press, 1996.

Smith, Red. "Larry Doby, Manager-in-Waiting." *New York Times* 30 September 1974: n.p.

Staff. "Doby Signing Wins Magnates' Approval." *Cleveland Press* 3 July 1947: p. 18.

Staff Special. "Disappointed Doby Is Not Vindictive." *Cleveland Plain Dealer* 3 October 1974: n.p.

Sudyk, Bob. "The Year the A.L. Signed Its First Black." *Cleveland Press* 29 November 1973: n.p.

United Press International. "Larry Doby, Ace Negro Infielder, Signs Contract with Cleveland." *New York Times* 4 July 1947: n.p.

Robinson's Legacy: Black Women and Negro Baseball

Gai Ingham Berlage

After World War II, the ban on blacks in Major League Baseball became a major issue in the black press. With over a million black soldiers having served in the war, black newspapers such as the Pittsburgh *Courier* wrote it was time for the integration of Major League Baseball. The slogan became "If he's good enough for the Navy, he's good enough for the majors."[1]

In 1945 Branch Rickey signed Jackie Robinson to play for the 1946 season for Brooklyn Dodger Montreal farm team. The following spring, 1947, Robinson was moved up to Brooklyn. Blacks everywhere were ecstatic. At long last Major League Baseball was going to be integrated and black players finally would be able to prove that they were as good as if not better than many white players.

One unintended consequence of Jackie Robinson's integration of Major League Baseball was that three black[2] women, Marcenia "Toni" Stone, Mamie "Peanut" Johnson and Connie Morgan, had a chance to play Negro League baseball.[3] This window of opportunity for women lasted only two years, 1953 through 1954, and the women had no impact on the image of baseball as a male domain. Financial concerns rather than ideological ones led to their recruitment. The question of sexism in baseball was never an issue.

Jackie Robinson's signing with the Brooklyn Dodgers was a victory against racism, but for the owners of the Negro Leagues teams it was a financial disaster. In 1947 the entire Negro League, especially the eastern

Negro National League teams, suffered revenue losses when fans deserted them to see Jackie Robinson and other blacks play in the majors. Even the Kansas City Monarchs, who had won the World Series in 1946 and still had the legendary Satchel Paige, saw a decline in attendance. As Hilton Smith, a star of the Kansas City Monarchs, stated, "All the people started to go Brooklynites. Even if we were playing here in Kansas City, everybody wanted to go over to St. Louis to see Jackie. So our league really began to go down, down, down."[4] Black fans willingly spent five hours on the train to see Robinson in the Dodger line up against the St. Louis Cardinals. According to Negro League historian, Donn Rogosin, Monarchs owner, J.L. Wilkinson, grew so disgusted with black fans that he sold his interest to Baird and left baseball in 1948.[5]

After 1947, the East-West game was the only vital aspect of Negro League baseball. After the recruitment of Jackie Robinson the East-West game provided black fans with the opportunity to see future black major league stars. In 1947, 48,112 fans attended the game. By 1952 the number had dwindled to 18,279.[6] Nineteen fifty-three attracted the smallest crowd since World War II. Many sportswriters estimated the crowd around 7,000. John Johnson, sports editor of the Kansas City *Call*, declared "East-West Game Faces Death in Chicago."

By 1953, little was left of Negro League baseball, the Negro National League was gone, having disbanded in 1948. Only four teams remained in the Negro American League, the Indianapolis Clowns, the Kansas City Monarchs, the Birmingham Black Barons and the Memphis Red Sox. In 1949, there had been ten teams.

Integration of the major leagues, however, wasn't the only reason that the Negro Leagues were losing attendance. Professional football and basketball were becoming popular and drawing away fans. Television was changing viewing patterns, as more people stayed home to watch major league games from their living rooms rather than go out to the ballpark. Predominantly white minor league baseball was also adversely affected. After the war, attendance at minor league games declined from 42 million to 15.5 million. Many teams found they couldn't compete financially.[7] The All American Girls Baseball League, founded by Philip K. Wrigley in 1943, closed its doors in 1954.

Hard times called for innovation and Syd Pollock, owner of the Indianapolis Clowns, a Negro American League team, was an expert in mixing entertainment with baseball. The Clowns, referred to in the black press as the "Funmakers," were the Harlem Globetrotters of baseball. In the 1930s and 40s, the Clowns were known as much for their comedy team of Spec Bebop, a dwarf, and King Tut, as they were for their baseball. Several players also clowned on the field. If the team were ahead by several runs, Goose Tatum of Harlem Globetrotter basketball fame, the first baseman, might catch a few grounders with a huge mitt that he wore on his foot. Pepper Bassett, the catcher, might play a few innings sitting in a rocking chair behind homeplate.[8] In 1953 the Clowns comedy department claimed, besides King Tut and Spec Bebop, Boogie Woogie Paul, a one man "Spike Jones" type band entertainer.[9] The Clowns successfully combined clowning with high caliber, professional baseball. Hank Aaron was a member of the team in 1952.[10] In 1950 and 1951 the Clowns were the top team in the Negro American League in the East.[11]

In 1953 with waning attendance, Pollock's new gimmick was to hire a woman ball player, Toni Stone,[12] and bill her as the first woman to ever play in the Negro Leagues. It is ironic that Stone because of economics got to play men's Negro League baseball but because of racism couldn't get a try-out with Wrigley's All-American Girls' Baseball League. In the 1940s when she wrote the AAGBL for a try-out, she received no reply.[13] The AAGBL probably didn't respond because they were only interested in white women who fit Philip K. Wrigley's image of the All American Girl.

Pollock's new female star, Toni Stone, at age twenty-seven was no newcomer to men's baseball. She had been playing professional ball since 1947 when she barnstormed with the San Francisco Sea Lions, an integrated white and black semi-pro team. A couple of years later, when the team was barnstorming in New Orleans she jumped teams, deserting the Sea Lions to play for the Black Pelicans, a Negro minor league team. Stone claimed that she jumped teams because she thought Harold "Yellowhorse" Morris, the owner of the Sea Lions, was cheating her financially. A short time later, she switched teams again, and began playing for the New Orleans Creoles, another Negro minor league team. In 1949, the Creoles were paying her $300 a month. Each time she switched she made more money. To be in such demand, she had to have been more than just a novelty. Otherwise these teams could have obtained another woman at less cost. Stone's batting average of .265 with the Creoles is testimony to her skills.[14] In 1950 *Ebony* magazine, in its section on "Speaking of People," cited Stone as "one of the best performers in the Negro Texas League."[15]

In 1953, Pollock claimed that he was paying Stone $12,000 to play for the Indianapolis Clowns. He was quick to point out that he was paying his female phenom more than Jackie Robinson made when he first signed with the Dodgers. He maintained that her salary was based on her skills rather than her drawing power. He claimed that on signing her he was deluged with booking requests.[16] How much he actually paid her is debatable. One writer claims that her actual salary was about $350 a month. He also claims that Pollock wrote A.P. Alberga, Stone's husband, a letter stating that for publicity reasons "we must overrate her and keep saying she's tops in all departments."[17]

There is no doubt that Toni Stone was hired as a gimmick to draw crowds, but she was not just window dressing. She had no trouble competing on an equal footing with the men. In her first time at bat for the Clowns she batted in two runs.[18] In 1953 she played in 50 of the 175 Clowns games and maintained a .243 batting average. A fairly consistent but not a powerful hitter, she recorded only singles with the exception of one double.[19]

But according to Buster Haywood, the Clowns manager, Stone looked so good because she played in mostly non-official games. Haywood said that he considered Stone more of a novelty than a real player and, therefore, he played her mostly in non-league or barnstorming games. Was this just sexism on his part? Obviously this is a question that can't be answered. In Haywood's mind, Stone's signing was "mostly a show." He did admit that she knew the fundamentals and would have been a top player in a woman's league.[20]

It is difficult to determine how good a ball player Toni Stone really was. There are no official records. The information is mostly anecdotal. However, it is known that she played against some top black ball players. While with the Clowns she played against Ernie Banks of the Monarchs who went on to become a Hall of Famer with the Chicago Cubs.[21]

Some Clowns had difficulty accepting the fact that a woman could play a "man's game." After all, baseball symbolized the black male community. According to Stone, a few even told her to "go home and fix (her) husband some biscuits."[22]

Most, however, adjusted to having a woman on the team and came to admire her skills. Typical of the attitude transformation of the players is that of Clowns' shortstop, Rube Williams. Williams admitted that at first he found it funny to be "working with a girl on second. I have to fight against the feeling I might knock her down with a hard throw. But I let her have it, however. The kid is good, I mean, real good. Main thing about her is that she's always there to take my throws. She's fast on grass-cutters and balls that take a bad hop."[23]

An article in *Ebony* magazine in 1953 gave her a mixed review. It said, "Her excellent fielding and accuracy make up for lack of power in throwing arm."[24] However, William Beverly, a veteran Negro League Baseball player, doesn't recall any lack of power. His comment was, "She could tear the glove off your hand just like a man."[25]

Ironically, *Ebony*'s statement that Stone had a weak throwing arm is the same limitation that Effa Manley, co-owner of the Newark Eagles, thought Jackie Robinson had. "He (Jackie Robinson) didn't have the greatest arm in the world, but in the infield you need not be able to throw too hard."[26]

Physically Stone was strong and fast. She was clocked at eleven seconds for 100 yards. At 5 feet 7½ inches, 148 pounds, in a uniform, she looked like one of the men. She also insisted on being treated like one. When Pollock suggested she play in shorts, she refused and insisted on wearing the same uniform as the men. As she said, "I know what I am doing and what I am in for. I don't want anyone playing me 'easy' because I am a woman and I don't plan to play easy against them. I am here to play the game."[27]

The only concession to her sex was that she used the umpire's dressing room and shower rather than the team dressing room. The rest of the time she stayed with the team. She traveled on the team bus and on the road stayed in the same hotels and rooming houses.[28]

Stone admitted she felt like a "goldfish" when she first reported for spring training in Norfolk, Virginia with the Clowns.[29] However, when a reporter from *Ebony* magazine interviewed her, she radiated enthusiasm and optimism. She said, "I've got my own ideas. Who knows? Maybe I'll be the first woman to play major league baseball.... There's always got to be a first in everything. Before 1946 nobody thought Negroes would be in the major leagues."[30] Unfortunately, she was wrong. The highlight of her professional career was a hit off legendary pitcher Satchel Paige in 1953.

Stone's career with the Indianapolis Clowns, however, was short-lived. In 1954, Syd Pollock sold her contract for an undisclosed amount to the Kansas City Monarchs and hired two new women to replace her. Connie Morgan took over Stone's position at second base and Mamie "Peanut" Johnson became the first female pitcher in the Negro League.[31] Reportedly Pollock paid Morgan $10,000 and Johnson $5,000.[32]

Future Hall of Famer Oscar Charleston, the new manager of the Clowns, claimed he personally scouted Morgan and that she was one of the most sensational women players he had ever seen. He proclaimed that she threw across the diamond on par with many major leaguers.[33] How much scouting he did is questionable. According to Morgan,[34] she replied to a newspaper ad asking for ball players to try-out for the champion Indianapolis Clowns. Her reception with the players was very different from that of Stone. By now the players were used to having a woman and were delighted with the extra publicity. Morgan claimed that they treated her like a sister and watched out for her.[35]

Morgan, at nineteen and 5 feet 4 inches, was much younger and smaller than Toni. She was also less experienced. She had played five years with the North Philadelphia Honey Drippers, an all girl baseball team. Although her batting average with the Honey Drippers was an impressive .368, the competition was not as intense.[36]

However, Morgan received excellent press. A photo in *The Call*, the Kansas City black newspaper, showed her getting pointers from Brooklyn Dodger, Gil Hodges. The caption noted that Hodges had seen Morgan work out with Jackie Robinson's All-Stars the previous fall and that he believed that she had "terrific promise."[37]

Mamie Johnson, the other female player for the Clowns, began playing at the end of the regular 1953 season. On a month long barnstorming tour, she had regularly pitched an inning or so. *The Call* reported that she averaged a strike out per inning against Negro League Stars.[38]

Both Morgan and Johnson were featured players in the opening games of the 1954 Negro American League season, and it was hoped that they, like Stone, would draw large crowds. In regular season play, Morgan received more playing time and publicity than Johnson did. In Monarchs/Clowns games competition between the two second basewomen, Stone of the Monarchs and Morgan of the Clowns were often highlighted.

In the Clowns' first game of the season, May 16th against the Birmingham Black Barons, an article in the Kansas City *Call* declared that rookie second baseman Morgan "electrified over 6,000 fans ... when she went to far right field to make a sensational stop of a scorcher labeled 'base-hit'...." Her hitting was not quite as sensational. The two times she came to bat she walked.[39]

In May even before the Kansas City Monarchs' first official home game, John Johnson, sports editor of the Kansas City *Call*, touted the July 11 double header to be played in Yankee Stadium between the Clowns and the Monarchs. Here was a chance for Harlem fans to see the three female phenoms — "infielder, Miss Toni Stone, formerly with the Funmakers, and now with the Monarchs, plus the new sensations of the Clowns, infielder Connie Morgan and Mamie "Peanut" Johnson, the first and only female hurler to ever pitch in the Negro Professional League Circuit."[40]

In the same article, Johnson called "Peanut" Johnson a female "Satchel Paige" and said that she had held the Monarchs scoreless against the Clowns. In retrospect, the Mother's Day game between the Monarchs and Clowns seems contrived much like the Harlem Globetrotters record against the Generals. Only the women seemed to excel. Toni Stone was the only Monarch player to reach first base. Johnson, however, threw a pickoff toss to first baseman Speed Merchant who tagged her out.

In 1954 the Clowns and Monarchs spent a great deal of time

barnstorming playing exhibition games against each other. The intensity of these games may have differed significantly from those of the official NAL schedule. The majority of the women's playing time was in exhibition games. Regular season games were still of a high enough professional quality that the Philadelphia Phillies signed two Monarchs players, Fran Herrera and Hank Mason, at the end of the 1954 season.[41]

When the Indianapolis Clowns opened with a home game against the Kansas City Monarchs on May 30th in Blues Stadium, the press release emphasized that both teams had a female player, Connie Morgan with the Clowns and Toni Stone with the Monarchs. No mention was made of Mamie Johnson.[42] The Kansas City *Call*, the black newspaper, in the many weekly articles during the 1954 season on the Indianapolis Clowns, makes no mention of her pitching after the Mother's Day exhibition game.

The 1954 Indianapolis Clowns/Kansas City Monarch Program contains pictures of Johnson, Morgan, and Stone. Under Johnson's picture, it states, "Peanuts for her size and weight, pound for pound throws as hard as many men pitchers. She not only pitches but is used in utility roles." Her nickname "Peanut" came from her size. At 5'4" and 120 pounds, she was the smallest player on the team. The only reference to her past athletic accomplishments is that she played sports with boys, even football, at Long Beach High School.

The Monarchs/Clowns opening game May 30th was broadcast for the first time on radio station KPRS. Chuck Moore did the live play-by-play coverage. The game was to have been the biggest event of the season. Fans were expected from a two hundred mile radius to come and see the game and the opening day festivities. The game was an annual tradition that black families looked forward to and many arrived early in the morning to get good seats. Families brought picnic baskets and made it a day's event.

The Monarchs Booster Club arranged a one half mile parade with over seventeen marching units and more than four hundred participants. The Boosters Club predicted a crowd of more than 20,000 fans to top the previous season's opening day attendance of 18,205 paid admissions.

All the major black newspapers sent their sports editors. Russ Cowan of the Chicago *Defender*, Bill Nunn of the Pittsburgh *Courier*, John Johnson of the Kansas City *Call*, as well as others, were in the press box. Unfortunately, due to rain most fans stayed home, and the opening day parade and other festivities were postponed until the following Sunday, June 6th. The official count of paying fans was 7,131.[43]

On June 6th, beside the postponed parade and other events, Monarch player William Bell and his bride, Itaska Parker, were to exchange marriage vows between the 5th and 6th inning of the game. Still, only 6,458 paying fans came to the game.[44] Even adding together the two Sunday admissions, the attendance numbers still fell below the predicted 20,000 for the opening game. Attendance figures were a real problem. Continuation of the NAL was totally dependent on black fans patronage. There were no corporate sponsors.

John Johnson, sports editor of *The Call,* wrote a depressing article as to the future of the league. The June 25th headline read, "No Big Names Left in Negro Baseball." Johnson said that he was startled to discover that there were no longer any well-known names in the NAL. In fact, the two best known players might be women, Toni Stone of the Monarchs and Connie Morgan of the Clowns, and they had the worst batting averages in the league. According to Johnson, as of June 25th, with nineteen times at bat, Toni Stone had two hits for an average of .105 and Miss Morgan with fourteen times at bat, recorded one safety for an average of .071. The Monarchs, the 1953 NAL Champions, were now ranked in last place behind the two new teams to the league that had all new recruits.[45]

With so many black players now in the majors or on major league farm teams, interest in Negro League Baseball was at an all time low. The majors had recruited all the good players and many unknowns were drafted out of high school. The Monarchs were still training new young ball players but their team was now composed of minor league rather than major league talent.

The 1954 Major League World Series between the New York Giants and the Cleveland Indians had six black players. Willie Mays, Monte Irvin, and Henry Thompson played for the Giants and Larry Doby, Al Smith and Dave Pope for the Indians. The Major League All-Star Game in July, besides Willie Mays, had two other black stars, Jackie Robinson and Roy Campanella of the Brooklyn Dodgers.

Serious Negro League Baseball now had too much competition, both from Major League Baseball and other competing barnstorming teams with major leaguers. In the fall of 1954 Cool Papa Bell took a barnstorming team with top black major league players through the Midwest, south, southwest and Mexico. Campanella's All Star team toured the Far East, Latin America and several U.S. cities. Black baseball as a purely professional game had out-lived its time.[46]

The NAL obituary was being written. At the end of the 1954 season, the reigning champions, the Indianapolis Clowns, quit the NAL to barnstorm independently. This was a severe blow to the viability of the league. The Clowns had been in the NAL for thirteen years and had won four of the last five championships.

At the end of the 1954 season, both the Monarchs and the Clowns released their female players. *The Call* made no mention of the fact that Toni Stone and Mamie Johnson were leaving the league. An October 29th article, however, states that Connie Morgan is ending her fifteen month career with the Clowns in order to go to secretarial school. The writer says that she wants to pursue her real ambition "to become a top-flight worker in a business office." The writer notes that she was a star attraction from Key West, Florida, to Canada, hitting out a "tattoo of hits" during her brief career.[47]

From the publicity that Stone and Morgan received as late as August 27th, the public would never have guessed that the women were soon to be released. An article in *The Call* states that the two women are to play in the Clowns/Monarchs game in Columbia, Missouri, August 29th. The writer declares, "These two ladies (Stone and Morgan) prove that we can no longer refer to them as the weaker sex. They field well and can hit the long ball."[48]

Throughout the 1954 summer Toni Stone and Connie Morgan had received good press. An article in *The Call* on July 11 stated, "The girls (Toni Stone and Connie Morgan) have displayed amazing ability in playing the men's game. They handle their chances in the field speedily and they take their cuts at the ball at the plate." Another *Call* article, August 20, cited the excellent fielding of Clowns second basewoman Connie Morgan. "Miss Connie Morgan ... figured as the pivot-man in a key double play that halted a possible Monarch's rally." The same article states that the win kept the Clowns in first place in the NAL.

Based on these articles, lack of skills was not the reason for the release of Stone and Morgan. Perhaps, Mamie Johnson was released for mediocre pitching ability. Stone claims that she quit because the Monarchs didn't give her enough playing time, not that her contract was not renewed. Morgan and Johnson both admit they left because their contracts were not renewed. However, the real reason for their release was economics. They hadn't brought the necessary crowds to justify their contracts.

Syd Pollock foresaw the demise of professional Negro League Baseball. He decided that the Clowns could attract more fans and make more money by concentrating on comedy and playing only exhibition games. Pollock stated, "We want to concentrate more on having the team and its comediennes get in more of their stunts such as 'shadowball,' 'pepperball' and other fun-making specialties, including pantomime and laugh provoking features."[49]

Pollock, a smart businessman, probably made the right decision financially. The women players were lucky to be released at the end of the 1954 season and not to have been exploited as part of the new comedy show. Perhaps Pollock no longer considered them enough of a novelty, when women wrestlers made their debut in Kansas City in 1953. Women wrestlers became the new sensation and drew large crowds.

The February 20, 1953, edition of *The Call* announced that the first interracial wrestling championship between white champion Mildred Burke and black challenger Babs Wingo in Kansas City drew a crowd of 8,972. On May 15, Babs Wingo returned to battle another black wrestler, Ethel Johnson. Over 7,000 fans watched. On April 1954 four black women appeared in a wrestling show at the Municipal auditorium and attracted 9,000 fans. In December Wingo and Johnson received top billing beside famous male wrestler Gorgeous George. Wingo and Johnson were billed as the top black feminine stars.[50]

In 1955 the Clowns, now totally independent from the NAL, played exhibition games against the New York Black Yankees in major league stadiums across the country, as well as in smaller ones. The Clowns continued their tradition of combining clowning with athletic skills.

Pollock, no doubt, saw the financial future of the Clowns as similar to that of the Harlem Globetrotters. In 1955 the Harlem Globetrotters basketball team garnered tremendous media coverage when they hosted a benefit game to raise money for the U.S. Olympic basketball team. CBS televised the game to over 25.5 million TV households. It was the Globetrotters' 29th season and their crowd appeal was growing. In 1952 they had set an attendance record when they played before 75,000 in Berlin's Olympic Stadium.[51] Pollock hoped his baseball Clowns could do the same. The Clowns died out in the 1970s, long after the other Negro teams had ceased to exist. The Globetrotters, however, are still playing basketball.

In 1955 the remaining four NAL teams — the Kansas City Monarchs, the Birmingham Barons, the Memphis Red Sox and the Detroit Stars — continued to play legitimate baseball and lost money. Gate receipts could not keep up with expenses. With integration of the Major Leagues, there was no longer a need for the Negro Leagues. As sports editor John Johnson aptly noted, Negro baseball, once a necessity, had now become a relic of the Jim Crow period.[52] The NAL and the Monarchs had become another causality of major league baseball.

For all intents and purposes, Negro League Baseball ceased to operate after 1955. Hiring Toni Stone, Connie Morgan and Mamie Johnson had been a last ditch effort at survival. The window of opportunity for women disappeared. Unfortunately, women playing in the Negro Leagues had no effect on the sexist attitudes of Major League Baseball administrators.

In 1952 when Eleanor Engle, a white stenographer, was signed to play shortstop for the Harrisburg Senators, a minor league team, baseball commissioner Ford Frick quickly ruled women ineligible. George Trautman, the head of the minor leagues, called the signing of a woman "a travesty" and declared that any club that even attempts to "go through the motions" of signing a woman player "will be subject to severe disciplinary action."[53] That decision was not questioned in 1953 or 1954. No minor league team in 1955 picked up the contracts of Toni Stone, Mamie Johnson or Connie Morgan. Women players merely vanished and were soon forgotten. Financially they were no longer needed for their drawing power as novelty entertainment. The door of opportunity closed and has virtually remained closed. The opportunity that Jackie Robinson created was short-lived. Integration of Major League Baseball may have helped to eliminate racism but not sexism.

Notes

1. Quoted in Janet Bruce, *The Kansas City Monarchs: Champions of Black Baseball* (Lawrence: University Press of Kansas, 1985), 98.
2. The term black rather than African American is used since this was the usage at the time of the Negro Leagues.
3. Kansas City's *The Call*, a weekly African American newspaper, regularly reported on Kansas City Monarchs baseball games. Much of the playing data on Toni Stone, Connie Morgan and Mamie Johnson cited in this paper is derived from articles written during the 1953 and 1954 seasons.
4. Quoted in Bruce, 116.
5. Donn Rogosin, *Invisible Men: Life in the Negro Leagues* (New York: Atheneum, 1987), 218.
6. Bruce, 145.
7. Bruce, 118.
8. Rogosin, 141–149.
9. "Clowns Signs Two Top Sophomores," *The Call*, 20 March 1953, 10.
10. Rogosin, 149.
11. Dick Clark & Larry Lester (eds.), *The Negro Leagues Book* (Cleveland: SABR, 1994), 163.
12. More biographical information on Toni Stone can be found in Gai Ingham Berlage, *Women in Baseball: The Forgotten History*, Westport, CT: Praeger, 1994, and Barbara Gregorich, *Women at Play: The Story of Women in Baseball,* NY: Harcourt Brace, 1993.
13. Riley, 23.
14. James A. Riley, "Lady at the Bat," *The Diamond*, March/April 1994, 23; Ron Thomas, "Baseball Pioneer Looks Back: Woman Played in Negro Leagues," *San Francisco Chronicle*, 23 Aug. 1991, C3.
15. "Speaking of People: Lady Ball Player on Male Team," *Ebony* (1 Sept. 1950), 4.
16. Unidentified article in NBHFL file on Toni Stone.
17. Doug Grow, "A League of Her Own: Tomboy Stone Is Dead at 75," *Star Tribune*, 5 November 1996, B7.

18. Diane DuBay, "From St. Paul Playgrounds to Big Leagues, Stone Always Loved Baseball," *Minnesota Women's Press*, 3–16 Feb. 1988.

19. Al Marvin, "Clowning Helps Keep Indianapolis Clowns Integrated," *The New York Times*, 30 May 1971; "Monarchs Win NAL Championship: Rav Neil Cops '53 Batting Title," *The Call*, 25 Sept. 1953, 12.

20. Thomas, C3.

21. Ross Forman, "Black Woman Was Alone in Own League," *USA Today*, 2 July 1992, 2C.

22. Thomas.

23. "Woman Player Says She Can 'Take Care of Self' in Game," *Ebony*, June/July 1953, 48.

24. "Woman Player...." 50.

25. Claire Smith, "Belated Tribute to Baseball's Negro Leagues," *The New York Times*, 13 August 1991, B9.

26. John Holway, *Blackball Stars: Negro League Pioneers* (Westport, CT: Meckler, 1988), 185–186.

27. "Woman Player...." 50.

28. "Woman Player...." 50.

29. "Female Player Remembered by Major League Baseball," *Jet*, 1 June 1992, 50.

30. "Woman Player...." 50.

31. Bruce, 118.

32. "Clowns Sell Girl Player, Toni Stone to Monarchs then Hire 2 Other Girls," *The Call*, 12 March 1954, 12.

33. "Clowns Sell Girl Player..."

34. Telephone interview by author with Connie Morgan, July 23, 1995.

35. Lynn Ford, "Send in the Clowns, er, Indians," *The Indianapolis Star*, 3 June 1995.

36. 1954 Indianapolis Clowns/Kansas City Monarchs Program.

37. Photo, *The Call*, May 28, 1954, 10.

38. "Clowns Sell Girl Player...."

39. "Clowns' Girl Second Baseman Thrills Birmingham Fans with Speedy Plays," *The Call*, May 28, 1954, 10.

40. "Complete Plans for Monarch and Clowns to Play a Twin-Bill in Yankee Stadium," *The Call*, 21 May 1954, 10.

41. "Philadelphia Phillies Reported Signing Two Monarchs: Herrera and Mason," *The Call*, 15 Oct. 1954, 10.

42. "This Date in Bush Stadium History," *The Indianapolis Star*, 10 June 1995.

43. "Visiting Scribes to Cover Game," *The Call*, 21 May 1954, p. 11; "Monarch Boosters Club to Present Its Annual Pre-Game Exhibition June 6," *The Call*, 4 June 1954, 10. "Mrs. L.A. Otey, Willie Huggins Win Monarch Crowd Guess Prizes," *The Call*, 18 June 1954, 12.

44. "Monarch Player to Wed During Game of June 6," *The Call*, 28 May 1954, 11.

45. "No Big Names Left in Negro Baseball," *The Call*, 25 June 1954, 12.

46. "Cool Papa Bell to Take a Team on Tour," *The Call*, 16 July 1954, 10; "Campanella Plans Barnstorm Tour," *The Call*, 16 July 1954, 10.

47. "Clowns Girl Player Returns To School," *The Call*, 29 October 1954.

48. "Clowns, Monarchs To Columbia, August 29," *The Call*, 27 August 1954.

49. "Indianapolis Clowns Quit Negro American Loop," *The Call*, 28 Jan. 1955, 11.

50. "Challenger and Champion," *The Call*, 20 Feb. 1953, p. 11; "Negro Girl Wrestlers Battle Like Tigers," *The Call*, 15 May 1953, 11; "Four Negro Girl Wrestlers Please," *The Call*, 2 April 1954, 11; "Top Negro Wrestlers to Appear on Gorgeous George, Red Berry Mat Card," *The Call*, 7 Dec. 1954, 10.

51. "Pro Harlem Globetrotters to Play TV Benefit Tilt to Aid Olympic Amateurs," *The Call*, 25 Feb. 1955, p. 11; "Trotters to Play in TV Game Saturday," *The Call*, 11 March 1955, 10.

52. John I. Johnson, "Sport Light: Hand Writing on the Wall," *The Call*, 23 Sept. 1955, 10.

53. "Baseball: No (Wo)man's Land, Trautman, Frick Put Law Barring Women into Book," *Harrisburg Patriot,* 24 June 1952.

Ten Years After:
The Baseball Establishment,
Race, and Jackie Robinson

Ron Briley

In September 1956, *The Sporting News*, speaking on behalf of Organized Baseball, printed a self-congratulatory editorial lauding the sport's tenth year of racial integration. The paper observed that with over forty "Negro" players on major league rosters, "their place in the game is secure." On a rather smug note, *The Sporting News* reported that while challenges to racial segregation in the schools often resulted in violent confrontations, baseball offered a model for peaceful reconciliation of racial strife. The editorial concluded, "The National Game does not presume to advise other segments of the population or other sports, on how to handle this complicated and emotional problem. It merely points with satisfaction to its own record of gradual, voluntary, and peaceful advance toward the complete fulfillment of its code that a player should not be judged on the basis of creed, connections or color, but on the basis of ability alone."[1]

The baseball establishment in 1956 was especially proud of Afro-American players such as Harry Simpson of the Kansas City A's, who, after leading his team in runs-batted-in, had no problems reaching terms for a new contract with Kansas City management. In an interview with reporters, Simpson expressed his gratitude to baseball for giving him an opportunity, insisting that all Afro-American ball players should be appreciative of baseball's racial policies. Simpson stated, "Here I am making more than a great percentage of the men of my race. Here I am on a ball club where I've been given every chance in the world to make good. What more could I possibly want? That's everything there is." *The Sporting News* was appreciative of the sentiments espoused by Simpson, editorializing, "Naturally, the good things of the game seem especially gratifying to a big leaguer who, as a boy, probably assumed his color would make it impossible for him even to enjoy them. But Simpson's words would have been every bit as valid had he made no mention of his race. They apply with just as much force to all big leaguers, regardless of nationality, background, or pigmentation."[2]

However, these noble sentiments were less than apparent on the playing field as in 1956 the roster of major league teams contained approximately only forty players of Afro-American descent. That year only thirteen Afro-American players were added to major league rosters, and clubs such as the Philadelphia Phillies, Detroit Tigers, and Boston Red Sox had no black players. Like Southern reaction to the Supreme Court's 1954 Brown decision on school desegregation, the baseball establishment did not exactly move with all deliberate speed to integrate the sport. Baseball officials explained their actions by citing such concerns as the reaction of Southern white players to black teammates, the many minor league clubs in the South, spring training facilities in the South, potential racial conflict among spectators, and the quality of black athletes.

These excuses constituted a rather feeble effort to conceal the continued racism within the baseball establishment. Accordingly, historian Ben Rader maintained that by the mid–1950s, "... many if not all clubs had unwritten understandings to restrict the total number of blacks. Driven in part by the profit motive, the owners tried to calculate whether increasing the number of black players would result in more wins and thereby increase attendance or whether it would adversely affect the identification of white fans with their teams and thereby reduce attendance and revenues." In a similar vein, Robinson biographer Jules Tygiel argued, "Baseball's failure to integrate more rapidly reflected not only a persistent hostility to blacks, but prevailing racial attitudes and assumptions, and widely shared player development strategies. Many teams stalwartly resisted desegregation. Other moved haltingly, bypassing established Negro League stars in favor of young prospects and demanding higher standards of performance and behavior from black players than white." Black athletes such as Curt Flood, who starred for the St. Louis Cardinals and later gained notoriety by challenging baseball's reserve clause, insisted that white ownership was most concerned with sexual politics and interracial dating between Afro-American ballplayers and white women.[3]

Thus, there was an assumption within the baseball community that unacknowledged racial quotas existed for some teams. Indeed, many teams in 1956 had only one black athlete, as was the case of the New York Yankees and Elston Howard. In an article on Howard, reporter Dan Daniel made it clear that more than playing ability was evaluated as a factor in the advancement of Afro-American athletes in the major leagues. Reflecting widespread racial stereotyping within the baseball establishment, Daniel's reporting raised no protest when he observed that Howard stayed with the Yankees not only because he was a fine player, but also because the Afro-American athlete was "quiet, well-behaved, and a fine asset to the off-the-field tone of the club." Daniel praised Howard for raising no objection when he could not stay with the team at the Emerson Hotel in Baltimore due to city segregation ordinances. Concluding on what could certainly be interpreted as a racist tone, Daniel wrote, "The Yankees would like to find another Negro player. But they insist that he be of the Howard stamp, and that is not going to be easy. In fact, at the moment, it's impossible."⁴ In addition to indulging in racial stereotypes regarding character, the Yankee management seemed to accept a double standard based on race. While Howard was expected to always demonstrate exemplary behavior, and the Yankees refused to call up Afro-American Vic Power from the minor leagues, the "party" antics of white stars such as Mickey Mantle, Billy Martin, and Whitey Ford were tolerated.

While management continued to display condescending attitudes regarding race, racial taunts had not disappeared from the playing field. In a late August contest between the Brooklyn Dodgers and Milwaukee Braves, Jackie Robinson fired a ball into the Braves dugout, narrowly missing the head of pitcher Lew Burdette, who turned down a challenge by Robinson to fight. Burdette had called the Afro-American athlete a "watermelon head." However, *The Sporting News* reporter covering the incident failed to describe the taunting as racially motivated. Instead, he wrote, "It was assumed that the pitcher referred to Robinson's girth, which had been given prominent display in a photograph which appeared recently in a national sports publication."⁵ Even if commentators refused to acknowledge racist language, Robinson would no longer tolerate it.

While black players continued to struggle with segregated housing and racism on the playing field, the baseball establishment made clear its lack of understanding and commitment to racial segregation with the manner in which it handled the end of Jackie Robinson's illustrious career and the challenge of segregation with the Shreveport Sports of the Texas League.

By the conclusion of the 1956 season, in which the New York Yankees edged Brooklyn for the World Series championship, it was apparent that the illustrious career of Jackie Robinson was winding down. Battling injuries and health problems, Robinson's playing time in 1956 was limited to 117 games. However, his games played, batting average, home runs, and runs batted in were all improvement over his 1955 marks.[6] Thus, many in baseball were shocked to learn on the morning of December 13, 1956 that Brooklyn had traded Robinson to their fierce National League rivals, the New York Giants, for cash and journeyman pitcher, Dick Littlefield. In an official statement, Robinson stated that he was disappointed and having to comfort his crying son, Jackie, Jr. However, trades were part of baseball, and he spoke of his relationship with the Brooklyn club in diplomatic terms, stating, "There are no hard feelings. The Brooklyn club had to protect its own best interests. I thought I helped Brooklyn last year and didn't figure to be traded." Robinson concluded that he would wait until January 10, 1957 to inform Giants owner Horace Stoneham whether he would retire or play for the Giants.[7]

Dodger fans were outraged. The *New York Times* quoted one Brooklyn partisan as proclaiming, "I'm shocked to the core. This is like selling the Brooklyn-Battery Tunnel. Jackie Robinson is a synonym for the Dodgers. They can't do this to us." (Of course, this fan did not realize the Robinson trade was only the beginning of Dodger management's betrayal of Brooklyn.) Despite the antagonism from the Dodger faithful and Robinson's hint that he might retire, the baseball establishment's assumption was that business would go on as usual. Giants owner Stoneham did not believe Robinson would leave the game. Instead, Robinson, whom Stoneham labeled the "greatest competitor I've ever seen in baseball," would play first base for the Giants in 1957. Referring to Jackie Robinson, Jr.'s, tearful reaction to the trade, *The Sporting News* insisted, "Jackie, Sr., being an adult, recognizes the expediency that exists in this world with which he must cope and has displayed no tear-stained-face to the public. He is now a Giant and will play ball for the Giants with the same fiercely competitive spirit he displayed for so long as a Dodger. That is the only way Robinson knows how to play."[8] However, when Robinson engaged in a bit of his own expediency regarding the announcement of his retirement, *The Sporting News* and baseball establishment yelled foul.

While Brooklyn fans were dismayed with the trade, Robinson was less surprised and was already making plans for his departure from the game. Robinson did not get along well with Dodger manager Walter Alston, and his relationship with the front office deteriorated when Walter O'Malley maneuvered to force Branch Rickey out of Brooklyn. From a peak figure of $39,000, Robinson's salary suffered slight reductions for each of his last three seasons in Brooklyn. In his memoirs, Robinson commented unfavorably on the racial views of O'Malley, alleging that the Dodger President perceived him as an "uppity Nigger."[9]

Accordingly, on December 10, 1956, Robinson met with William Black, President of Chock Full o'Nuts, a fast-food restaurant chain in the New York City area. Black, whose employees were predominantly Afro-American, offered Robinson a position as vice-president in charge of personnel at an annual salary of fifty thousand dollars. That evening Robinson attempted to reach Dodger General Manager "Buzzy" Bavasi and inform him of his intentions. However, Bavasi, who was negotiating with the Giants, was unavailable. The next day, Robinson signed a contract with Black. That same evening, Robinson was told that he had been traded to the Giants. He did not advise Dodger officials that he had decided to retire from baseball and accept a position with Chock Full o' Nuts. The reason for Robinson's apparent duplicity was an exclusive contract for fifty thousand dollars which he had signed with *Look* magazine. The contract stipulated that Robinson's retirement would first be announced in a magazine exclusive.[10]

Yet, the story broke early before the magazine hit the newsstands. A few *Look* subscribers received advance copies, and *Look* executives scrambled to call a press conference for Robinson. When asked why he had chosen to work through a magazine deal and not keep his employer informed of his intentions, Robinson replied, "I had given my best to Brooklyn for eleven years and my debt to baseball has been paid." Buzzy Bavasi did not agree, insisting that Robinson owed an obligation to the Dodgers as well as the sportswriters of New York. Bavasi told reporters, "And this is the way he repays the newspapermen for what they've done for him. He tells you one thing and then writes another for money. You fellows will find out that you've been blowing the horn for the wrong guy." An angry Robinson retorted, "After what Bavasi said, I wouldn't play ball again for a million dollars."[11]

The New York press immediately weighed into the Robinson-Bavasi debate. Red Smith of the *New York Herald Tribune* rebuked Robinson for his lack of loyalty to the Dodgers, asserting, "But for the Dodgers, the Jackie Robinson of this last decade would not have existed. The fact that he gave them full value on the field and the fact that after eleven years they sold his contract without consulting him, these do not alter the fact that everything he has he owes to the club. His debt to the Dodgers had precedence over any agreement to sell a story to *Look*, and with his mind already made up at the time of the trade he was honor bound to speak up." Dick Young of the *New York News*, who often chastised Robinson, maintained that the Brooklyn great did not owe anything to reporters or the Dodgers.

Young was more upset that Robinson, in his *Look* press conference of January 6, had criticized baseball for lacking sentiment. Rallying to the defense of the national pastime, Young argued, "So Robinson should have quit, which certainly is his privilege, without smearing the game that has earned him $500,000 in ten years. Baseball has as much sentiment as any business he can name, much more than the cream cheese sandwich business, for one." On the other hand, Joe Williams of the *New York World Telegram* insisted that Robinson would be a "dope" to not take *Look*'s lucrative offer. Seeking to take a more neutral position, *The Sporting News* editorialized that while Robinson had every right to sell his story, the Bible of Baseball preferred the "outstanding example" of dignified retirement established by Bob Feller, who announced his retirement several weeks before Robinson and had accepted a position as corporate spokesperson for the Motorola Corporation.[12]

In the much maligned *Look* article, Robinson simply maintained that his decision to leave the game was based on financial security for his family. He concluded the article by noting, "I know I'll miss the excitement of baseball, but I'm looking forward to new kinds of satisfaction. I'll be able to spend more time with my family. My kids and I will get to know each other better.... They won't have to look for me on TV."[13] However, shortly after his retirement, Robinson agreed to postpone assuming his duties with Chock Full o'Nuts, while he commenced on a speaking and fund-raising tour on behalf of the NAACP. Accordingly, Robinson's retirement was also related to the athlete's decision to make a larger commitment and contribution to the burgeoning civil rights movement. Commenting upon the athlete's statement that he was ready to accept responsibility to his race and country, Robinson biographer Arnold Rampersad wrote, "Most immediately, he was making this sacrifice in order to aid black people living under Jim Crow down south."[14]

On December 8, 1956, two days before he met with William Black, Robinson received the prestigious Spingarn Medal, awarded annually "for the highest achievement of an American Negro." Ed Sullivan, columnist and television celebrity, presented the gold medal at a New York dinner sponsored by the NAACP. Among the previous recipients present were Ralph Bunche, W. E. B. DuBois, and Thurgood Marshall. The award citation placed Robinson's contributions in historical perspective, proclaiming, "The entire nation is indebted to him for his pioneer role in breaking the color line in Organized Baseball. Through sheer ability and exceptional competitive zeal, he won popular acclaim of sports lovers of all races and demonstrated that there were no fore-ordained racial restrictions upon the ability to play the National Game. He opened the doors of the major leagues for Negro stars whose skill, zest, and stamina have entered the national sport."[15]

Perceived as a symbol of opportunity and struggle for Afro-Americans, Robinson could hardly refuse when NAACP Executive Secretary Roy Wilkins asked the athlete to chair the organization's 1957 Freedom Fund drive. While a novice as a public speaker, under the tutelage of veteran NAACP organizer Franklin Williams, Robinson became a successful orator and fund raiser, proudly pointing out that the 1957 tour was able to garner a million dollars for the NAACP coffers. Echoing the sentiments of Martin Luther King, Jr., Robinson argued that Afro-Americans were out of patience and could no longer wait for equal rights. He told a Chicago audience, "We have waited almost one hundred years for these rights. In my view, now is the time for Negroes to ask for all of the rights which are theirs."[16]

It is worth noting the courage which Robinson displayed in embracing the cause of the NAACP. In the late 1950s, opponents of racial integration attempted to brand the civil rights organization as a subversive tool of the Communist Party and Soviet Union. For example, appearing before the Louisiana Joint Legislative Committee on Segregation, Afro-American Manning Johnson, who had been a minor Communist Party official in New York, attacked Martin Luther King, Jr., and the NAACP. The vitriolic Johnson described King as a "dastardly misleader who is taking his race down the road of violence, bloodshed, revolution, and possible communism in the South." In concluding his testimony, Johnson denounced the NAACP as a "communist vehicle designed to initiate the overthrow of the government."[17]

However, sport coverage of the Robinson speaking tour failed to acknowledge his courage and determination. Instead, publications such as *The Sporting News* focused upon baseball questions Robinson fielded during press conferences. The Robinson image projected by *The Sporting News* was not the crusader for racial equality, but rather a hot-headed commentator who antagonized fellow players and baseball executives. For example, at a speaking engagement in Waukegan, Illinois, Robinson stated that too much night life cost the Milwaukee Braves the 1956 National League pennant. Braves players replied to the criticism by labeling Robinson a "rumor monger." Braves shortstop Johnny Logan maintained that Robinson was "just popping off to keep his name in the headlines." As if a man whose mission to raise a million dollars for an institution under attack needed the publicity of alleged night life in Milwaukee.[18]

On a more serious note, Robinson was quoted as describing former teammate Roy Campanella as "washed up." An angry Campanella retorted that he was tired of Robinson "popping off." The burly catcher criticized Robinson for demonstrating a negative attitude toward baseball, asserting, "Instead of being grateful to baseball, he's criticizing it. Everything he has he owes to baseball. That beautiful house of his, and this new job of his, too. Does he think those people would have had anything to do with him if he had never played baseball." The two men initially quarreled over Campanella's failure to join Robinson in challenging segregated housing for the black Brooklyn ball players.[19] The antagonism between Campanella and Robinson reflected a debate within the Afro-American community about the necessity of pushing for racial integration going back to the days of Booker T. Washington and W. E. B. DuBois.

But Campanella's complaints failed to silence Robinson who observed that it was "strange" that no Afro-American players could make the major league rosters of Detroit, Philadelphia, and Boston. While speaking in Detroit, the former Brooklyn star further acknowledged that he was puzzled by the fact that "for some reason there are no Negro players on the fields of Detroit. Detroit is a great sports town. But you can't help but wonder about the absence of Negro players in both football and baseball."[20]

While Robinson insisted that he was speaking honestly, seeking a better nation for all Americans, former playing field opponents of Robinson continued to label the Dodger great a trouble-maker. Giants pitcher Sal Maglie, no stranger to baseball rhubarbs, was quoted as saying Robinson was unpopular with the players due to self-promotion. Maglie believed Robinson, who had expressed interest in managing, would never be given the reins of a major league club. Maglie concluded, "I don't think any ball club would take a chance on Jackie, because you just couldn't get anybody to play for him after the way he's been rapping other players."[21]

Despite business success, political involvement, and a respected role in the civil rights movement, one of Robinson's greatest disappointments was that he was never allowed to try his hand at piloting a major league franchise. Writing in 1972, Robinson observed, "I felt that any chance I might have had of moving up to an administrative job with the Dodgers or any other team was mighty slim. Had I been easy going, willing to be meek and humble, I might have had a chance. But this fact has not changed much even today. There are many capable black athletes in the game who could contribute greatly as managers or in other positions of responsibility, but it just isn't happening."[22] In fact, Robinson never lived to see his dream of an Afro-American manager, for Frank Robinson was not named to manage the Cleveland Indians until 1975, three years after the death of the pioneering Dodger great.

While Robinson was displaying his courage on the civil rights front, the baseball establishment was demonstrating its timidity in fighting segregation. In July, 1956, the Louisiana state legislature approved House Bill 1412, which, among other measures to ensure continued racial segregation in the state, prohibited blacks and whites from participating in interracial sporting events anywhere in the state. Despite protests from the NAACP and some concern by the business community regarding the economic consequences of this legislation, Governor Earl Long, explaining that he was "just a poor little old man going along with the majority," signed the legislation, which was to go into effect on October 15, 1956. *Newsweek* predicted that national condemnation of the athletic segregation statute would result in the shuffling of football and basketball schedules, while in baseball the Shreveport Sports would be expelled from the Texas League due to the number of black players on league rosters.[23]

While the forecast of *Newsweek* proved somewhat accurate in regard to intercollegiate basketball and football, professional baseball was not as adamant in its opposition to segregation. While major league exhibition games scheduled for Louisiana in the spring of 1957 were canceled, the segregationist Shreveport Sports baseball club retained its good standing in the integrated Texas League. While Commissioner Ford Frick was silent on the issue, the segregation problem was placed in the hands of Texas League President Dick Butler, who said he would seek a compromise solution, assuring that there would be no legal challenge by organized baseball to the Louisiana interracial sports ban. Finding a middle ground would not be easy. Art Routzong, general manager of the Houston Buffaloes, announced that his team would play the best players possible, regardless of race. However, he did put forth the idea that Houston might be willing to withdraw black players, if Shreveport would reciprocate by benching equivalent starting players. Crusty Bonneau Peters, long time President of the Shreveport franchise (an independent club with no major league working agreement), sounded a bit like Arkansas Governor Orville Faubus when he shunned compromise, asserting, "If these clubs want to play at Shreveport, they'll just have to play under the laws of Louisiana. I'm not going to do anything about it."[24]

Engaging in delicate diplomacy, League President Butler orchestrated an agreement which essentially catered to the obstinate Peters. Clubs with black players on the roster would be allowed an extra man above the league-imposed player limit of eighteen. Franchises such as Houston and Dallas, who each had five black roster players, were to be placed at a considerable competitive disadvantage when they journeyed to Shreveport. This agreement, or sellout, allowed *Sporting News* correspondent Jack

Gallagher to portray the January 20, 1957 annual midwinter meeting of Texas League management as conciliatory. According to Gallagher's report, "Only minor business occupied the directors, thus portraying the Texas League as one circuit without problems — a rarity in these times."[25]

Despite the baseball establishment's lack of understanding and sensitivity in responding to the retirement of Robinson, along with a shortage of courage in confronting racial segregation in Shreveport, *The Sporting News* continued to extol the sport's race record. In a May 22, 1957, editorial, the paper reminded readers, "The Negro in Organized Ball is so completely taken-for-granted these days that it must be difficult for younger fans to recall the time little more than a decade ago, when both majors and minors raised an invisible but effective barrier on the color line."[26]

Those who maintained that baseball was color blind pointed to a June 13, 1957, confrontation between Larry Doby, the first Afro-American player to integrate the American League, and New York Yankee pitcher Art Ditmar. In the first inning of the game at Comiskey Park, Ditmar brushed Doby back with a high and tight fast ball. After sprawling in the dust, Doby charged the mound and landed a left hook to the jaw of Ditmar. The Chicago and Yankee dugouts emptied, and a full scale brawl ensued. Following the game, Doby and teammate Walt Dropo, along with the Yankees Billy Martin and Enos Slaughter, were fined by League President Will Harridge. Shirley Povich of *The Washington Post* described the fight as historic for the sport of baseball. Povich wrote, "The Doby-Ditmar episode had special significance because for the first time a Negro player was daring to get as assertive as the white man whose special province Organized Ball had been for nearly a hundred years.... There is no intent here to condone what Doby did; merely to point out the consequences fell far short of Civil War or succession or a violent sense of outrage except among Ditmar's Yankee teammates who dashed to his assistance, but in no more anger than if his attacker had been a white player." While the fisticuffs between Doby and Ditmar did prove that black and white players could have altercations on the field without setting off race riots in the stands, Povich went too far in the conclusions he drew from the fight. Povich asserted, "There's no call now to brief the Negro player who is breaking into the big leagues. The chances are that any discrimination in his mind are more fancied than real. Anyway, the novelty of the Negro player in the majors long since wore off. They are no longer a gate attraction because of the color of their skin. Its the glint of their batting averages and other skills that count."[27]

Tell that to Larry Doby, who continued to endure segregation and Jim Crow during the White Sox's spring training in Tampa, Florida. Doby had to find housing with black families as he could not stay at the team hotel, and black players were given meal money to eat on their own. Accordingly, Doby told biographer Joseph Thomas Moore, "Not many people realize this, but I was segregated in spring training for 10 out of 13 years, right through the spring of 1959. Now do you see what I mean when I say that there were constant reminders that I was black? Was I imagining things when I was segregated? Does anyone think that the prejudice which caused segregation in the South didn't exist in the North?"[28]

A similar gap between myth and reality was evident in descriptions of Hank Aaron's 1957 pennant-winning home run for the Milwaukee Braves. On September 23, Aaron clubbed an eleventh inning home run giving the Braves a four to two victory over the St. Louis Cardinals. The first National League pennant for the Milwaukee club set off impromptu street parades in the brewing capital, while Aaron's teammates carried him off the field on their shoulders. According to *The Sporting News*, this moment represented the democratic spirit of baseball. Aaron was depicted as exemplifying the Horatio Alger success epic of America in which any individual, regardless of race or social class origin, may obtain success through hard work, drive, and determination. *The Sporting News* wrote, "A few years ago, Henry Aaron, one of a large family of children, was just another Negro boy playing softball on the sandlots of Mobile, Alabama. Now he is a national figure, a star on a pennant-winning team, the hero of the flag-clinching game, a World's Series participant, his name familiar to every follower of baseball. More than that, he is a popular member of the Braves, acclaimed and respected by his fellow players and by fans with no thought of his color. For, as the pennant-clinching scene proved again, outstanding achievement depends only on ability, and not on race, creed or background, in the real fellowship of sports."[29]

Notwithstanding the democratic credo endorsed in *The Sporting News* editorial, Aaron's baseball career demonstrated that discrimination and racial bigotry were still major factors in American society and the sport of baseball. The perception of being treated as an interchangeable commodity to be transferred from Milwaukee to Atlanta for the 1966 season weighed heavily upon Aaron. Even though Milwaukee had a relatively small Afro-American population, and its own history of racial discrimination,[30] Aaron, who grew up in Alabama, was not eager to return to his native region. In his memoirs Aaron, who finished his playing career with the Milwaukee Brewers, insisted that he never got over the trauma of the Braves departure from the Wisconsin city.

Aaron needed reserves of character and talent as he dealt with the challenge of life in Atlanta. He and his wife were able to purchase a beautiful home, although, of course, it was located in a segregated neighborhood.

As a prominent Afro-American player, Aaron received several hate letters a week, in addition to hearing the racial insults hurled in his direction at the ballpark. Aaron's wife Barbara was even arrested when she tried to drive into the stadium, as a white guard, who did not recognize her, stopped the car, pulled his gun, and verbally abused her. The charges were dropped after intervention from the mayor's office. Aaron responded the only way he knew, with his bat. In his memoirs, Aaron asserted, "I knew that, as a black player, I would be on trial in Atlanta, and I needed a decisive way to win over the white people before they thought of a reason to hate me. And I believed that the way to do all of this was with home runs."[31] Aaron's decision to let his bat do the talking culminated in the surpassing of Babe Ruth's career home run mark, which, ironically, seemed to increase the racial abuse to which the Braves outfielder was subjected.

The reality of the discrimination encountered by players such as Hank Aaron, Larry Doby, and Elston Howard; the failure of Organized Baseball to challenge segregation in Shreveport; the criticism of Jackie Robinson as a rabble rouser following his baseball career and commitment to the civil rights struggle; and the slow progress of racial integration in the major leagues (Franchises in Boston, Detroit, and Philadelphia had no black players on their major league rosters), all indicate that baseball ten years after Jackie Robinson was hardly a model of racial integration and toleration. Baseball spokespersons, such as *The Sporting News*, who assumed that baseball had put racial issues behind it by the 1956 and 1957 seasons, were as much out of step with the changes occurring in America as those in Congress who assumed the rather innocuous Civil Rights Bill of 1957 would satisfy those courageous individuals mounting assaults upon Jim Crow and racism in America. For in 1956–1957 the Civil Rights movement was just beginning to gather steam, and much sacrifice would be needed to topple the structure of Jim Crow. While Organized Baseball congratulated itself for integrating some black players, the sport remained silent about Shreveport and much of the discrimination in spring training sites. On the other hand, black players such as Robinson, Doby, and Aaron knew the movement for equality was only gathering momentum ten years after Robinson began his career with the Dodger organization.

And where are we today fifty years after Jackie Robinson? There is much about baseball and American society of which Robinson would probably be proud. The kind of overt racism to which Robinson was subjected is no longer tolerated in American society, and it is most appropriate that Organized Baseball is honoring Robinson's memory. Robinson was also a businessman, and he would welcome a growing black middle class; however, the overall economic gap between rich and poor, where black

Americans are over represented, continues in grow in America. And it is easy to assume that Robinson would be most concerned with the discrepancy between the number of young Afro-American males, ages eighteen to twenty-four, in penal institutions as opposed to educational institutions. The number of Afro-American managers in baseball has increased in recent years, but after expressions of concern following the racist comments of Dodgers' executive Al Campanis on the fortieth anniversary of Robinson's Dodger career, baseball management has not been forthcoming with opportunities for Afro-Americans in the executive suite. And the percentage of Afro-American players in baseball is down to seventeen percent, as black athletes increasingly turn to careers in football and basketball. As we honor Jackie Robinson's fiftieth anniversary, it is no time to be overly self-congratulatory. Just as baseball and America in 1956–1957 had a long way to travel in regard to an egalitarian society, we still have a distance to go. But as we proceed in our endeavors to achieve a just society let us not grow complacent, and let us always keep in mind the courageous legacy of Jackie Robinson.

Notes

1. *Sporting News*, September 9, 1956.
2. *Ibid.*, November 21 and 28, 1956. For additional information on Harry "Suitcase" Simpson, see: Larry Moffi and Jonathan Kronstadt, *Crossing the Line: Black Major Leaguers, 1947–1959* (Jefferson, North Carolina: McFarland, 1994), p. 65–67.
3. On the progress, or lack thereof, of major league baseball integration, see: Moffi and Kronstadt, *Crossing the Line*; Ben Rader, *Baseball: A History of America's Game* (Urbana: University of Illinois Press, 1994), p. 152–153; Jules Tygiel, *Baseball's Great Experiment: Jackie Robinson and His Legacy* (New York: Random House, 1983), p. 285–286; and Curt Flood with Richard Carter, *The Way It Is* (New York: Trident Press, 1970), p. 100–102.
4. On Elston Howard, see: *Sporting News*, February 1, 1956; Elston Howard, "It's Great to Be a Yankee," *Ebony*, 10 (September, 1955), p. 50–54; Barry Stainback, "Have the Yankees Held Back Howard?," *Sport*, 32 (December, 1961), p. 46–47; and Moffi and Kronstadt, *Crossing the Line*, p. 133–136.
5. *Sporting News*, September 5, 1956. On Lew Burdette, see: Bob Wolff, "Burdette, the Dodger Baiter," *Sport*, 16 (April, 1984), p. 24–31.
6. John Thorn and Pete Palmer, eds., *Total Baseball: The Ultimate Encyclopedia of Baseball* (New York: HarperPerennial, 1993), p. 1, 182.
7. *Sporting News*, December 19, 1956; *New York Times*, December 14, 1956; and "If You Can't Beat Him," *Time*, 68 (December 24, 1956), p. 42.
8. *New York Times*, December 14, 1956; *Sporting News*, December 19 and 26, 1956; and "After Ten Years," *Newsweek*, 48 (December 24, 1956), p. 49.
9. For Robinson's perspective of O'Malley, see: Jackie Robinson, *I Never Had it Made* (New York: G. P. Putnam's Sons, 1972), p. 100–115.
10. For Robinson's negotiations with William Black and *Look* , see: David Falkner,

Great Time Coming: The Life of Jackie Robinson from Baseball to Birmingham (New York: Simon & Schuster, 1995), p. 249–251; Arnold Rampersad, *Jackie Robinson: A Biography* (New York: Alfred A. Knopf, 1997), p. 303–309; and Robinson, *I Never Had It Made*, p. 130–134.

11. *Sporting News*, January 16, 1957; and *New York Times*, January 7, 1957.

12. *Sporting News*, January 16, 1957.

13. Jackie Robinson, "Why I'm Quitting Baseball," *Look*, 21 (January 22, 1957), p. 99–102.

14. Rampersad, *Jackie Robinson*, p. 316–317.

15. *New York Times*, December 9, 1956; and *Sporting News*, December 19, 1956.

16. For Robinson's Freedom Foundation tour, see: Robinson, *I Never Had It Made*, p. 137–146; Falkner, *Great Time Coming*, p. 253–262; and Rampersad, *Robinson*, p. 314–330.

17. For the public hearings of the Louisiana Joint Legislative Committee on Segregation, see: *Shreveport Times*, March 7, 8, 9, and 10, 1957. For background information on Manning Johnson, see: Harvey Klehr, *The Heyday of American Communism* (New York: Basic Books, 1984), p. 400–401 and 471–472.

18. *Sporting News*, January 23, 1957.

19. *Ibid.*, February 6, 1957. For the Robinson-Campanella relationship, see: Robinson, *I Never Had It Made*, p. 110–111; and Rampersad, *Robinson*, p. 291–292. For additional background information on Campanella, see: "Big Man From Nicetown: Roy Campanella," *Time*, 66 (August 8, 1955), p. 50–55; and Roy Campanella, *It's Good To Be Alive* (Boston: Little, Brown, 1959).

20. *Sporting News*, February 27 and 6, 1957.

21. *Ibid.*, February 6, 1957. For the temperamental Maglie, see: Robert W. Creamer, "An Angel of Darkness Named Sal the Barber," *Sports Illustrated*, 2 (June 6, 1955), p. 43–44; and Millan J. Shapiro, *The Sal Maglie Story* (New York: Julian Messner, 1957).

22. Robinson, *I Never Had It Made*, p. 130.

23. "Segregation Snafu," *Newsweek*, 48 (July 30, 1956), p. 79–80.

24. *Sporting News*, October 24, 1956. The Louisiana law which went into effect on October 15, 1956 prohibited racially-mixed athletic contests in the state, providing penalties for participants which would range from sixty days to one year in jail and fines from $100 to $1,000.

25. *Sporting News*, January 30, 1957. Preseason Texas League rosters included five black players at Houston and Dallas, while San Antonio and Austin each counted two Afro-American players, and one each at Fort Worth and Tulsa. The Shreveport and Oklahoma City franchises listed no black players.

26. *Sporting News*, May 22, 1957.

27. *Ibid.*, June 26, 1957.

28. Joseph Thomas Moore, *Pride Against Prejudice: The Biography of Larry Doby* (New York: Praeger, 1988), p. 112.

29. *Sporting News*, October 2, 1957.

30. Joe William Trotter, *Black Milwaukee: The Making of an Industrial Proletariat, 1915–45* (Urbana: University of Illinois Press, 1988).

31. Henry Aaron with Lonnie Wheeler, *I Had a Hammer: The Hank Aaron Story* (New York: HarperCollins, 1991), p. 179–184.

Nine Principles of Successful Affirmative Action: Branch Rickey, Jackie Robinson, and the Integration of Baseball

Anthony R. Pratkanis and Marlene E. Turner

For most Americans, April 10, 1947, began just like any other Thursday. Commuters went off to work; shopkeepers opened their stores for business; farmers planted their spring crops; children went off to school perhaps dreaming of playing Major League baseball or, at least, of playing a little ball at recess. The news of the day was just like the news of any other day — a border dispute in Poland, geologists claiming that Antarctica was gradually warming, a world trade conference in Geneva, and a telephone operator strike in New Jersey. The weather forecast called for a sunny day with highs in the upper 50s in Brooklyn, New York.

Around 11:00 A.M., a crowd of baseball fans began to gather on the steep cobblestone slope of Bedford Avenue just outside of Ebbets Field in Brooklyn. Later, the biggest crowd of the spring — 14,282 paying fans plus a few youngsters looking in through a gap under the metal gate in right-center — would be on hand to see the Brooklyn Dodgers play their top Minor League ball club, the Montreal Royals (the 1946 Champions of the International League), in one of the last exhibition games of the pre-season. The crowd was abuzz with the big sports story of the day: Baseball Commissioner Happy Chandler had announced a one-year suspension of Dodger manager Leo Durocher for "accumulation of unpleasant incidents which can be construed as detrimental to baseball." Dodger fans commiserated about the injustice of the action. Perhaps a few fans were discussing a short article in the *New York Times* reporting "of particular interest would be the performance of Jackie Robinson, Negro star, who is expected to play first base for the International League champion Royals. Dodger officials are considering whether to shift Robinson's contract to the Brooklyn club."[1] No black individual had played white Major League baseball since 1887.

The game began at 2 P.M. with the playing of the United States National Anthem. Robinson's first at bat in Ebbets field came in the top of the first; he received what the *New York Times* called a "warm and pleasant reception" from the fans. As Robinson was batting in the top of the fifth, Mr. Branch Rickey, President of the Dodger ball club, gave his assistant Arthur Mann a note to take up to the press box. At the top of the 6th, Red Barber, the Dodger announcer, read the statement for the fans listening to the game on the radio:

> The Brooklyn Dodgers today purchased the contract of Jackie Roosevelt Robinson from the Montreal Royals. He will report immediately.

Branch Rickey

With these 19 words, Mr. Rickey announced to the public what historian Jules Tygiel calls baseball's great experiment and what we view as the first, largely successful, affirmative action program in human history.[2] We define affirmative action as the proactive removal of discriminatory barriers and the promotion of institutions leading to integration of in- and out-groups. In other words, affirmative action is the inclusion of an out-group that has a history of exclusion (such as black Americans and baseball) and the promotion of positive relations between the members of the groups.[3] In our previous article, we reviewed the history of black American exclusion from the game of baseball and looked at some of the reasons why Mr. Rickey and Mr. Robinson inaugurated history's first affirmative action program.[4] In this article, we look at just how they did it and why their efforts were such a success.

How did Mr. Rickey integrate his Brooklyn Dodger ball club?[5] For over 40 years, social psychologists have been studying how best to implement desegregation programs. This research has taught us that the best way to accomplish the goal of integration is to change directly the institutions and social patterns that support discrimination; attitude change will follow from the resulting behavior change. Our thesis is that many of the principles discovered by social psychologists are illustrated in Mr. Rickey's hiring of Jackie Robinson. We have identified nine principles used to integrate the '47 Dodgers — principles that can still be used today to improve the effectiveness of affirmative action programs.

1. Create the Psychology of Inevitable Change

One factor that increases the likelihood of successful integration is the feeling that change is inevitable — the out-group member (in this case, black Americans) will be joining the in-group members (white Major Leagues) in the very near future and there is nothing that can be done to prevent it. This principle was identified by social psychologists studying the desegregation efforts of the 1950s and 1960s. For example, in a case analysis of communities implementing school desegregation, Thomas Pettigrew found that violence often occurred in cities (for example, Little Rock and Clinton) where authorities hinted that desegregation was reversible; peaceful integration generally occurred in towns (such as Norfolk and Winston-Salem) where leaders made it clear that the decision was irreversible.[6]

How does the psychology of the inevitable work to reduce prejudices? In 1944, Gunnar Myrdal argued that race relations in America are guided by a moral dilemma: on the one hand, the American Creed demands that all people be treated as equal, but, on the other hand, cultural mores and norms prescribe that some people should receive inferior treatment.[7] For in-group members, this dilemma results in a sense of moral uneasiness and ambivalence or what can be termed cognitive dissonance. In everyday life, this dissonance can be reduced by avoiding the issue, avoiding the out-group, denigrating the out-group (stereotyping), adopting symbols of the American Creed, and politely deferring to local norms and the "way things are done."

However, Myrdal's moral dilemma cannot be avoided when a change in the norms supporting prejudice is enacted; it must be faced squarely. There are two routes for resolving the dissonance: increased prejudice and resistance to change (violence), or reduced prejudice and rejection of the norm of prejudice. The position of leaders is the key to determining which route will be taken. When leaders openly oppose or half-heartedly support affirmative action, then opposition and even violence can result. In contrast, support for affirmative action closes off this route; to reduce dissonance, the in-group member is motivated to scrutinize his or her prejudice and to alter negative stereotypes. The inevitability of change encourages in-group members to bring their attitudes in line with the new reality.

The psychology of the inevitable can be seen in how Red Barber came to terms with a Negro player coming to the Dodgers. Mr. Rickey required the full support of Barber — the official voice of the Brooklyn Dodgers. He took Barber into his confidence early in March of 1945. According to Barber, Rickey broke the news during lunch at Joe's Restaurant; after some small talk, Rickey's voice grew serious, "I'm going to tell you something only the board of directors of the Brooklyn ball club and my family knows." He looked Barber straight in the eyes and fixed his attention.

> I'm going to bring a Negro to the Brooklyn Dodgers. I've got my best scouts searching for the best Negro players. They think they are searching for the Brown Dodgers. They don't know that what they are really searching for is the first black player I can put on the white Dodgers. I don't know who he is or where he is, but, he is coming.[8]

Barber recalls that Rickey spoke those last words very slowly, very intently, very positively.

Red Barber was stunned by the announcement. He was born in Mississippi, raised in Florida, and had been taught a strict code of relationships with black Americans. His first words to his wife when he got home were, "I'm going to quit." Red Barber felt he could not work with a team where one or more of the players were black. However, after his initial anger, Barber began to think. As he put it:

> There is a force on this earth called economic determinism. That force whispered to me that at Brooklyn I had the best sports announcing job not only in the country, but in the world. If I threw it away, what would I do? I didn't quit. I made myself realize that I had no choice in the parents I was born to, no choice in the place of my birth or the time of it. I was born white just as a Negro was born black. I had been given a fortunate set of circumstances, none of which I had done anything to merit, and therefore I had best be careful about being puffed up over my color.[9]

Mr. Rickey also used the psychology of the inevitable to help change the attitudes of the Dodgers players. One of the more colorful stories involved then Dodger manager Leo Durocher. During spring training of 1947, Durocher found out that some Dodger players — Dixie Walker, Eddie Stanky, Kirby Higbe, Bobby Bragan, and others — were drawing up a petition to warn that they would never play with Robinson. At first Durocher decided to wait until Mr. Rickey returned from a trip; however, the idea of a petition gnawed at Durocher. Tossing and turning in bed, unable to sleep, Durocher resolved to take action. He told his coaches to round everyone up for a team meeting in the kitchen. Once the team had assembled, Durocher came in his pajamas and bright yellow bathrobe; his words were quick and to the point:

> I hear some of you fellows don't want to play with Robinson and that
> you have a petition drawn up that you are going to sign. Well, boys,
> you know what you can to with that petition. You can wipe your ass
> with it. I hear Dixie Walker is going to send Mr. Rickey a letter ask-
> ing to be traded. Just hand him the letter, Dixie, and you're gone.
> GONE! I don't care if a guy is yellow or black or if he has stripes like
> a fuckin' zebra. I am the manager, and I say he plays.[10]

(Little wonder that Rickey was disturbed when Durocher was suspended just before the start of the '47 season. He was ably replaced by Burt Shotton. Durocher returned to the helm in '48).

The next night, Mr. Rickey called the players to his hotel suite. He began the meeting with a lecture on Americanism. Several of the players felt ashamed and gave ground. Others did not. Mr. Rickey then offered to trade any player who didn't want to be on the team with Robinson. Dixie Walker sent a letter to Rickey asking for a trade. (At the time, Walker was one of the most popular Dodgers and was nicknamed "The People's Cherce.") True to his words, Rickey worked out a deal with Pittsburgh. But, Walker, realizing the inevitable, reversed his decision and asked for his letter back. Rickey canceled the trade (see Principle 7 below). Kirby Higbe also wanted to be traded and persisted in his opposition to Robinson. Rickey sent Higbe to the last place Pirates for close to $200,000 in cash. (As late as 1967, Higbe continued to believe what he did was right.) Mr. Rickey dragged his heels on a third trade involving Bobby Bragan; he felt that Bragan was working through emotional difficulties. Events would prove him correct (see Principle 7 below). In 1965, Bobby Bragan sat next to Jackie Robinson at the funeral of Mr. Rickey. As Bragan puts it: "We shook hands warmly. I don't think either of us thought anything about it, or of the past. It was a new time. I changed. Jackie changed. The world changed."[11]

The spring training petition was not to be the last attempt to ban Robinson. In early May of 1947, three players from the St. Louis Cardinals began to organize a strike. They would not take the field against the Dodgers when they came to St. Louis with Jackie Robinson; further, the Cardinal players were trying to enlist the support of players on other teams. When National League President Ford Frick found out about the plan, he issued the following statement to the players:

> If you do this you will be suspended from the league. You will find that
> the friends you think you have in the press box will not support you,
> that you will be outcasts. I do not care if half the league strikes. Those
> who do will encounter quick retribution. All will be suspended and I
> don't care if it wrecks the National League for five years. This is the
> United States of America and one citizen has as much right to play as

another. The National League will go down the line with Robinson no matter the consequences. You will find, if you go through with your intentions, that you have been guilty of complete madness.[12]

President Frick's statement put a quick end to the strike.

Many of the participants in baseball's great experiment understood the power of authority to create the psychology of the inevitable. Often in this paper we refer to Branch Rickey as Mr. Rickey. In a 1946 interview, Rachel Robinson, Jackie's wife, noted: "We always called him *Mr.* Rickey. Everyone did. I think we wanted to hold him in that position of respect and honor. Part of his power was maintaining that mystique about himself."[13]

2. Establish Equal Status Contact with a Superordinate Goal

At the time Rickey was making the final plans to bring a black American to baseball, some were of the opinion that blacks and whites could not get along in close interpersonal relationships. Intergroup contact would inevitably result in strife — the races just could not get along. Casual observation may lead some to believe that conflict between races must occur.

However, conflict need not inevitably result. In the early 1950s, social psychologists and sociologists identified what has been termed the equal status contact hypothesis. Gordon Allport stated it as follows: Positive intergroup relations are most likely to occur when members from the two groups (a) possess equal status, (b) seek common goals, (c) are cooperatively dependent on each other, and (d) interact with positive support of authorities, laws, or customs.[14]

There is much support for this equal status contact hypothesis. For example, Morton Deutsch and Mary Evans Collins found that whites' attitudes towards blacks showed less prejudice if blacks and whites were assigned to share the same building in a public housing complex; such positive attitudes did not occur if buildings were segregated.[15] In a dramatic experiment, Muzafer Sherif first created social conflict among boys attending a summer camp merely by creating artificial groups (Rattlers and Eagles) and placing them in competition. The conflict was reduced by giving the groups a superordinate goal (i.e., joining together to bring water to the camp, to rent a movie, and to start a stalled truck).[16]

Research leading to the equal status contact hypothesis was begun in the 1940s. Branch Rickey was privy to the thinking of social scientists of the time. Dan Dodson — a New York University sociologist and a member of the Mayor's Committee on Unity — became a Rickey confidant. He gave Rickey the following advice: "Don't worry about the attitudes of people who are asked to accept new members. When relationships are predicated on the basis of goals other than integration — in the Dodger case, winning the pennant — the people involved would adjust appropriately."[17]

In Rickey's mind, baseball offered the unique opportunity to test out social scientists' theories about integration. In many ways, the typical ball club does or (more often) can meet Gordon Allport's four conditions. Each playing position has more or less equal status; teams seek a common goal (the pennant); each player is mutually dependent on teammates to reach the goal (it is easier to score an RBI with runners in scoring position; put-outs require a co-ordinated infield); Rickey's managers could provide the positive support of authority (see Principle 1).

The task of Dodger management was to keep the team on track towards its superordinate goal — a task that should be routinely performed by every manager. Dodger management reminded the white players of how close they came in 1946 to going to the World Series (losing out to the Cardinals in the final week of the season) and that the missing component just might be filled with Robinson's speed on the base paths. As Durocher repeatedly told the white players in spring training, "He'll put money in your pocket, boys. Money in your pocket." In other words, the chances of going to the Series were much improved with Robinson.

The results of equal status contact can be seen in the behavior of Dixie Walker (a leader of the petition drive). A short time into the 1947 season, Walker approached Robinson in the batting cage and spoke his first words to him in a deep Southern accent, "Ah think you'd be better able to handle that curve ball if you didn't stride so far."[18] That afternoon, Robinson, taking the advice, hit a line drive double, a bunt single, and a single up the middle. He thanked Walker quietly in the clubhouse. Walker later showed the rookie Robinson how to hit behind the runner. When asked why he did it, he replied, "I saw things in this light. When you're on a team, you got to pull together to win."[19] At the end of the 1947 season, Walker commented that it was Robinson who had put the Dodgers in the race.

3. The Pee Wee Reese Principle: Puncture the Norm of Prejudice

One factor that maintains and perpetuates prejudice is norms. A norm is a rule or expectation used to guide and direct social behavior (e.g., whites don't play baseball with blacks; women can't handle top management positions). Norms can prescribe what "ought" to happen in a social situation and can describe how most people will act in a setting. Norms gain their power from the belief (sometimes mistaken) that everyone else believes and performs the norm (pluralistic ignorance) and from the belief that social sanctions will result if the norm is transgressed.[20]

Numerous social psychological studies have demonstrated the importance of social norms in maintaining prejudice. For example, Thomas Pettigrew found that conformity to social pressures was a key determinant of prejudice in the South.[21] Ralph Minard documents a case where black and white coal miners followed a pattern of complete integration below ground, but were almost completely segregated above ground where the norms differ.[22]

The power of social norms can be illustrated in Clay Hopper's (manager of the International League Montreal Royals) reaction upon learning that Jackie Robinson was being assigned to his club for the '46 season. Hopper did not protest because Robinson couldn't play, or because he hated blacks, or because he felt he couldn't manage what might be a racially charged situation. Instead, he pleaded with Mr. Rickey: "Please don't do this to me. I'm white and I've lived in Mississippi all my life. If you're going to do this, you're going to force me to move my family and home out of Mississippi."[23] A year later, we might add, it was Clay Hopper who urged Mr. Rickey to promote Robinson to the Majors; in Hopper's mind, Robinson was ready and had proved all he could prove in the minors.

Although norms are powerful and persistent, they can be changed. A series of classic studies by Solomon Asch illustrates how the presence of even one dissenter can shatter the power of group pressure and norms.[24] In his studies, a group of seven "subjects" were shown sets of three lines differing in length and were asked to choose the one line that was the same length as a standard. Unbeknownst to the real subject (who always selected last), the other "subjects" were really confederates of Asch and were instructed to unanimously pick a wrong line on key trials. The results showed that the real subject yielded to the group influence on a substantial number of trials. However, when Asch gave the real subject a partner — either another naive subject or a confederate instructed to pick the correct line — conformity was reduced by 75 percent.

When Rickey hired Robinson he took the first step toward breaking the norms of prejudice. Others also displayed their support for the hiring. For example, Brooklyn fans began wearing "I'm for Robinson" buttons around Ebbets field. Sportswriters such as Louis Effrat and Arthur Daley wrote sympathetic articles for the New York Times. Pirate Hank Greenberg supported Robinson when Pittsburgh fans began to verbally abuse Jackie.

(Greenberg — a Jewish American — had received similar treatment a few seasons earlier.) The heavyweight champion Joe Louis came to a Dodger game to shake Jackie's hand.

However, one Dodger stands out in his actions to break the norms of prejudice — Harold "Pee Wee" Reese. A ten-time National League All-Star, Reese batted a career .269 and often led the league in fielding at his short-stop position. When Robinson was moved to second, they made an unbeat-able double play team. Many may consider Pee Wee Reese as an odd choice to be a civil rights leader. Reese, born in Ekron, Kentucky, was a South-erner who learned the racial code of conduct at a quite early age.

In spring training, Reese refused to sign the petition against Robin-son. His actions surprised teammates and petition organizers; they expected that a Southern boy would know better. Perhaps Bobby Bragan (a petition-organizer) best understood what Pee Wee's actions meant:

> Those early days were awfully tough on Jackie. I remember times on the train when nobody would sit with him or talk with him. Pee Wee always seemed to be the first to break the tension. He kidded Jackie before anybody else did and made him a part of the team. He was probably the first Dodger to have a meal with him off the field. Pee Wee was a real leader on our club, and when he started being friendly with Jackie, everybody started being friendly. In the beginning, Jackie was alone at the dining table. By the middle of the year you couldn't get a seat at the dining table with him, there were so many guys.[25]

One incident involving Reese and Robinson has reached the status of legend. Early in the 1947 season, the Dodgers traveled to Crosley Field in Cincinnati, Ohio to play the Reds. (Robinson later describes the incident as happening in Boston; Reese doesn't even remember the event, but recalls Jack recalling that it took place in Cincinnati; Reese also remembers that such incidents were quite common, especially in that first year.) The ball-park was jammed with thousands coming up from Reese's boyhood home of Kentucky. Many of Reese's friends and relatives despised him for play-ing on a team with a black man. The crowd hurled racial slurs — "get the nigger off the field; Robinson the watermelon eater; Reese the nigger lover." The hatemongering continued into the bottom of the first when the Dodgers took the field. Mr. Reese left his shortstop position and walked the 120 feet over to first base where Robinson stood. He smiled at Robin-son; Robinson smiled back. Tapping his glove, Reese spoke a few words to Robinson. All eyes were on the pair at first base. Pee Wee then placed his right arm around Jack's shoulder as chums often do. There was absolute silence in the stands. Mr. Reese's action not only punctured the norm of anti-black racism, but also broke another common myth: that all whites are racists and incapable of change.

In 1984, Harold Reese was elected to the Baseball Hall of Fame. The last line of his Hall of Fame plaque lists this accomplishment: "Instrumental in easing acceptance of Jackie Robinson as baseball's first black performer."

4. *Practice Nonviolent Resistance*

The story of the first meeting between Robinson and Rickey has been told many times. Clyde Sukeforth, one of Rickey's most trusted assistants, had been scouting Negro Major League talent under the guise that Mr. Rickey planned to form the Brown Dodgers in a new Negro league. Mr. Rickey kept his true intentions secret because of considerable opposition in the past to hiring black Americans to play baseball. However, when Mr. Rickey asked him to bring Robinson to Brooklyn and then added the comment, "if he can't come to New York, arrange a time for me to go out to the Midwest to meet him," Sukeforth realized that this would be no routine meeting.

Jackie Robinson met Mr. Rickey for the first time on August 28, 1945, in Rickey's Brooklyn office. Branch Rickey stared intently at Robinson, studying his every movement. Robinson recalls the moment, "His piercing eyes roamed over me with such meticulous care I almost felt naked." Robinson stared back as if he were trying to get inside the man. Rickey broke the ice with a question about Robinson's family. Jackie responded that he was planning to marry his girlfriend Rachel. Rickey was pleased, because he knew Robinson would need all the family support he could get. Then Rickey broke the news, "The truth is you are not a candidate for the Brooklyn Brown Dodgers. I've sent for you because I'm interested in you as a candidate for the Brooklyn National League club. I think you can play in the Major Leagues. How do you feel about it?" Robinson was skeptical; black Americans had been led on before. Indeed, in April of 1945, Jackie Robinson, along with black Americans Sam Jethroe and Marvin Williams, had participated in a sham try-out with the Boston Red Sox.

Rickey continued, "I know you're a good ballplayer. My scouts have told me this. What I don't know is whether you have the guts." Robinson bristled at the implication that he was a coward. Rickey told him that he wished that all that mattered was the boxscore — that maybe someday that would be all that counted. However, right now that wasn't all that mattered. For the next three hours, he described the situations that Robinson would face as a black man entering an all-white league. He told him about the segregated hotels and restaurants; he told him what his wife would hear in the stands; he told him the abuse he would take on the field. Rickey, always the actor, would get up into Robinson's face and yell insults and racial slurs. Robinson recalled, "His acting was so convincing that I found myself chain-gripping my fingers behind my back." Rickey brought the tension to a climax: "Suppose a player comes down from first base — you are the shortstop — the player slides, spikes you high, and cuts you on the leg. As you feel the blood running down your leg, the white player laughs in your face, and sneers, 'How do you like that, nigger boy?'" Robinson asked, "Mr. Rickey, do you want a Negro who's afraid to fight back?" Rickey's answer, "I want a ballplayer with guts enough not to fight back." Rickey then reached into a desk drawer and pulled out a copy of Giovanni Papini's *The Life of Christ* and read a section on nonviolent resistance. He told Robinson there was only one way to break the color bar, "You cannot retaliate; you cannot answer a blow with a blow; you cannot echo a curse with a curse." He looked Robinson straight in the eye and asked, "Can you do it?" Robinson stared straight back and answered, "Mr. Rickey, I've got to do it."

When Mr. Robinson left the office that day, he had made two commitments to Branch Rickey: (a) for three years he would not return violence with violence and (b) that he would play for the Dodger's top farm club in Montreal. Robinson honored both commitments. The color bar was officially broken.

Branch Rickey's nickname was the Mahatma after the Indian civil rights leader Mahatma Gandhi. Nonviolence was a guiding principle of Rickey's life. For example, just before the start of the 1947 season, Rickey met with black civic leaders and impressed upon them that any violence would set back race relations. The motto became, "Don't spoil Jackie's chances." Why did Mr. Rickey place so much emphasis on nonviolent resistance?

Branch Rickey was afraid of a spiral of violence. A white person would attack a black; the black person would respond; then more white persons would attack until a full-scale riot broke out. Black Americans would inevitably take the blame, "See, they can't get along."

Branch Rickey had every reason to expect a spiral of violence. Between 1900 and 1949, there were 33 major race riots in the United States — most in the North and many near baseball towns. At least two of these riots must have stuck out in Rickey's mind. On July 2, 1917, the second worst race riot in American history occurred in East St. Louis, Illinois. Nine whites and at least 39 blacks died in the violence; estimates of the number of blacks who died varies because the bodies of many black Americans were mutilated and burned beyond recognition, making an exact count difficult.

Seeking refuge, thousands of black Americans crossed one of the three bridges over the Mississippi River into St. Louis, Missouri. Mr. Rickey had just begun his managerial career with the St. Louis Cardinals. In 1943, the fourth worst race riot in American history took place in Detroit, Michigan (with nine whites and 25 blacks killed). One of the triggering events for this riot was the promotion of three black assembly line workers. Coming just as he was making plans to hire a black American, the location of (a baseball town) and the reason for (black employment) the Detroit riot were probably not lost on Mr. Rickey. Nonviolence was one way that Mr. Rickey saw to prevent a spiral of violence.

But nonviolence is more than just breaking the spiral — it changes the dynamics of social interaction. Nonviolent resistance is not just passive acceptance of the status quo. Rather, it shows an irrevocable commitment to a course of action and to change. Nonviolent action says, "No matter what you do to me, I will not hurt you; I will, however, continue to move to the new goal of racial equality." Nonviolent resistance also switches the locus of responsibility for what happens to others. Robinson was not to blame for any incidents. When Robinson was mistreated, it became the responsibility of the Dodger team to stand up for him. Finally, nonviolence (compared to violence) made it easier for the "enemy" to be converted to the cause (see Principle 7 below).

The value of nonviolent resistance can be seen in a study by Morton Deutsch.[26] In his study, an accomplice of the experimenter and a real subject played a two-person game that permitted altruistic, cooperative, individualistic, defensive, and aggressive behavior. Subjects won varying amounts of money by cooperating, attacking, or ignoring the other player. The results showed that when the accomplice played a nonviolent resistance strategy (i.e., cooperate if the other player cooperated and play defensively when attacked) both players gained more money compared to other possible strategies (i.e., passive, deterrence, etc.). Further, practicing nonviolent resistance resulted in the accomplice being perceived as fair and cooperative.

The value of Mr. Rickey's nonviolent resistance can also be observed on the playing field. Perhaps the most dramatic event occurred late in the season, on August 20, when the Dodgers were playing the fourth game of a series with the Cardinals. In the opening game, Joe Medwick had spiked Robinson's left foot. Two games later, Robinson barely removed his leg in time to avoid an Enos Slaughter spike. In the top of the seventh of game four, Slaughter — a man known for his opposition to blacks in baseball — hit a grounder that was tossed to Robinson at first. Robinson took the throw with his foot on the inside of the bag. This time Slaughter's spike came down hard on the back of Jackie's leg, missing the Achilles tendon (and thus ending Robinson's career) by an inch. The cut on Robinson's leg was eight inches above the ankle — a location that is hard to argue as an accidental spiking. The Dodger teammates led by Hugh Casey came out in mass to protest. Several Dodger players threatened the Cardinals with "dire consequences" if the attacks continued. Nonviolent resistance by Robinson had changed the social dynamics, preventing a spiral of violence and increasing the cohesion of the Dodger ball club.

For a long time, the principle of nonviolent resistance stirred not only Robinson's teammates to action, but sportswriters as well. Red Barber is of the opinion that Enos Slaughter's entrance into the Hall of Fame was delayed by this spiking incident because many sportswriters (including himself), knowing what he had done to Robinson, could not bring themselves to cast a vote for Slaughter. (Slaughter agrees with Barber's assessment.)

5. Create Empathy

One effective means of attitude change is to reverse perceptions and present the world through another's point of view. The ability to experience empathy — feeling the emotion of others — is perhaps a uniquely human trait. Seeing the world as another sees it provides an opportunity to receive new information and to challenge old ways of viewing matters. Observing another's pain often results in empathy which predisposes the observer to take altruistic action.[27] Interestingly, when whites have black friends, they are more likely to support affirmative action.[28] Part of Mr. Rickey's success was his ability to get the Dodgers to see the world through Robinson's eyes and to feel his pain.

The Dodgers' baptism by fire occurred on April 22 when the Philadelphia Phillies came to town for a three-game series. It was a very cold day in Brooklyn with temperatures in the low 40s; the fans sat frozen in their seats. On the field, things were quite a bit hotter. Ben Chapman (manager of the Phillies) started screaming out racial slurs at Robinson.[29] "Hey nigger, why don't you go pickin' cotton?" Soon his team joined in: "Hey, coon, do you always smell so bad?" and then they would flap their hands as if something stunk. The slurs continued inning after inning and into the second game of the series. "Hey, darkie, you shouldn't be here in the big leagues — they need you back home to clean out the latrines." Robinson called it the worst experience of his life; he cursed Mr. Rickey and his experiment under his breath. But Robinson stood firm and took the abuse.

And the attack continued. "If that black-lipped nigger was a white boy, he'd a been sent to Newport News a long time ago." Feelings on the Dodger bench were tense. Imagine what it must have been like for the white Dodger players that day. Most likely, they had never experienced prejudice directly before and now they were getting the full treatment. "Hey nigger lovers, they are waiting for your black boy back in the jungle. Hey snowflake, which one of the white boys' wives you shacking' up with tonight? Hey, you carpetbaggers, how's your little reconstruction period getting along?"

Towards the end of the second game, the white Dodgers could not continue to take the pressure, and they exploded with rage. Eddie Stanky was the first off the bench; he screamed at the Phillie bench, "What kind of men are you anyway? You're all chicken! Why the hell don't you pick on someone who can fight back. You know Robinson can't fight back — knock it off and just play ball!" Dixie Walker joined in. Yes, this was the same Eddie Stanky and the same Dixie Walker who two months earlier were heading a petition drive against Robinson. It was the same Eddie Stanky who told Robinson on his first day of work, "I don't like you, but we'll play together and get along because you're my teammate." Stanky's support of Robinson diminished the intensity of the Phillies attack, although it still continued over the next few years. Unfortunately, after this blatant racial attack, death threats directed at Mr. Rickey and Mr. Robinson increased. Many commentators link the two events.

For the record, it should be noted that Robinson was not completely silent during the series; he spoke the language every baseball fan understands — with his bat. In game one, Robinson broke the ice with a hit in the bottom of the 6th. With the score tied 0–0 in the bottom of the 8th, Robinson reached first on an infield hit. As Reiser was striking-out, Robinson stole second and reached third on a catcher throwing error. Dixie Walker then walked. Gene Hermanski took an 0–2 count to 3–2 and then lined a drive to center. Brooklyn won 1–0 with Robinson scoring the lone run. In game 2, Robinson walked and then scored on a Reiser double. Robinson bunted, then scored on a bases loaded single by Carl Furillo. Dodgers won 5–2. In game 3, Robinson reached first on an error; he scored the go-ahead run off of a Dixie Walker hit. Dodgers won 2–0. The Brooklyn fans brought out their brooms; the Dodgers swept the three game series from the Phillies.

Branch Rickey was beside himself with glee and could not resist the opportunity to gloat over the win and to lecture Ben Chapman. As he put it,

> The Chapman incident did more than anything to make the other
> Dodgers speak up in Robinson's behalf. When Chapman and the others

poured out that string of unconscionable abuse, he solidified and unified thirty men, not one of whom was willing to see someone kick around a man who had his hands tied behind his back. Chapman created in Robinson's behalf a thing called sympathy, the most unifying word in the world. That word has a Greek origin — it means "to suffer." To say "I sympathize with you" means "I suffer with you." That is what Chapman did. He caused men like Stanky to suffer with Robinson, and he made this Negro a real member of the Dodgers.[30]

6. Individuate the New Group Member

One problem that occurs when an out-group member joins an in-group is the continued categorization of the new member in terms of out-group stereotypes — the person is not "Jackie Robinson" but a Negro ballplayer. The continued use of such labels and categories can pose a number of problems for integration.[31] It is easier to attack a vague category (especially one that has been denigrated) than it is to hurt a real flesh and blood human being. When group identities are salient, in-group favoritism (perceiving the in-group to be better than the out-group; rewarding the in-group over the out-group) is common.[32] The stereotype serves to organize perceptions about the out-group member in what is termed the ultimate attribution error: negative acts by out-group members are seen as caused by permanent dispositions, whereas positive acts are attributed to situational factors or luck.[33]

One special problem for the first in-group members entering a newly desegregated setting is their solo or token status. Rosabeth Kanter has marshaled considerable evidence to show that tokenism is a particularly painful psychological state.[34] The solo receives close scrutiny and attention by the in-group members. In-group members have a tendency to exaggerate evaluations of the performance of the solo and to see the solo as playing a special, often stereotypic, role in the group.[35]

One way to reduce categorization and token effects is to encourage the treatment of the new group member as an individual. For example, researchers have found that typical in-group favoritism was reduced when an out-group acted as individuals and signed their names in notes sent to the in-group.[36] Similarly, other researchers have reduced prejudice in children by having them learn and memorize the names of out-group members and by having the children make judgments on how out-group members were similar and different from each other.[37]

Rickey felt that through the "intimacy" of baseball and the heat of competition, the white Dodgers would come to know and like Robinson.

(Dixie Walker's remarks to Robinson on his batting stance demonstrate this point.) However, baseball fans would not have the opportunity to interact personally with Jackie. Rickey called on his friends in the media to "introduce" Robinson to the fans. Stories by Arthur Mann and *New York Times* writers Louis Effrat and Arthur Daley portrayed Robinson as an individual of accomplishment. (Of course, not all sportswriters were connected to Rickey and not all followed suit; even a supporter of Rickey, such as Mann, was not above poking fun in private circles at the effort by Rickey to hire Robinson.)[38]

Here is how Effrat first described Robinson to the Brooklyn fans:

> A native of Georgia, Robinson won fame in baseball, football, basketball, and track at the University of California at Los Angeles before entering the army as a private. He emerged a lieutenant in 1945 and in October of that year was signed to a Montreal contract. Robinson's performance in the international League, which he led in batting last season with an average of .349, prompted President Branch Rickey of the Dodgers to promote Jackie.[39]

The article was accompanied by a picture of Clay Hopper congratulating a smiling Jackie Robinson. Indeed, after the early 1947 season, sportswriters often failed to mention Robinson's race as well as the race of other black stars such as Larry Doby and Roy Campanella. Interestingly, sportswriters continued to mention the race of black pitchers such as Don Newcombe, perhaps because "pitcher" is a leadership position.[40]

In 1950, Jackie Robinson contributed greatly to the individuation effort by personally starring in the film *The Jackie Robinson Story*.[41] The film features a likable and determined Jackie Robinson facing the torrent of racism in his first years in the league. We see the young Jackie develop his love of baseball, his first meeting with Mr. Rickey, Robinson's exclusion from facilities during spring training, how he learned the new position of first base, and the unwavering strength of character of his mother, Mallie Robinson. Even the most casual of viewers is left with two impressions: (1) Jackie Robinson is truly a great American hero, and (2) it would be nice to have the Robinsons — Rachel and Jackie — over for a barbecue this weekend. Do you think they are available?

7. *Offer Forgiveness and Redemption*

In many ways, Mr. Rickey's introduction of Jackie Robinson to the Dodgers and white America can be viewed as one elaborate cognitive dissonance experiment — forcing white Americans to confront Myrdal's dilemma. First, through the psychology of the inevitable, he placed pressure on white Americans to change their prejudices. Next, he blocked off negative, but typical, routes for dealing with Myrdal's dilemma such as derogating Robinson, bolstering negative stereotypes, and hatemongering. Finally, he needed to provide a positive means of coming to terms with racism. Mr. Rickey's devotion to Christ provided just such a mechanism — forgiveness and redemption.

In Mr. Rickey's Methodist theology, redemption meant the renewal and transformation of the person; you loved the sinner, but hated the sin. Forgiveness meant more than just a formal apology; indeed, it often did not involve an apology. When Mr. Rickey saw signs that an oppositional white player was "coming around," he would immediately place that player in a new role of authority — a position that would involve interacting with and serving black Americans. Social scientists refer to this process as cooptation.[42] Cooptation provides the opponent with a new role, complete with new information, role expectations, and social pressures, that increases identification with the organization's goals.

A case in point is Bobby Bragan. A lifetime .240 hitter over seven seasons, Bragan was the Dodger's second string catcher and considered expendable. Mr. Rickey could have easily gotten rid of him after Bragan's participation in the petition drive. According to Rickey's confidant, Arthur Mann, Mr. Rickey recognized unusual courage in the man; he felt Bragan needed time to think and that someday he would learn that he was wrong. Bragan remained a Dodger for the 1947 season (although he spent some time in the minors). In 1948, Mr. Rickey appointed Bragan manager of the Dodger farm club in Fort Worth. The Bragan-led club won the pennant and play-offs in 1948 and the pennant in 1949. Mr. Rickey's confidence was not lost on Bragan. As he put it, "Mr. Rickey paid me the ultimate compliment when he hired me after my playing days were over to work in the Dodger farm system."[43] Bragan also took great pride in his coaching of black ball players.

> When I was a manager in the Dodger organization, I helped Tommy Davis, and later on I really worked hard with Maury Wills. I made him into a switch hitter, and he got to the Majors and became the great base stealer and fine player he was. I'm very proud of that.[44]

Hank Aaron acknowledges that Bobby Bragan made him a complete player by encouraging him to steal. Hall of Famer Monte Irvin, one of the first black Americans to play for the New York Giants, described it this way: "After a year or so, Bragan realized how wrong his attitude was. Later he went out of his way to help black ballplayers."[45]

Mr. Rickey was not above using even the bitter Chapman incident to promote his cause. After the Phillies attacked Robinson and the other Dodgers, there was a public outcry against Chapman. Fans seated near the Phillies dugout wrote protest letters to Commissioner Happy Chandler. Chapman's actions were deplored in the black press and by some white sportswriters. Walter Winchell attacked Chapman on his national Sunday radio broadcast. Worried about his and the Phillies image, Chapman issued a statement that he was riding Robinson just like he would any rookie. Few believed him. Mr. Rickey then took the opportunity to stage a photo of Chapman with Robinson. The photo of both men in uniform holding a bat appeared in the sports section of every major paper. There is little doubt that Chapman's "apology" lacked sincerity. (Robinson considered it one of the most difficult things he had ever done.) Nevertheless, Chapman had once again served Mr. Rickey's purposes; Chapman's photo with Robinson demonstrated to a nation that even the most hardened can change.

8. Undo the Perception of Preferential Selection

Many white Americans doubted Jackie Robinson's ability to make it into the National league. The pitcher Bob Feller stated: "If he were a white man, I doubt they would even consider him big league material." When Robinson had an off-day because of a sore shoulder, a reporter commented: "Had he been white, the Royals would have dropped him immediately." Larry MacPhail — Rickey's nemesis as general manager of the New York Yankees — stated in 1946 that the level of Robinson's ability "were he white, would make him eligible for a trial with, let us say, the Brooklyn Dodgers' Class B farm at Newport News." MacPhail also believed blacks, in general, could not make it in the white leagues without considerable training. As he put it, "A Major League player must have something besides natural ability. He must also have a competitive attitude and discipline," implying that blacks lacked these latter abilities.

The fact that Jackie Robinson was perceived as preferentially selected for the Dodgers should alert us to one potential problem of affirmative action — it can lead to the (mis)perception that the recipient was hired just because he or she was black (or a woman, etc.) and therefore can't do the job. The perception that Robinson was preferentially hired is ridiculous. In 1946, with the Montreal Royals of the International League (the top farm league), Robinson won the batting championship with a .349 average, was a terror on the base paths, scored 113 runs, was selected league

M.V.P., and went on to lead the club to the league pennant and victory in the Little World Series. If Robinson was not qualified for his chance in the Majors, then no other Minor League player that year was qualified.

Social psychologists have identified three general reasons why affirmative action can be (mis)perceived as preferential selection. The first is racism. As the quote from MacPhail indicates, some believed that blacks lacked certain abilities to play baseball (they were inferior on some dimension). If they lacked the ability, then why did they get the job? The answer: it must be preferential selection. Audrey Murrell and her colleagues find that whites were more accepting of affirmative action for the elderly and for the handicapped than for blacks.[46] Second, some affirmative action procedures may be seen to violate the norms of universality and procedural justice or fairness.[47] Finally, white resistance to affirmative action is higher among those whites who feel relatively deprived, or perceive that they have not gotten all that they deserve from life.[48] In such cases, attitudes towards affirmative action serve a self-protection or scapegoating function — the dissatisfied individual comes to blame blacks for his or her problems.[49]

The perception of affirmative action as preferential selection can have negative consequences for the recipient of affirmative action. Considerable research has shown that women who feel they were preferentially selected for a desired position gave lower self-evaluations of their abilities and skills, and that, under certain conditions, preferential selection can result in poorer performance.[50] It should be noted that Robinson was particularly sensitive to racial slurs that attacked his ability — that is, implied he was preferentially selected. As if to stress the point, he titled his autobiography, *I Never Had It Made.*

To account for the negative consequences of preferential selection, we have developed a model of affirmative action as help.[51] Sometimes help can be supportive and result in positive consequences for the recipient — for example, when the help conforms to social norms and removes barriers to success that have been erected through no fault of the recipient. On the other hand, help can be self-threatening — for example, when the help conveys to the recipient that he or she lacks ability or that the help was unfairly awarded. In such cases, the help results in negative self-evaluations and defensive behavior.

We have used this model to generate a number of specific actions that can be taken to reduce and eliminate the negative consequences of the perception of preferential selection. Many of these actions were intuitively taken by Branch Rickey and his assistants. Some of these measures include: (a) establish unambiguous, explicit, and focused qualifications criteria to be used in the selection decision (the baseball boxscore); (b) be certain that selection procedures are perceived as fair (Robinson paid his dues in the minors); (c) provide specific information testifying to the competencies of the new hire (Rickey's and Durocher's confidence in Robinson's ability; Robinson's season with Montreal); (d) emphasize the recipient's contributions to the team (Durocher claimed Robinson would get the Dodgers in the pennant drive); (e) develop socialization strategies that deter feelings of helplessness (the Minor Leagues and Dodgertown); (f) reinforce the fact that affirmative action is not preferential selection (Rickey repeatedly told Robinson that he would have to make it on his own — in the boxscore and with his teammates — and not to depend on Rickey for help); and (g) refocus the helping effort away from the recipient by identifying and communicating the social barriers preventing integration (everyone knew about the color bar).

9. Identify and Remove Institutional Barriers

Out-groups are excluded from the in-group by more than just interpersonal prejudice; certain institutional practices can also operate to restrict the choices and rights of an out-group.[52] Such practices can be subtle and unintended or blatant and intentional. For example, institutional barriers can include such things as inferior schools in areas populated by minorities, the lack of daycare for working parents, limited job opportunities in poor areas, a heavy reliance on standardized tests for admission decisions, laws restricting new housing, insisting on traditional career paths, the flow of information in "old boy" networks, and tracking out-groups into certain careers, among other practices.

One institution that posed a particular problem for Mr. Rickey was the segregated housing and dining facilities in many towns. Black ballplayers were not allowed to stay in hotels nor to eat in restaurants. Some clubs attempted to solve this problem by serving players box lunches on the team bus; others moved their spring training from Florida to Arizona which was still segregated, but to a somewhat lesser extent.

Mr. Rickey took a more radical solution. In 1947, the Dodgers held spring training in Havana, Cuba — a racially desegregated country. Given the cost of hotels and transportation, this was an expensive move on the part of the Dodgers. Ironically, Kirby Higbe — one of the petition drive organizers — made a major contribution to Mr. Rickey's effort; the money Mr. Rickey received from the sale of Higbe went to pay for the extra cost of holding spring camp in Cuba.

In 1948, Rickey opened "Dodgertown," fulfilling his dream of a college of baseball that provided a safe haven from segregation. In Dodgertown, black and white players could room together, eat together, and train together without the pressure of local segregation laws.[53] Of course, when the players stepped out of Dodgertown into the surrounding Vero Beach, Florida community, they still felt the sting of racism. Complete integration could only occur with the full dismantling of the Jim Crow laws of segregation. It is interesting to note that, long after the repeal of segregation, Dodgertown and its many imitators are still in operation because such camps were found to be useful in creating team cohesion. There is a lesson to be learned: the creative removal of institutions serving as barriers for the out-group can also improve the lot of the in-group.

Concluding Remarks: A Final Boxscore

What did Mr. Rickey and Mr. Robinson accomplish? Today, roughly 18 percent of all professional baseball players are black (down from a high of 30 percent in 1975).[54] Many of the games' greatest stars are black Americans.[55] It would be wrong, however, to conclude that Mr. Rickey and Mr. Robinson eliminated racism from baseball. Even superstar players such as Hank Aaron have been routinely "treated" to both subtle and blatant racial abuse, and black Americans are still frequently excluded from the ranks of managers and baseball's front offices.[56] However, Mr. Rickey and Mr. Robinson have left us a legacy for addressing the racism we still encounter today; they gave us nine principles of successful affirmative action.

Jackie Robinson played for the Brooklyn Dodgers for ten years — a period baseball writers call the golden Brooklyn decade. In that ten-year period, the Dodgers won the National League Pennant six times, won the World Series in 1955, took opponents to the wire in two races, and only once finished as low as third. In 1948, black Americans Roy Campanella and Don Newcombe joined the Dodgers. Together with Jackie Robinson, Gil Hodges, Pee Wee Reese, Preacher Roe, and Duke Snider, they formed the nucleus of one of baseball's greatest teams.

Mr. Rickey stayed with the Dodgers for three more seasons after 1947. After building dynasties in St. Louis and Brooklyn, Rickey moved to Pittsburgh in 1951 to become the Pirates' general manager and vice-president. Rickey built an outstanding farm system at Pittsburgh which would later win the World Series in 1960. In October of 1955, he retired from baseball at the age of 73. Always the innovator (and perhaps inspired by his years of watching Robinson get beaned), Rickey developed the modern batting helmet which became standard Major League equipment in 1957. Despite poor health, Rickey continued to study America's race relations and to speak out for integration. On one occasion in late 1956, Mr. Rickey was speaking to an audience in Washington, DC when he felt faint and lost his vision. He clutched the podium for three minutes until his vision returned, apologized to his audience for the embarrassing silence, and then continued with his plea for the integration of America. In 1957, he was appointed chair of a Presidential commission to promote racial harmony and justice (a precursor to the Equal Opportunity Employment Commission). As he was receiving an award, Mr. Branch Rickey had a heart attack; he died a short time later on December 9, 1965 at the age of 83. Two years later Rickey received baseball's highest honor. The plaque in the Hall of Fame reads:

> Wesley Branch Rickey
> St. Louis A.L. 1905–1906–1914
> New York A.L. 1907
>
> Founder of farm system which he developed for St. Louis Cardinals and Brooklyn Dodgers. Copied by all other Major League teams. Served as executive for Browns, Cardinals, Dodgers and Pirates. Brought Jackie Robinson to Brooklyn in 1947.

Jackie Robinson was named Rookie of the Year in 1947 and National League M.V.P. in 1949. He stole home an exciting 19 times (five times in one season). He was named to the National League All-Star team for six consecutive years. In the fall of 1947, he finished second to Bing Crosby in a poll as the most popular man in America. Robinson retired from baseball after the 1956 season and before the club moved to Los Angeles. He became vice-president of Chock Full O' Nuts — a fast food chain that employed many black Americans. Despite his bout with diabetes, Jackie Robinson also continued his struggle for civil rights. He was active in the Harlem YMCA, he promoted black capitalism through the Freedom National Bank, he refused a token membership at an exclusive "white" golf club (preferring to wait two hours for a time at the public course), and he continued to speak out against racism through his column in the *New York Post* as well as in other forums. In 1962, Mr. Jack Robinson received baseball's highest honor — election to the Hall of Fame. When he received his award, he asked three persons to stand beside him — his mother, Mallie, his wife, Rachel, and his friend, Branch Rickey. The plaque in Cooperstown reads:

> Jack Roosevelt Robinson
> Brooklyn N.L. 1947–1956
> Leading N.L. batter in 1949. Holds fielding mark for second baseman

playing 150 or more games with .992. Led N.L. in stolen bases in 1947 and 1949. Most Valuable Player in 1949. Lifetime batting average .311. Joint record holder for most double plays by second baseman, 137 in 1951. Led second basemen in double plays 1949–52.

Fittingly, the plaque does not mention the achievement for which Mr. Jackie Robinson is most remembered.

Portions of this paper were presented at the Baseball Hall of Fame's Fifth Cooperstown Symposium on Baseball and American Culture on June 10, 1993 in Cooperstown, NY. We thank Elliot Aronson, Susan Finnemore Brennan, Nancy Carlson, Jonathan Cobb, Ken Fuld, David Morishige, T. Douglass Wuggazer, and Dan Ziniuk for helpful comments and discussion.

Notes

1. "Dodgers to Play Royals," *New York Times,* April 10, 1947, p. 32.

2. J. Tygiel, *Baseball's Great Experiment: Jackie Robinson and His Legacy* (New York: Vintage Books, 1983).

3. T. F. Pettigrew, *Racially Separate or Together?* (New York: McGraw-Hill, 1971).

4. A. R. Pratkanis & M. E. Turner, "The Year Cool Papa Bell Lost the Batting Title: Mr. Branch Rickey and Mr. Jackie Robinson's Plea for Affirmative Action," *NINE: A Journal of Baseball History and Social Policy Perspectives,* Vol. 2, No. 2 (1994): 260–276.

5. We base our account on the following excellent descriptions of Robinson's introduction to the white Major Leagues: M. Allen, *Jackie Robinson: A Life Remembered* (New York: Franklin Watts, 1987). M. Alvarez, *The Official Baseball Hall of Fame Story of Jackie Robinson* (New York: Simon & Schuster, 1990). R. Barber, *1947 — When All Hell Broke Loose in Baseball* (New York: De Capo, 1982). L. Durocher, *Nice Guys Finish Last* (New York: Pocket Books, 1976). G. Eskenazi, *The Lip: A Biography of Leo Durocher* (New York: William Marrow, 1993). H. Frommer, *Rickey and Robinson: The Men Who Broke Baseball's Color Barrier* (New York: Macmillan, 1982). P. Golenbock & P. Bacon, *Teammates* (San Diego: Harcourt Brace Jovanovich, 1990). A. E. Green (Director), *The Jackie Robinson Story Starring Jackie Robinson* [Film] (New York: Goodtimes Home Video Corp., 1950). R. Kahn, *The Boys of Summer* (New York: Harper & Row, 1972). A. Mann, *Branch Rickey: American in Action* (Boston: Houghton Mifflin, 1957). J. R. Robinson, *I Never Had it Made* (New York: G. P. Putnam & Sons, 1972). J. R. Robinson & C. Dexter, *Baseball has Done It* (Philadelphia: J. B. Lippincott, 1964). F. Sabin, *Jackie Robinson* (Mahwah, NJ: Troll, 1985). G. Schoor, *The Leo Durocher Story* (New York: Julian Messner, 1955). R. Scott, *Jackie Robinson* (New York: Chelsea House, 1987). M. J. Shapiro, *Jackie Robinson of the Brooklyn Dodgers* (New York: Pocket Books, 1967). D. Snider, *The Duke of Flatbush* (New York: Zebra Books, 1988). J. Thorn & J. Tygiel, "Jackie Robinson's Signing: The Real, Untold Story," in J. Thorn & P. Palmer (Eds.), *Total Baseball: The Ultimate Encyclopedia of Baseball,* 3rd ed. (New York: Harper Collins, 1993), pp. 148–153, and especially, Tygiel, 1983.

6. T. P. Pettigrew, "Social Psychology and Desegregation Research," *American Psychologist,* 16 (1961): 1045–112; for a review see E. Aronson, *The Social Animal,* 6th ed. (New York: W. H. Freeman, 1992).

7. G. Myrdal, *An American Dilemma* (New York: Harper & Row, 1944).

8. Barber, 1982, pp. 50–52.

9. Barber, 1982, pp. 63–64.

10. For details see Barber, 1982; Tygiel, 1983.

11. Quoted in Allen, 1987, p. 103.

12. Quoted in Barber, 1982, p. 175.

13. Quoted in Tygiel, 1983, p. 48.

14. G.W. Allport, *The Nature of Prejudice* (Reading, MA: Addison-Wesley, 1954).

15. M. Deutsch & M. E. Collins, *Interracial Housing: A Psychological Evaluation of a Social Experiment* (Minneapolis, MN: University of Minnesota Press, 1951).

16. M. Sherif, "Experiments in Group Conflict," *Scientific American,* 195 (1956): 54–58.

17. Quoted in Tygiel, 1983, p. 195.

18. Quoted in Allen, 1977, p. 132.

19. Quoted in Tygiel, 1983, p. 195.

20. R.B. Cialdini, C.A. Kallgren, & R.R. Reno, "A Focus Theory of Normative Conduct," in M. P. Zanna (Ed.), *Advances in Experimental Social Psychology,* Vol. 24 (San Diego, CA: Academic Press, 1991), pp. 201–234. T. F. Pettigrew, "Normative Theory in Intergroup Relations: Explaining Both Harmony and Conflict," *Psychology and Developing Societies,* 3 (1991): 3–16.

21. T.F. Pettigrew, "Regional Differences in Anti-Negro Prejudice," *Journal of Abnormal and Social Psychology,* 59 (1950): 28–36. See also T. F. Pettigrew, "Personality and Sociocultural Factors in Intergroup Attitudes: A Cross-National Comparison," *Journal of Conflict Resolution,* 2 (1959): 29–42.

22. R.D. Minard, "Race Relations in the Pocahontas Coal Field," *Journal of Social Issues,* 8 (1952): 29–44.

23. For more discussion see Tygiel, 1983, pp. 103–104.

24. S. E. Asch, "Opinions and Social Pressure," *Scientific American,* 193 (1955): 31–35.

25. Quoted in Allen, 1987, pp. 102–103.

26. M. Deutsch, *The Resolution of Conflict* (New Haven, CT: Yale University Press, 1973).

27. M. D. Storms, "Videotape and the Attribution Process: Reversing Actors' and Observers' Points of View," *Journal of Personality and Social Psychology,* 27 (1973): 165–175. C. D. Batson, *The Altruism Question: Toward a Social-Psychological Answer* (Hillsdale, NJ: Lawrence Erlbaum, 1991). M. L. Hoffman, "Moral Internalization: Current Theory and Research," in L. Berkowitz (Ed.), *Advances in Experimental Social Psychology,* Vol. 10 (New York: Academic Press, 1977), pp. 86–133.

28. M. R. Jackman & M. Crane, "Some of My Best Friends are Black...: Interracial Friendships and Whites' Racial Attitudes," *Public Opinion Quarterly,* 50 (1986): 459–486.

29. We compiled this list of racial slurs hurled at Robinson from sources listed in Note 5. Most observers of the incident comment that published accounts do not adequately describe the abuse and have been edited to remove the more offensive remarks.

30. Quoted in Frommer, 1982, p. 137.

31. D. A. Wilder, "Social Categorization: Implications for Creation and Reduction of Intergroup Bias," in L. Berkowitz (Ed.), *Advances in Experimental Social Psychology,* Vol. 19 (New York Academic Press, 1986), pp. 291–355.

32. M. B. Brewer, "In-Group Bias in the Minimal Intergroup Situation," *Psychological Bulletin,* 86 (1979): 307–324. H. Tajfel, "Experiments in Intergroup Discrimination," *Scientific American,* 223 (1970): 96–102.

33. T.F. Pettigrew, "The Ultimate Attribution Error: Extending Allport's Cognitive Analysis of Prejudice," *Personality and Social Psychology Bulletin,* 5 (1979): 461–476.

34. R. M. Kanter, *Men and Women of the Corporation* (New York: Basic Books, 1977). See also S. E. Taylor, "A Categorization Approach to Stereotyping," in D. L. Hamilton (Ed.), *Cognitive Processes in Stereotyping and Intergroup Behavior* (Hillsdale, NJ: Lawrence Erlbaum, 1981), pp. 83–114.

35. Of course, one way to reduce solo effects is to hire more members of the out-group. This is not always possible if the out-group is a numerical minority. An unpublished 1945 manuscript by Arthur Mann and some lost photos of Robinson with other black players to accompany the piece in *Look* magazine indicate that Rickey had planned to bring more black Americans to the Dodgers than just Robinson. Rickey rushed the news of the Robinson hiring before signing other black stars because he felt that political pressures were mounting to sign a black American. He thought the integration of baseball would run smoother if it was perceived to be a voluntary effort. For an intriguing account see Thorn & Tygiel, 1993.

36. D.A. Wilder, "Reduction of Intergroup Discrimination Through Individuation of the Out-Group," *Journal of Personality and Social Psychology,* 36 (1978): 1361–1374.

37. P.A. Katz, "Stimulus Predifferentiation and Modification of Children's Racial Attitudes," *Child Development,* 44 (1973): 232–237.

38. See Tygiel, 1983, pp. 92–93.

39. L. Effrat, "Royals' Star Signs With Brooks Today," *New York Times,* April 11, 1947, p. 20.

40. G. Waterman, "Racial Pioneering on the Mound: Don Newcombe's Social and Psychological Ordeal," *NINE: A Journal of Baseball History and Social Policy Perspectives,* Vol. 1, No. 2 (1993): 185–195.

41. Green, 1950.

42. J. Pfeffer, *Power in Organizations* (Boston: Pitman, 1981).

43. Quoted in Allen, 1987, p. 102.

44. Quoted in Allen, 1987, p. 103.

45. Quoted in Frommer, 1982, pp. 127–128.

46. A.J. Murrell, B. L. Dietz, J. F. Dovidio, S. L. Gaertner, & C. Drout, "Aversive Racism and Resistance to Affirmative Action: Perceptions of Justice are Not Necessarily Color Blind," *Basic and Applied Social Psychology,* 15 (1991): 71–86. See also J.F. Dovidio, J.A. Mann, & S.L. Gaertner, "Resistance to Affirmative Action: The Implications of Aversive Racism," in F.A. Blanchard & F.J. Crosby (Eds.), *Affirmative Action in Perspective* (New York: Springer-Verlag, 1989), pp. 83–102.

47. R. Barnes Nacoste, "If Empowerment is the Goal...: Affirmative Action and Social Interaction," *Basic and Applied Social Psychology,* 15 (1994): 87–112. L. Sigelman & S. Welch, *Black Americans' Views of Racial Inequality: The Dream Deferred* (Cambridge: Cambridge University Press, 1991).

48. J.R. Kluegel & E. R. Smith, *Beliefs About Inequality* (Hawthorne, NY: Aldine de Gruyter, 1986).

49. A. R. Pratkanis & A. G. Greenwald, "A Socio-Cognitive Model of Attitude Structure and Function," in L. Berkowitz (Ed.), *Advances in Experimental Social Psychology,* Vol. 22 (New York: Academic Press, 1989), pp. 245–285.

50. M. E. Heilman, M. C. Simon, & D. P. Repper, "Intentionally Favored, Unintentionally Harmed? Impact of Sex-Based Preferential Selection on Self-Perceptions and Self-Evaluations," *Journal of Applied Psychology,* 72 (1987): 62–66. T.F. Pettigrew & J. Martin, "Shaping the Organizational Context for Black American Inclusion," *Journal of Social Issues,* 43 (1987): 41–78. M.E. Turner, A.R. Pratkanis, & T.J. Hardaway, "Sex

Differences in Reactions to Preferential Selection: Towards a Model of Preferential Selection as Help," *Journal of Social Behavior and Personality*, 6 (1991): 797–814. M.E. Turner & A.R. Pratkanis, "Effects of Preferential and Meritorious Selection on Performance: An Examination of Intuitive and Self-handicapping Perspectives," *Personality and Social Psychology Bulletin*, 19 (1993): 47–58. For a review see M.E. Turner & A.R. Pratkanis, "Affirmative Action as Help: A Review of Recipient Reactions to Preferential Selection and Affirmative Action," *Basic and Applied Social Psychology*, 15 (1994): 43–69.

    51. See Turner & Pratkanis, 1994.

    52. J.M. Jones, *Prejudice and Racism* (Reading, MA: Addison-Wesley, 1972). J.M. Jones, "Racism in Black and White: A Bicultural Model of Reaction and Evolution," in P. A. Katz & D.A. Taylor (Eds.), *Eliminating Racism* (New York: Plenum, 1988), pp. 117–135.

    53. For a discussion see Tygiel, 1983, pp. 315–318.

    54. D. E. Albrecht, "An Inquiry Into the Decline of Baseball in Black America: Some Answers — More Questions," *NINE: A Journal of Baseball History and Social Policy Perspectives*, Vol. 1, No. 1 (1992): 31–41.

    55. For a listing of the accomplishments of black baseball players see A. Rust, *Get That Nigger Off the Field: The Oral History of the Negro Leagues* (Brooklyn, NY: Book Mail Services, 1992).

    56. H. Aaron, *I Had a Hammer: The Hank Aaron Story* (New York: Harper Paperbacks, 1991).

Baseball, Cricket, and Social Change: Jackie Robinson and Frank Worrell[1]

Michael Malec and Hillary Beckles

The philosopher Jacques Barzun (1954: 159) once said, "Whoever wants to know the heart and mind of the American had better learn baseball, the rules, the realities of the game…." By this he meant, in part, that we can understand a culture by observing its games, and because baseball is "the American pastime," a knowledge of this particular game could help explain the culture. C.L.R. James (1993: xxi), a scholar from the West Indies, once wrote, "What do they know of cricket, who only cricket know?" By this he meant that the game of cricket could be understood as more than just a game, but as "a metaphor for life" and, when played on the international level, as a "symbolic battle between the nations represented" (Kurlansky 1992: 282). This paper explores two games, baseball and cricket, and two men who played these games, Jackie Robinson and Frank Worrell, and uses these to illustrate how athletes and their games were instrumental in contributing to large-scale social change in two different cultures.

> The cricket [baseball] field was a stage on which selected individuals played representative roles which were charged with social significance (James 1993: 66).

In ways that were different yet similar, Jackie Robinson, a baseball player from the United States, and Frank Worrell, a cricket player from the

West Indies, both played roles that revolutionized their sports and introduced or symbolized significant changes in their societies.

On April 15, 1947, Jackie Robinson (1919–1972) became the first African-American in the modern Major Leagues of Baseball, ending more than sixty years of baseball's formal and informal racial segregation. A simple game, baseball, broke its "color barrier" a year before the U.S. Armed Services were fully integrated, seven years before school segregation was ruled unconstitutional, and nearly twenty years before the significant civil rights legislation of the mid–1960s was passed into law. When Robinson took his position on the field, the face of modern American sport was radically changed. At the end of his first season he was named "Rookie of the Year," and two years later, he was his League's "Most Valuable Player." In 1962, he became the first African-American admitted to baseball's Hall of Fame.

Robinson's effect on American society went far beyond the playing fields. Intelligent and articulate, passionate and committed, insistent on immediate social change but keenly aware of the need for a long-range plan, Jackie Robinson eventually became a leading spokesman in the battle against a variety of the ugly forms of racial segregation and discrimination in the U.S.A.

The color line in American baseball at the end of World War II seemed as firm and unyielding as did the color lines throughout the United States. In much of the South, blacks and whites were legally barred "from attending the same schools, riding in the same sections of trains and buses, receiving treatment in the same hospitals, and competing in the same athletic contests" (Tygiel 1983: 7). In the North, the laws were less severe, but the everyday folkways were not.

In the West Indies, racism, and the responses to it, took somewhat different forms. Historically, emancipation came to the Anglo-Caribbean in the 1830s, three decades before it came to the United States of America. The great Caribbean civil rights struggles of the 1930s preceded by three decades similar struggles in the U.S.A. And it is highly significant that the population of most of the cricket-playing Caribbean comprised a far larger proportion that was of African descent than was the case in the U.S.A.

In the West Indies, cricket teams were racially integrated well before Robinson was born. Indeed, there is no figure in West Indies cricket comparable to Jackie Robinson, that is, a figure who is recognized and acclaimed as the man who broke the racial playing barrier. However, the struggles within the West Indies to achieve racial equality in cricket and in society were no less massive, no less historically significant. But in the

West Indies, with its majority black populations, the struggle focused not on playing, but on leading. Although black West Indians had been playing alongside whites since the turn of the century, no black man had ever captained the West Indies team.[2] (North Americans need to know that the role of captain in cricket is far more important than the roles of captain or manager are in baseball or most team sports. The captain is both a player and a leader, a motivator and decision-maker, a strategist and tactician.)

At the time when Robinson was integrating baseball and the United States was slowly moving towards its modern civil rights era, the nations of the British West Indies were moving towards political independence. Along with political equality, they demanded all forms of social equality, including that of the captaincy of the national team. Those who controlled West Indies cricket, however, still maintained the colonial legacy of white superiority. "The whole point was to send ... black or brown men under a white captain. [This] ... would emphasize to millions of English people: 'Yes, [blacks] are fine players, but ... they cannot be responsible for themselves — they must have a white man to lead them'" (James 1993: 233).[3] Thus, in the West Indies, the fact that an integrated team was captained by a white man was a constant reminder, in the face of looming agitation for voting rights and self-rule, that blacks were assumed by whites to be incapable of leadership. The athletic career of the black West Indian, Frank Worrell (1924–1967), undid much of this colonial legacy.

Throughout Worrell's career as a professional cricketer he engaged and protested the established norms of the status quo as they pertained to ethnic relations, relations between players and officials, and the ideological implication of sport with respect to the rise and maturity of national society. His ascendancy in the post-war years as a distinguished player corresponded with the emergence of organized anti-colonial politics and the crises of colonial society. Great black players of the inter-war period, such as Learie Constantine (the first West Indian black cricketer to be knighted) and George Headley, had ensured that the cricket culture would become a site for the discourse of decolonization and democratic freedom. Within the distinct West Indian tradition, Worrell occupied a place which, in the immediate post-war years, proved seminal. In this sense Worrell was, like Robinson, a product of his time. He was the heir to a political circumstance that saw the attachment of the culture of sports to the emergence of national society, just as Robinson was heir to a social circumstance that led to new norms for racial interaction.

Both Robinson and Worrell were strong-willed, with a passionate distaste for racism and racist institutional practices. Indeed, as agents of social change, both men were seen by their antagonists as arrogant or insubordinate. As a teen, Robinson had a few run-ins with the police, and while in junior college he responded to a racial insult in a way that nearly escalated into a small race riot, and left him with a police record. While serving in the Army, a racial dispute stemming from his refusal to move to the back of a segregated public bus led to charges of insubordination and a general court-martial; he was subsequently acquitted.

It is well-documented how during his first year as a Dodger, Robinson had to learn to control his passion and to "turn the other cheek." As part of his self-restraint agreement with the team's management, he pledged that he would not respond to insult or intimidation, that he would suffer silently the slings and arrows of racism on the field and off. Branch Rickey and the Dodger management deemed it essential that Robinson conduct himself at all times as a perfect gentleman. They believed that his behavior, manners, and demeanor would help to defuse racially hostile crowds.[4] They also agreed that, after the first year, the reins would come off and Jackie would be free to respond to insults and to intimidate the intimidators, which he did.

From his earliest professional years, Worrell attracted the reputation for being uppity, insubordinate, arrogant, and self-willed. In the context of the Barbadian society that produced him, a society that saw itself as the Caribbean center of Englishness[5] and as an imperial power within the West Indian Empire, these traits had much to do with popular perceptions of his self-determination and his rejection of the ideological world of white supremacy.

For example, as a young cricketer playing for Barbados in regional contests, on a team led and dominated by members of the local white elite, Worrell rejected the policy of separate training for white and black players. Like Robinson, he also criticized the policy of separate travel facilities and accommodations for whites and blacks while on tour. He eventually so incurred the wrath of the local white business elite that he considered himself unemployable in Barbados. His biography tells of the young Worrell walking the length of Bridgetown's Broad Street (the principal commercial area), unable to find any gainful employment.

The white community succeeded in promoting a negative image of Worrell through the print media it owned and encouraged the black community to share its opinion. When this hostility prompted him to leave his native Barbados for Jamaica, he was booed by whites and blacks alike. Later, as a wider social understanding of his ideological postures developed, he received hero receptions on his return visits to Barbados.

In 1948, Worrell confronted the white officials of the West Indies

Cricket Board of Control over remuneration for the upcoming tour to India. He classified himself as a professional, and demanded to be paid £250 to tour. The white players on the team, mostly from planter-merchant families, were amateurs who neither needed nor demanded any salary. When he was denied the fee, Worrell refused to tour though he was considered the best batsman on the West Indies team. The West Indies cricket establishment sought to crush Worrell for his insubordination, but his popularity among fans in the islands (other than Barbados), and among players and fans in England, protected him from its wrath.

Robinson and Worrell faced other similar challenges. For example, both had to deal with the prospect of failure. If Robinson failed on the field, all black players would be set back in their quest for participation. If Worrell failed as a captain, it might be decades before another black were awarded that position. Consequently, those who sponsored and supported both Robinson and Worrell chose men who had the athletic talent and skill to succeed on the playing field. More important, perhaps, they selected men whose personalities, backgrounds, emotional states, and intelligence enabled them to withstand great pressure and overcome fierce resistance as they created new norms of integration and new standards of black achievement in their wider societies.

> Worrell [Robinson] was no accident. [James, quoted in Manley 1988: 147].

It was no accident that Worrell was the first black to captain the West Indies team: he was a highly skilled athlete, he was university educated (University of Manchester), he had a middle-class upbringing that served him well in non-sport social settings, and he had a burning distaste for discrimination in his sport and in his culture. Three of these four traits can be ascribed to Robinson as well. (Robinson, the grandson of slaves, was from a working-class background.)

Worrell was no accident, and neither was Robinson. The color line in American baseball at the end of World War II seemed as firm and unyielding as did the color lines throughout the United States. In much of the South, blacks and whites were legally barred "from attending the same schools, riding in the same sections of trains and buses, receiving treatment in the same hospitals, and competing in the same athletic contests"(Tygiel 1983: 7). Robinson excelled in sports in high school, junior college, and college before turning professional. He set a junior college record in the long-jump. (The record he broke had been held by his older brother, Mack. Mack also had won a silver medal in the 200 meter dash at the 1936 Olympics.) Jackie was the first four-letter athlete in UCLA's history, and it is of some interest that of baseball, basketball, football, and track, the former was probably Jackie's weakest! Worrell's career was more singularly focused on one sport, but those who saw him play football (soccer) attested to his high level of skill in that sport as well.

There is, however, another sense in which Worrell and Robinson were "not accidents." Although one can argue that the tide of history would have eventually produced the first black baseball player and the first black cricket captain, the timing of the tides that specifically produced Robinson and Worrell was not happenstance. Robinson did not appear on the scene and declare his intention to be the first black major league player. Rather, Robinson was identified, scouted, and selected by Branch Rickey, the general manager of the Brooklyn Dodgers, and a political conservative. As early as 1942 or '43, Rickey had developed a six-part plan to bring black players to the Dodgers (Falkner 1995: 104). His plan included: (1) securing the support of the Dodgers' directors and stockholders; (2) finding the player who would be the right man on the field; (3) finding the player who would be the right man off the field; (4) insuring a positive reaction from the press and the public; (5) obtaining the support and understanding of the black community; and (6) securing the cooperation of the other Dodger players. Rickey revealed his plan to the Dodgers' Board of Directors in 1943. He first met Robinson in 1945, and signed him to a professional contract. In 1946, Robinson played in the Dodgers' farm system, in Montreal. In 1947, Jackie Robinson made history in the United States.

> When the local whites started to play cricket, black Barbadians watched and the black middle class began not only to play, but to form clubs.... But the white upper classes continued to hold all the economic and political power and ... social prestige.... [James, quoted in Manley 1988: 147].

The histories of baseball in the United States and cricket in the West Indies share many traits. Both sports were initially controlled by whites. And while the early history of both games in the nineteenth century is primarily a history of white and middle-class players and white organizations, blacks and the working classes soon embraced both games. The U.S. Civil War era was the period of the "democratization" of baseball, and the post–Emancipation era in the West Indies had a similar effect on cricket. Ownership of both games was in the hands of wealthy whites, and this has remained so to the present day. But although ownership is a form of privilege, other positions of privilege and control, in both sports, did not remain exclusively white in the later half of the twentieth century.

By the early 1950s, the black West Indian majority had decided that Worrell was the obvious and logical choice as captain of the West Indies team. They resented the fact that less qualified whites were given the task. Public opinion, particularly in Jamaica and Trinidad, reached fever levels of outrage with respect to the issue of racial injustice, the future of colonial rule, and the popular call for democratic decolonization. The public campaign was led by the distinguished intellectual C.L.R. James. James wrote for *The Nation*, one of Trinidad's leading newspapers, and an organ of a major political party, the People's National Movement (PNM). James's writings were strongly political, and were aligned with the rise of Eric Williams (who was to become the first Prime Minister of Trinidad & Tobago) and the PNM. "The connections between cricket, culture, and politics in the West Indies are evident in any discussion of Williams and the PNM" (Stoddart 1995: 246). The issue was clear: The ascendancy of a black man, Worrell, to leadership of the regional cricket team would signal the end of white supremacy in the governance of the West Indies, and the conceptual abandonment of the colonial project. James knew this, Worrell knew this, and the people of the West Indies knew this too.

The white community of Barbados, and its supportive element within the black middle class, never welcomed or accepted Worrell, even while he was captain of the island's team, the star West Indian player, and later captain of the West Indies team.

Robinson and Worrell were similar in that both had their advocates, Rickey and James, respectively. But there was also an important difference: Robinson was selected by a white man more than he was campaigned for by the black population. Although many blacks had been working for "a" black player, it was Rickey who selected "the" black player. Worrell was championed by James, who was black, and, more importantly, was campaigned for by the black masses as both a symbol and as "the" individual who deserved the honor.

In 1958, Worrell was offered the job as West Indies Captain to engage in a test series against the Indian team in India and the Pakistan team in the West Indies. He refused because he held the view that the white establishment in the West Indies was willing to accept him as captain only against non-white teams and not against white teams. He was prepared to accept the leadership only against the Australians or the English. (As an aside, we note that India in the 1930s, and Pakistan in the 1940s, had captains of color. This perhaps suggests an attitude towards the imperial occupation of India that was different from the attitude towards the West Indies; the legacy of slavery might explain some of these attitude differences.)

Finally, in 1959, the year of his graduation from Manchester, Worrell was appointed captain of the West Indies team for the 1960 tour to Australia, and the 1963 tour to England. James noted that once Worrell had done a good job in Australia and had shown the world that black men would manage their own affairs with distinction, he (James) would be off to London to demand constitutional independence for the West Indies islands. "[When] Worrell took over the captaincy of West Indian cricket ... [he] changed the image of the game in the minds of West Indians and also the expectations ... with respect to the performance of the captain, team spirit and the behavior of the West Indian cricket hero" (St. Pierre 1995: 119–120). In 1962, the process of constitutional decolonization began with independence for Jamaica and Trinidad and Tobago. The linkage was clear. Cricket and National Society were symbolically represented in the person of Frank Worrell.

Although the West Indies team lost to Australia in the first series led by Worrell, he won the hearts of the Australians and fascinated the English cricketing world not only with his athletic talent, but also with his charm, wit, and warm personality. Worrell did not bring instant success to his team, but he laid a foundation on which the West Indies would, over the next decade, build themselves into the world's best cricket team, a distinction which it would hold into the 1990s.

Worrell's achievements in sport can partly be measured by the recognition that was bestowed on him by others outside of sport. He was appointed to the Senate in Jamaica; he was appointed Dean of Student Services at the University of the West Indies; and he was knighted by Queen Elizabeth in 1964. His face is on the Barbados five dollar note. No Barbadian had ever received such a constellation of honors (Manley 1988: 169). No West Indian athlete has ever done more to change the face of sport in the Caribbean region, and thereby change the entire region's attitudes toward race.

Prior to 1997, Robinson's societal achievements were not rewarded in the same way by his country. (He did appear on a U. S. postage stamp issued in 1982 as part of the "Black Heritage" series.) However, after baseball he did achieve some measure of success in business, was consulted on civil rights issues by both Presidents Kennedy and Nixon, and worked as a special assistant to New York Governor Nelson Rockefeller. His anniversary year, however, produced numerous tributes to the man who, more than any other athlete, changed the face of modern sport in the United States, and thereby greatly contributed to changing the entire society's attitudes toward race.

Both Worrell and Robinson deserve their places of honor in their respective sports. But both men are more fittingly celebrated for the changes that they helped produce in the larger arenas of history and culture. Neither man chose his destiny, but neither shirked his responsibility.

Notes

1. This chapter is revised and expanded from an earlier version (Malec and Beckles 1997).

2. Actually, the great George Headley captained the West Indies team in 1948 for one test match in Barbados because the white captain was ill. Headley was thus, technically, the first black man to captain the West Indies, although it was understood by all that this was a temporary measure with no seminal significance. Headley was probably the greatest West Indian player of his time and therefore the greatest casualty of the concept of white leadership.

3. This view is similar to that expressed by Al Campanis in his infamous remark, in 1987, that blacks lacked the "necessities" to occupy leadership positions in baseball and other sports.

4. In *Levels of the Game*, John McPhee (1969, 28–29) tells how the young Arthur Ashe was taught to behave on the court. His teacher was Dr. Robert Johnson, who held certain principles

> as absolute requirements — in his view — for an assault on a sport as white as tennis. Supreme among these was self-control — "no racquet throwing, no hollering, no indication of discontent with officials' calls." Since players call their own lines in the early rounds of junior tournaments, he insisted that his boys play any opponents' shots that were out of bounds by two inches or less. "We are going into a new world," he told them. "We don't want anybody to be accused of cheating."

Dr. Johnson wanted Ashe "to be psychologically prepared for any adversity," just as Rickey wanted Robinson to be prepared.

5. Non-Caribbean readers should know that in the British West Indies there is a very strong sense of national identity that varies from island to island. Depending on the context, Bajans (the popular term), Jamaicans, Trinidadians, etc., do not regard themselves as one "West Indian" people.

Bibliography

Barzun, Jacques. 1954. *God's Country and Mine.* Boston: Little, Brown and Company.
Beckles, Hilary McD. 1994. *An Area of Conquest.* Kingston: Ian Randle Publishers.

_____, and Brian Stoddart. 1995. *Liberation Cricket*. Manchester: Manchester University Press.

Falkner, David. 1995. *Great Time Coming*. New York: Simon & Schuster.

James, C. L. R. 1993 [1963]. *Beyond A Boundary*. Durham, NC: Duke University Press.

Kurlansky, Mark. 1992. *A Continent of Nations*. Reading, MA: Addison-Wesley.

Malec, Michael A. and Hilary McD. Beckles. 1997. "Robinson and Worrell: Athletes as agents of social change." *Journal of Sport and Social Issues* 21(4), pp. 412–418.

Manley, Michael. 1988. *A History of West Indies Cricket*. London: Andre Deutsch.

McPhee, John. 1969. *Levels of the Game*. New York: Farrar, Strauss & Giroux.

Stoddart, Brian. 1995. "Caribbean cricket: The role of sport in emerging small-nation politics," pp. 239–255 in Beckles and Stoddart, *Liberation Cricket*. St. Pierre, Maurice. 1995. "West Indian cricket — Part I: A socio-historical appraisal," pp. 107–124 in Beckles and Stoddart, *Liberation Cricket*.

Tygiel, Jules. 1984 [1983]. *Baseball's Great Experiment: Jackie Robinson and His Legacy*. New York: Vintage Books.

Part 3

THE LEGACY OF ROBINSON

The Black Knight: A Political Portrait of Jackie Robinson

Steven Wisensale

On July 18, 1949, Jackie Robinson appeared before the House Un-American Activities Committee to testify against Paul Robeson, another prominent black who was accused of being a member of the communist party. It marked a turning point in the lives of both men. For Robinson, it meant being catapulted into the political arena in which he would remain until his death 23 years later. For Robeson, an internationally-known opera star, and the first black to ever play Othello, it meant the end of his brilliant singing career. Ironically, just a few years earlier Robeson walked a picket line outside Yankee Stadium to protest segregated baseball.

Robinson's impact on Robeson's career in 1949 illustrates the complexity of his life during a crucial period in American history. Both were African-American men who had reached the pinnacle of their careers in a world dominated my whites. But opera was not baseball and thus Robinson found himself in a much more influential position to integrate a segregated society. After all, it was Robinson who came alone and arrived before the others. He came before Campanella and Newcombe, before Doby and Minoso, and before Mays and Aaron. He came before Banks, Clemente, Gibson, Brock, Stargell and all the other greats. He came before Rosa Parks and James Meredith, before Martin Luther King and Malcolm X, and before bus boycotts, freedom rides, and the March on Washington.

When baseball desegregated itself in 1947, the first American institution to do so voluntarily, Jackie Robinson was penciled into the lineup as the leadoff hitter for what was to become a whole new ball game. He stood at home plate years before an executive order desegregated the U.S. Army, before the U.S. Supreme Court integrated public schools, and before Congress enacted the Civil Rights Act of 1964.

Writing in *Take Time for Paradise*, Bart Giamatti emphasized the importance of an integrated game. "Late, late as it was, the arrival in the majors of Jack Roosevelt Robinson was an extraordinary moment in American history. For the first time, a black American was on America's most privileged version of a level field."[1] Martin Luther King put it more simply during a meeting with Don Newcombe. "You will never know how easy it was for me because of Jackie Robinson."[2]

The year 1997 marked the 50th anniversary of Jackie Robinson breaking major league baseball's racial barrier. Although remembered primarily for integrating baseball and for his athletic skills in a Dodger uniform, Robinson always appeared to be someone who was on a much broader and more important mission in life. "He used his athletics as a political forum," stated his widow, Rachel, in an interview with Peter Golenbock. "He never wanted to run for office, but he always wanted to influence people's thinking."[3] Perhaps that explains why Mrs. Robinson always stated that Jackie was an informal civil rights leader first and a ballplayer second.

Yet, despite numerous books and articles on Robinson the ballplayer, very few draw attention to his role as a political activist. Consequently, few Americans today are aware of his battles with the military, his appearance before the House Un-American Activities Committee to testify against Paul Robeson, his involvement with Martin Luther King, Roy Wilkins, and Thurgood Marshall during the civil rights movement, and the role he played in several presidential campaigns.

The purpose of this paper, therefore, is to paint a political portrait of Jackie Robinson. What were his major political views and which individuals (in baseball and out) were most influential in shaping them? To capture his political portrait, this presentation will focus on three significant episodes of his life: the Paul Robeson affair, his involvement in the civil rights movement, and his role in presidential campaigns.

The Paul Robeson Affair

The signing of Jackie Robinson in 1945 by Branch Rickey is legendary. Scouted closely while a member of the Kansas City Monarchs, Robinson spent the 1946 season in Montreal before joining the Dodgers in 1947. For Rickey, Robinson was a jewel. He neither smoked nor drank and, like

Rickey, he was born and raised in a strict Methodist home. He attended a major university and participated in four sports both with and against white athletes. He was combative, proud and courageous. On the field he excelled. Promising Rickey that he would "turn the other cheek" for at least two years and absorb the racial slurs and insults from opponents, Robinson devoted all of his energy to baseball in 1947.

In his first season *The Sporting News* named him Rookie of the Year — the first time such an award was given. His record spoke for itself: 42 successful bunts, 14 for hits, 28 sacrifices; 29 stolen bases; 12 home runs; and a .297 batting average. The editor of *The Sporting News*, J.G. Taylor Spink, commented on his accomplishment: "Robinson was rated solely as a freshman player — on his hitting, his running, his defensive play, his team value."[4] For ten seasons, from 1947 to 1956, he would lead the Dodgers to six National League pennants and one World Series championship.

It can be argued, however, that 1949 was the most significant year of his life — both on the field and off. On his way to his first and only MVP award, he would lead the league in hitting (.342) and stolen bases (37), hit 16 home runs and collected 124 RBIs as the Dodgers won the pennant by a game over the St. Louis Cardinals. It was also the year in which he became the first black to ever participate in a major league All-Star game.

Also, in June of 1949, Paul Robeson returned to the United States after completing a European tour. Robeson, the first black ever to play Othello on stage, had become a major critic of U.S. segregationist policies. Born in Princeton, New Jersey, in 1898, he was Phi Beta Kappa and valedictorian of his graduating class at Rutgers. He later received a law degree from Columbia University. On the athletic field he was equally impressive, earning fifteen varsity letters and twice being named a football All-American. Unable to find a job in a predominantly white world, he chose instead to pursue a musical career, concentrating primarily on opera.

By the mid–1940s his concerts became a combination of songs and messages, as he frequently spoke out on the plight of America's blacks. The Ballad of Joe Hill, a song about a union organizer, replaced famous arias. Before a packed audience at the Bolshoi Theater in Moscow he announced that he had changed the original words of "Ol' Man River" to mean "we must fight to the death for peace and freedom."[5] And, as the years passed, he became more closely associated with the American Communist Party.

A growing concern that the Communist Party was making inroads among America's blacks developed into paranoia. Robeson was confronted regularly with protesters at his concerts and twice, in Peekskill, New York, his appearance caused riots. In Harlem's Red Rooster Restaurant, Dodger pitcher, Don Newcombe, refused to shake his hand.[6] Meanwhile, the House Un-American Activities Committee continued its assault against "disloyal" Americans. In early July it opened its "Hearings Regarding Communist Infiltration of Minority Groups." Soon after they concluded, Paul Robeson was stripped of his passport and driven into obscurity. To this day, he remains the only two-time All-American who is not a member of the College Football Hall of Fame.

If life is a chess game, then Jackie Robinson's role in the summer of 1949 was to check Paul Robeson. In early July, Representative John S. Wood of Georgia and Chairman of the House Un-American Activities Committee, contacted Robinson and asked him to testify before his committee and "to give lie" to the statements of Paul Robeson.[7] It is not surprising that Robinson was chosen to testify. According to Alvin Stokes, a black investigator for the Committee, it was imperative to get someone of Robinson's stature to discredit Robeson.[8]

Robinson was clearly confronted with a dilemma. On one hand, if he testified he might be little more than a black pawn in a white man's game that pitted black against black. If he did not testify, however, Robeson's statement might be upheld as a view representative of all blacks, a view with which Robinson and millions of other blacks vehemently disagreed. Despite appeals from his wife not to testify, he was eventually won over by the more persuasive arguments of Branch Rickey who apparently decided that a public appearance of this nature was a necessity. Assisted by Lester Grange of the Urban League, Robinson wrestled vigorously with the content of his statement. "It must be placating, so that the white race will not be alienated," he said. "And of course, it must be strong enough so that it won't lose the colored audience, either."[9] He found himself suspended in what Carl Rowan referred to as "a patriot's purgatory."[10] On July 18, 1949, he presented his prepared statement before the House Un-American Activities Committee.

In essence, Robinson's appearance before the House Un-American Activities Committee was a checked swing. He lunged after Robeson's Paris statement and dismissed it as "silly" before quickly pulling back his bat and attacking American racism in general. Years later and shortly before his death he reflected back over his 1949 testimony: "I have grown wiser and closer to the painful truth about America's destructiveness. And, I do have an increased respect for Paul Robeson who ... sacrificed himself, his career, and the wealth and comfort he once enjoyed because, I believe, he was sincerely trying to help his people"[11] It was Paul Robeson who picketed Yankee Stadium in the early 1940s, demanding that baseball be integrated.[12]

The Civil Rights Movement

A year after his appearance before the House Un-American Activities Committee, *The Jackie Robinson Story* opened at neighborhood theaters across the country. Jackie played himself in the film, Ruby Dee played Rachel. Years later he would lament that it was made much too soon. Indeed it was! For Robinson's overall contributions to society went far beyond his display of outstanding athletic skills. Over the next two decades he actively participated in the civil rights movement and three presidential campaigns. He cultivated close friendships with Martin Luther King, Thurgood Marshall, Nelson Rockefeller, and Jesse Jackson while he feuded openly with Adam Clayton Powell, Malcolm X, and William F. Buckley. He wrote a regular syndicated column on political issues, appeared on Meet the Press, served as a corporate executive, was named to the directorship of a major bank, and was appointed to numerous boards and commissions in both the private and public sectors. He even contemplated running for Congress.

Throughout the 1950s and 1960s, a dormant America, most of which was satisfied with the status quo, was rudely awakened by sit-ins, freedom rides, and mass marches — all in the name of racial equality. Soon the unfamiliar became the familiar. There was Birmingham and Little Rock, Greensboro, and Selma. And there was Emmet Till and Medgar Evers, James Meredith and Viola Liuzzo. While Congress passed three civil rights bills and a voting rights act, the nation was stunned by urban riots and the assassination of four of its most prominent leaders: John Kennedy, Malcolm X, Martin Luther King, and Bobby Kennedy. Still to come was the pain and agony of the Vietnam War.

Through it all, Jackie Robinson immersed himself in the cause, molded his political views, fortified his basic principles, and acted upon his most cherished beliefs. When he retired from baseball in 1956 he immediately entered the business world as a vice-president of personnel for Chock Full O' Nuts, a New York restaurant chain. Under the tutelage of owner William Black, he not only learned how to manage a private enterprise (a skill that he would later apply successfully to other business ventures) but he was also given the opportunity to continue his quest for racial equality nationwide. He advocated strongly for black capitalism.

In 1957 he was named chairman of the NAACP Freedom Fund Drive and traveled around the country to recruit new members and raise money for the civil rights organization. In April of that year he appeared as a guest on NBC's *Meet the Press* and discussed two matters in particular: civil rights ("we're moving too slow") and baseball's reserve-clause (he supported it).[13]

By 1959 he had discovered another outlet for expressing his views. Writing a syndicated newspaper column three days a week, he explored a variety of topics that ranged from lynchings in Mississippi to substandard housing in Harlem. In one column he announced that he was politically independent but being wooed by both parties.[14] In another column he accused the Red Sox of racism because they failed to bring Pumpsie Green (their only black with major league skills) north after spring training.[15] But his subjects would soon broaden and include other issues.

Although he had met Martin Luther King as early as 1955 (after King's home was firebombed), it was not until the early 1960s that he developed a close working relationship with the famous civil rights leader, as he accompanied him on numerous speaking tours. However, when King openly opposed the Vietnam War and attempted to blend the peace movement with the civil rights movement, Robinson retreated. "Isn't it unfair for you to place all the burden of blame on America and none on the communist forces we are fighting?" he asked King in a public letter.[16] Eventually, however, after his son returned from the war, Jackie began to view U.S. involvement there from a different perspective. He became particularly concerned about the disproportionate number of poor blacks who were being dispatched to the war zone.

Relentless, Robinson's assaults on racism continued. In 1968 he was one of the primary organizers to block South Africa's admission to the Olympic games. In 1970 he testified before the Senate Small Business Subcommittee and criticized the Nixon Administration's anemic efforts to encourage black capitalism. And, shortly before his death in 1972 he attacked baseball for its reluctance to hire black managers, coaches, and front office personnel. Unlike many professional athletes who find the transition from the playing field to mainstream society difficult, Robinson appeared to thrive on it, never permitting an opportunity to pass to remind people of the evils of racism.

The Presidential Campaigns

Robinson's involvement in the civil rights struggle led him naturally toward the political arena. As more blacks demanded greater power, their votes increased in value. Not surprisingly, politicians aggressively sought out well-respected role models who could deliver black votes. Jackie Robinson, in particular, was considered to be a prize catch for any would-be candidate. By 1959, however, he still maintained his political neutrality, though he was actively recruited by both parties. A year later things would change.

The presidential election year of 1960 would prove to be pivotal for blacks in particular and the nation in general. Aware of its significance, Robinson sought the presidential candidate whom he thought most clearly understood the racial issue and best represented the cause of civil rights. He initially chose Hubert Humphrey, a liberal Democrat. "I had campaigned for Senator Humphrey in the Democratic primaries because I had a strong admiration for his civil rights background as mayor of Minneapolis and as a Senator. I had heard him publicly vow that he was pledged to be the living example of a man who would rather be right morally than achieve the presidency."[17] His choice of Humphrey, however, would be short-lived. Following his defeat in the West Virginia primary, the Minnesota Senator ended his quest for the presidency, leaving Robinson to choose between Kennedy and Nixon.

In the spring of 1960 Jackie traveled to Washington to meet with both presidential candidates. "Finally, I didn't think it was much of a choice but I was impressed with the Nixon record on rights," he would write years later. "And when I sat with him in his office in Washington, he certainly said all the right things."[18] Also, he was later given the impression that Nixon would appoint a black to his cabinet if elected. On the other hand, he found Kennedy courteous but uncomfortable with him.

> My very first reaction to the Senator was one of doubt because he couldn't or wouldn't look me straight in the eye. My second reaction, much more substantial, was that this was a man who had served in the Senate and wanted to be president but who knew little or nothing about black problems and sensibilities. I was appalled that he could be so ignorant of our situation and be bidding for the highest office in the land.[19]

According to Harvey Frommer's account in *Rickey and Robinson: The Men Who Broke Baseball's Color Barrier* (1982), Jackie was also upset because the Massachusetts Senator had offered him money for his support.

Clearly, Robinson did not find it easy defending his decision to join the Republican party but his reasoning appeared sound. If blacks do not play an active role in both parties, he argued, they will eventually be ignored by the Republicans and taken for granted by the Democrats. Such a combination, he emphasized, would leave blacks both powerless and vulnerable. His reasoning would be severely tested in 1964.

Still licking their wounds from a devastating loss in 1960, the Republicans' reaction was consistent with that of a party out of power and uncertain of its mission. It nominated an extremist. In August of 1964 at the Cow Palace in San Francisco, Barry Goldwater accepted his party's nomination and promptly delivered his famous "extremism in pursuit of liberty is no vice" speech. Robinson, who worked the convention floor in support of Rockefeller's nomination, and who was shocked when the delegates booed his candidate loudly in front of a national television audience, responded both quickly and harshly. He referred to Goldwater as "anti–Negro, anti–Jewish, and anti–Catholic" and predicted that he would be defeated soundly in November. His greatest fear, that the Republican party would become a party for "whites only," was becoming a reality.

In 1966 Rockefeller appointed Robinson to be a special assistant for community relations. Two years later, he resigned, just a few days after his party nominated Richard Nixon for president. Distraught over a report that the South "had a veto" over the party's nomination for vice-president, he announced that he was leaving Rockefeller's staff and that he would be campaigning for Democrat Hubert Humphrey. In a front page article in the *New York Times*, he expressed his feelings in baseball terms: "I don't know of anything that hurt me more than the nomination of Richard Nixon and the rejection of Governor Rockefeller," he said. "It made me feel like I felt when Bobby Thomson hit a home run that beat us out of the pennant in 1951."[20]

By 1971 Jackie's disillusionment with white politics had even penetrated his relationship with Nelson Rockefeller. He became dismayed over the Governor's cuts in education and welfare and his implementation of a one-year residency requirement to qualify for welfare. "He seems to have made a sharp right turn away from the stand of the man who once fought the Old Guard Establishment so courageously," he wrote of his former boss and mentor in 1972.[21]

So after years of fighting for civil rights and campaigning for presidential candidates, the Black Knight from Brooklyn with the pigeon-toed gait and the graying hair found himself stranded on second — "far out at the edges of the ordered world at rocky second — the farthest point from home. Whoever remains out there is said to 'die' on base," writes Bart Giamatti. "Home is finally beyond reach in a hostile world full of quirks and tricks and hostile folk. There are no dragons in baseball, only shortstops, but they can emerge from nowhere to cut one down."[22] For Robinson, the shortstops came in the form of John Kennedy, Barry Goldwater and Richard Nixon.

In the numerous books and articles written about Robinson over the years, one may conclude that he learned three important lessons that can be passed on to succeeding generations. First, he learned and believed that people could change for the better. A Jim Crow army was integrated, reluctant Dodgers accepted him, and Malcolm X overcame a life of crime and drugs. Second, he learned the importance of mentors and role models in shaping one's life. The three most important teachers in his life, other than his wife Rachel, were Branch Rickey, William Black, and Nelson Rockefeller. And third, he learned that one should never be satisfied with the status quo. Most important he learned the power of questions. "Why can't I sit in the front of the bus?" he asked in 1949. "Why don't the Yankees have more black ballplayers ?" he asked in 1953. "Why doesn't John Kennedy know more about the plight of black people?" he asked in 1960. "And how can the Republicans ever hope to recruit blacks after rejecting Rockefeller?" he asked in 1968.

When Robinson appeared at Riverfront Stadium on October 15, 1972, it was, for him, the bottom of the ninth. Prior to the start of the second game of the World Series, Robinson was presented a special award by Commissioner Bowie Kuhn commemorating the 25th anniversary of the breaking of baseball's color barrier. But in accepting the honor he used the opportunity to make his position clear one last time. A polite and gracious "thank you" was not good enough. "I'd like to see a black manager," he said while millions watched on national television. "I'd like to live to see the day when there's a black man coaching third base."[23]

It was to be the last major public appearance of his life. Nine days later he succumbed to a heart attack at his home in Stamford, Connecticut. Reverend Jesse Jackson delivered the eulogy at his funeral. "He was the Black Knight in a chess game," shouted Reverend Jackson from the pulpit as he delivered the eulogy. "He was checking the king's bigotry and the queen's indifference. He turned a stumbling block into a stepping stone ... and his body, his mind, his mission cannot be held down by a grave."[24]

Notes

1. Bart Giamatti, *Take Time for Paradise: Americans and Their Games* (New York: Harcourt, Brace, and Jovanovich, 1989), p. 64.

2. Peter Golenbock, *Bums* (New York: Pocket Books), p. 280.

3. *Ibid.*, p. 178.

4. Michael Delnagro, "It's 40th Anniversary of Robinson's Historic Debut," *The Sunday Observer-Dispatch*, April 5, 1987, p. 4b.

5. Edwin Hoyt, *Paul Robeson: The American Othello* (New York: The World Publishing Company, 1967), p. 176.

6. *Ibid.*, p. 161. Two additional sources on the Paul Robeson affair are Duberman's *Paul Robeson*, published by Knopf in 1988, and O'Reilly's *Racial Matters: The FBI's Secret File on Black America*, published by the Free Press in 1973.

7. Ronald Smith, "The Paul Robeson-Jackie Robinson Saga and a Political Collision," *The Journal of Sports History*, 1979, pp. 5–27.

8. *Pittsburgh Courier*, July 16, 1949, p. 2.

9. Bill Roeder, *Jackie Robinson* (New York: A.S. Barnes and Company, 1950), p. 154.

10. Carl Rowan, *Wait Till Next Year* (New York: Random House, 1960).

11. Jackie Robinson, *I Never Had it Made* (New York: G.P. Putnam and Sons, 1972), p. 98.

12. Ronald Smith, op. cit., 1979. Another source for the actions of the House Un-American Activities Committee is Eric Bentley's *Thirty Years of Treason: Excerpts from Hearings before the House Committee on Un-American Activities*, 1938–1968, published by Viking Press in 1971.

13. Robinson appeared on *Meet the Press* on April 14, 1957. A transcript of his appearance is available from NBC News, 4001 Nebraska Avenue, N.W., Washington, DC 20016.

14. *The New York Post*, May 8, 1959, p. 92. Robinson wrote a regular column (three times a week) for the *New York Post* for about a year, between 1959 and 1960.

15. *New York Post*, May 27, 1957, p. 96.

16. Jackie Robinson, op. cit., 1972, p. 224.

17. *Ibid.*, p. 148.

18. *Ibid.*, p. 148.

19. *Ibid.*, p. 149.

20. *New York Times*, August 12, 1968, p. 1.

21. Jackie Robinson, op. cit., 1972, p. 220.

22. Bart Giamatti, op. cit., 1989. p. 93.

23. Jackie Robinson, October 15, 1972. This appearance and statement prior to the start of the second game of the World Series at Riverfront Stadium in Cincinnati, was Robinson's last public appearance of his life.

24. Eulogy delivered by Reverend Jesse Jackson at Robinson's funeral in October 1972.

Jackie Robinson as Media's Mythological Black Hero

Doug Battema

In Ken Burns' *Baseball*, scholar Gerald Early noted that "1997 will mark the fiftieth anniversary of Jackie Robinson breaking the color barrier in baseball. I believe in that year at some point every single American should get down on his or her knees for five minutes and thank God that Jackie Robinson was here because he made this country a better place."[1] These two sentences suggest an interconnection among America, baseball, Christianity, democracy, multiracialism — and the position of Jackie Robinson at the critical point where those concepts intersect. Remembering Robinson, Early suggested, ensures a continuous access to those concepts; by embracing Robinson and such ideals, the institutions affording us with both a communal and an individual identity will continue.

Left unspoken in Early's words are the consequences of not remembering Robinson and the institutions associated with him without this sort of hagiographic glow. Worse, we may become unwilling or unable to remember Robinson. If Robinson is the repository of our communal faith in America, baseball, Christianity, and democracy, then forgetting him will mean the loss of that faith, and the loss of ourselves. Therefore, Robinson is at the center of who we are today, or at least who we wish to become. Robinson thus may be understood as the central focus of a myth we circulate among ourselves — myths implying not false stories or untrue statements, but myths in the sense that anthropologists and folklorists traditionally define them. Alan Dundes described a myth as "a sacred narrative explaining how the world and man came to be in their present form

[sic]."[2] Joseph Fontenrose expanded on that definition by noting that, "whatever the origin of myth-telling, whatever its purpose, myths acquire an ideological character: they often provide a rationale for institutions and customs.... When institutions change, myths and beliefs change; new justifications are needed, and rival parties and factions produce conflicting myths and beliefs."[3]

Several scholars — most notably Bruce Lincoln,[4] Theodore van Baaren,[5] and Raymond Firth[6] — demonstrated how these myths and justifications operate in other societies and at other points in history. Others, such as Roland Barthes, Gregor Goethals and James Carey, have referred to the various mass media and other cultural artifacts as vehicles of mythic narratives.[7] I submit that we can look at media representations of Jackie Robinson as myths, as ideologically charged narratives particular to 20th century America.

Yet the America most of these narratives about Robinson encourage us to enter is a particularly white America. It is an America wherein whiteness is invisible and unequal power relations are construed as acting fairly and often naturally. If Robinson is at the center of who we are or wish to become, how are we encouraged to see ourselves through him? How are we to consider our relationship with others and with our America? What are the terms on which Robinson appears, and how do those terms shift and remain stable over time?

In my Master's thesis,[8] I examined portrayals of Jackie Robinson across a range of media during the last 50 years. This paper asserts that Robinson has been most prominent in mass media texts, the site of our collective imagination, in American societies dominated by a conservative consensus that strives to efface systematic and systemic racism by recalling America's putative ability to transcend this racism and include African-Americans on an equal basis.

This conservative nostalgia for a golden age that never was prides itself on including Robinson then while ignoring problems now. Robinson appears less frequently and less prominently when this conservative consensus is explicitly challenged, as when other figures and ideologies were given center stage during the struggle for civil rights in the late 1950s and early 1960s.

America holds up Robinson as its hero to justify its claims that this nation is no longer racist and that whatever racism used to exist was a vestige of slavery peculiar to the South, not a prejudice common to all white Americans. The rhetorical connections between Robinson and America tend to contain and constrain racial division and to imply that even if America is and has always been dysfunctional because of its systematic and systemic racism, we have no legitimate means of correcting this problem. No means, that is, except by expressing a renewed faith in the same institutions — baseball, democracy and — that have produced this dysfunctional America, the same institutions that manifest themselves in our narratives about Robinson.

Robinson in the 1940s and 1950s

Robinson's entry into the segregated major leagues in the wake of World War Two was hailed, particularly by the black press, as a moment of fundamental change. The war against European racism had been fought and won, and the *Pittsburgh Courier*'s "Double-V for Victory" campaign had only one front remaining: the domestic front. Journalists cited Robinson's incorporation into the white major leagues as a key moment in the assault on that domestic front, casting his signing by Branch Rickey and the Brooklyn Dodgers as a great victory for blacks and for democracy, largely because of the affiliation between America and baseball. The *New York Times* heralded Robinson's signing in October 1945 by noting, "For the first time in the long history of organized baseball a Negro player officially has been taken into its ranks."[9] The black teams with which Robinson played were apparently not an acceptably "organized" social group to white America, whereas white teams signified official order and "major-league" quality — the pinnacle of white American civilization. Mentioning Robinson's college credentials and military service clinched his worthiness, marking him as little different from — if not superior to — many white Americans and major-league players. The possible objections from "some sections of the United States where race prejudice is rampant" and, specifically, players "from certain sections of the South," would be ignored — implying that race prejudice did not appear in the North or other regions of America.

In the black press, too, Robinson's signing suggested that "[d]emocracy has finally invaded baseball, our great national pastime" and was "a step toward a broader spirit of democracy in baseball and will do much to promote a friendlier feeling between the races."[10] W. Rollo Wilson of the *Philadelphia Tribune* called Robinson "the right type to be sent up to Organized Baseball" from the ostensibly inferior Negro Leagues,[11] emerging from the apparent chaos of black baseball to a white America that would achieve its democratic ideal by becoming racially diverse.

The media frequently attributed Robinson's success to his quintessential Americanness, to the characteristics that made him "the right type."

To readers of both the *New York Times* and *The Baltimore Afro-American*, both *Time* and *Ebony*, Robinson was a family man, an "[e]x-Sunday School teacher,"[12] a respected veteran, a baseball player, a normal middle-class American willing to suffer in noble silence for his cause and his country — to demand nothing more than an equal chance that was not yet guaranteed. Any hint of radical politics or belligerence was suppressed in the early years of his career: no publication mentioned his court-martial, Robinson refused to respond to racial taunts, and Robinson evidently respected American law — even, for a time, the Jim Crow laws he so hated — so as to disrupt racism in an acceptable manner. In 1948, Robinson defended the largely-segregated white major leagues against the Negro Leagues, charging in *Ebony* that Negro League problems ranged from "the low salaries paid players and sloppy umpiring to the questionable business practices of many of the team owners."[13]

Before HUAC in 1949, Robinson professed his love for America despite its racism, demonstrating a Christian forgiveness that he, self-defined as a "religious man," could express in America — "a privilege ... some countries do not give."[14] Just as the Dodgers implied that race prejudice existed only within "certain sections of the South," Robinson implied that possibility for racial progress existed only within an ostensibly free, capitalist, Christian America. For the moment, Robinson secured his own citizenship rights in America because of his involvement in white baseball. Though white Americans denied other blacks the same rights, *de facto* if not *de jure*, Robinson claimed that this problem would be "licked" in time if the country maintained its present course. Robinson demonstrated his faith in capitalism, citing a pay raise he intended to request; his stated commitment to military service demonstrated his willingness to risk his life for the American democracy that professed but did not practice equality regardless of race. He set aside his stated displeasure about speaking in order to do his duty, to serve the country as best he could by providing a strong voice in support of America and democracy despite its current and correctable flaws. He became clearly and consistently identified with a collection of values and qualities that promised a transcendence of current problems.

Mass media outlets essentially cast Robinson in a role as the ideal, the mythic archetype, for both white and black Americans — a role that Robinson effectively sanctioned. By embracing him as a black baseball player, America could envision itself as moving toward a racially inclusive democracy — a black *and* white America — even if the rest of baseball and most other institutions remained segregated — a black *or* white America. Placing him in the ideological center enabled the white media to decry the death threats Robinson received in Cincinnati during 1947 as coming from "insane" and "ugly" extremists.[15] These apparently un–American agitators focused solely on his non-whiteness rather than on his other mediated qualities — each quality overdetermined and emphasized to demonstrate how well he fit in with that era's image of the ideal American.

The terms of Robinson's inclusion may be best illustrated in two moments from *The Jackie Robinson Story* (1950). The first showed the overt connection between Robinson and the United States, overlaying the American flag on Robinson as he stands in his living room, wearing his U.S. Army uniform, talking with his mother, and taking his baseball glove from his duffel bag. In just a few seconds, Robinson was visually linked with America's greatest institutions: baseball, the family, the home, the military, the country itself. Rejecting Robinson meant, implicitly, rejecting these institutions. The second moment, appearing at the end of the film, depicted Robinson delivering his anti–Communist speech before HUAC in 1949. Robinson declared that "democracy works for those who are willing to fight for it," a notion underscored by the constant presence of the Statue of Liberty, the symbol of America's willingness to absorb the tired, hungry, poor and oppressed, the symbol of American possibility, which was superimposed on the image of Robinson. "America the Beautiful" played while Robinson demonstrated his fitness as a citizen in a closing montage that traced his development from a young black boy walking down a dirt road to a bona fide American hero. Robinson, a narrator explained, lived in a nation that gave "every child has the opportunity to become president ... or play baseball for the Brooklyn Dodgers." That these are not equally influential positions, or that such access may not be open to "every child" then (or now), did not matter: Robinson's actions fulfilled the latent promise of an idealized, mythical America.

Advertisements for the film reinforced the underlying Americanist ideology: "If you are a lover of fair play and clean sportsmanship — if you believe in the right of a guy to win on merit alone — which is the American way of doing it — then you will thrill to 'THE JACKIE ROBINSON STORY,'"[16] blared one *New York Times* ad. The *Times* film review noted that "Mr. Robinson's trail-blazing career is reenacted with manifest fidelity and conspicuous dramatic restraint ... a story of which all Americans with respect and gratitude, may be proud, too."[17] *The Baltimore Afro-American* not only proclaimed the film "one of the greatest documentary motion pictures ever produced"[18] but also identified it as "the American story — American in the sense that it shows what is possible without 'pull,' without having been born with a 'silver spoon in one's mouth.'"[19] Robinson's story contained what Bruce Lincoln referred to as authoritative or paradigmatic truth: a truth that was taken as self-evident and verifiable by everyone in society.[20] Robinson proved that the American dream had no color barrier.

Robinson became more controversial, and less popular among some sportswriters and some fans, during the 1950s as he spoke out more frequently and stridently on racial inequality. Nonetheless, *Ebony* nominated the decade as "the Jackie Robinson era," a time when "the climate in human relations in America is much more pleasant ... than it was a decade ago."[21] Despite his occasionally fiery and outspoken nature, by the time of his retirement both the black and white presses continued to portray him as the symbol of a peacefully integrated America, a story of success, a "national symbol" held up as the model American who had earned a deserved "acceptance and respect."[22]

Robinson in the 1960s and 1970s

Despite these intrinsic linkages with America and democracy, however, Robinson faded from the public view from the late 1950s through the late 1970s. While not absolutely silenced — he remained active in the NAACP, in business, and in politics — Robinson's actions gained less attention from the media, especially beyond the New York area. With other, more dramatic events occurring in the civil rights movement and in the field of race relations, with the spotlight on other black baseball stars, and with the questioning of American democracy and liberalism from both the political right and left, the same associations between America and Jackie Robinson that had made him such a popular figure in the 1940s and 1950s rendered him a much less effective symbol for the 1960s and 1970s.

The shift seems to have taken a decisive turn around 1963, with the events in Birmingham, Alabama, and the assassination of John F. Kennedy. Prior to this year, Robinson had received intermittent but substantial attention for his civil-rights work, his first autobiography, and his Hall of Fame induction. Robinson reacted to the brutality in Birmingham by forming a fund-raising group in New York, sending telegrams to President Kennedy and, a few days later, visiting Birmingham with boxer Floyd Patterson. While possibly effective, these actions were less media-friendly than the events in Birmingham themselves; the civil rights movement and the white backlash, rather than the person of Robinson, was the front-page story. His symbolic presence appeared to carry significantly less weight than in the decade before. The death of Kennedy a few months later signaled the end of Camelot, the beginning of an era in which the optimistic faith in American possibility and progress was questioned. If America itself was not slain with this act, its reputed innocence began to unravel. Both Robinson and America had changed from what they had seemed to be in the 1950s, and the gap between their ideal forms spread rapidly.

By 1969, when Robinson informed a *Times* reporter that "I wouldn't fly the [American] flag on the Fourth of July or any other day.... When I see a car with a flag pasted on it I figure the guy behind it isn't my friend,"[23] his statement generated barely a ripple of media attention. The nation's self-image had already been tarnished, and Robinson was no longer the nationally significant symbol he once had been. The extent to which media outlets overlooked Robinson was also manifest in the media's and major-league baseball's failure to commemorate the 25th anniversary of his breaking the color barrier in 1972. Even participating in the first-ball ceremonies in that year's World Series gained little attention in print or on television, despite several pointed remarks Robinson made about the dearth of black managers and executives.

Robinson's death a few weeks later brought him back into the headlines as the "pioneer" who "made history in 1947" and "opened the door of baseball to all men" while keeping "baseball in perspective" as a mere metaphor for life.[24] *The Times* claimed that Robinson had taken on "the historical task of sweeping a host of mental cobwebs from the minds of millions of white Americans, many of whom were probably unaware of their own bigotry and racism," while proving himself "an authentic all-American who made a memorable impact for good on his country and his time."[25] The *Philadelphia Tribune* noted that Robinson was "a maker of history, not merely a man who was part of history," who encouraged economic unity as the way to integrate blacks "in the mainstream of the American economy."[26] Robinson had apparently succeeded in excising racism from millions of white American minds to the point where this seemed to be an archaic problem rather than a modern one, even if his strategy of integration had not yet brought blacks into an equal economic or social position.

Yet Heywood Hale Broun articulated what appeared to be the conventional wisdom of the time, given the relative silence that surrounded Robinson for most of two decades. A week after Robinson's death, Broun noted that "[t]ragically, [Robinson] believed in the basic validity of the [Horatio] Alger fantasy, and ... fought towards its triumphant last chapter, trying to drag a whole race behind him. Toward the end of his life some members of his race differed sharply with Jack's essentially integrationist philosophy. He was called an Uncle Tom."[27] Though Broun believed that Robinson was "gallant," he also appears as a romantic, if not quixotic, figure; the integrated America he longed to create was as unrealistic and impractical as the "Alger fantasy." The media silence surrounding Robinson returned within a week of his death.

Robinson in the 1980s and 1990s

During the 1980s and 1990s, however, we have seen a public rehabilitation of faith in American democracy, a desire to return to 1950s-style "normalcy" and the traditional "family values" popularized by politicians. Dave Anderson, in 1987, noted a similar trend with respect to Robinson, declaring that "[t]he reincarnation of Jackie Robinson resumes."[28] This "reincarnation," effected mostly in white-oriented media, also rearticulated Robinson's public image to appeal to contemporary sensibilities and to assert that real progress had been made and will continue to be made on this same trajectory.

Part of this reincarnation involved moving the moment of fundamental change in America prior to the civil rights movement of the 1960s, bypassing some of the questions asked and advances made during that era. The reincarnation began in part with the 1981 Broadway play "The First"— at the time the most expensive musical ever produced — which, according to the play's producer, tried to highlight Robinson's "'self, a sense of dignity, a sense of his pride, his ability to practice non-violent retaliation'" and thereby create a "national moment."[29] Celebrating the peaceful and nonviolent nature of Robinson's entry into white society and America's transformation into an apparently equal, biracial nation downplayed the antagonism that characterized race relations, both in the 1940s and in the 1980s. The play was an abject failure, but the subject matter was not: a *Times* reviewer noted that the story "obviously has some good things going for it. We bring into the theater with us emotions ready and waiting to be tapped all over again."[30] These emotions were not named, but they may apply equally to the emotions about a rhetorical Reaganesque America or about Robinson's actual accomplishments — the differences *appear* difficult to distinguish.

Robinson's accomplishments, noted the *Times* in 1987, predated and presaged the civil rights movement: "seven years before the Supreme Court ordered the schools integrated, years before black people could share restaurants, buses and depots with whites, years before Martin Luther King Jr. marched and dreamed.... Jack Roosevelt Robinson marched alone."[31] Robinson fought the seminal battle to overcome racial tension, providing a nonviolent precursor to the events of the 1950s and 1960s which implicitly served as a model for King — a heroic individual effort without institutional support that can and should be emulated today. William Safire elaborated on Robinson's significance, indicating that the ballplayer taught politicians a powerful lesson: "failure to show concern for minority feelings is now seen as a sign of political ineptitude." Because Richard Nixon rejected Robinson's advice during the 1960 presidential campaign and failed to provide "a gesture of respect" to Martin Luther King, Jr., Safire claimed, the 1960s were marked by "eight wilderness years" of Democratic rule, racial tension and sociopolitical chaos, chaos that apparently ended when Nixon gained the White House.[32] Robinson became the primary figure around which a civilized, orderly nonracist America could be constructed in the 1980s: one must provide a public gesture to mollify "minority feelings," though that gesture may mask true feelings or sentiments and may have no substantive content.

The 1990 made-for-cable-TV movie *The Court-Martial of Jackie Robinson* also reconstructed Robinson as a seminal American figure, affecting American social practices even before reaching the Dodgers' attention. The film depicted Robinson as very assertive, skeptical, and independent, avoiding the charges of "Uncle Tom-ism" that had occasionally been leveled at him during the 1960s, putting another spin on the Robinson myth appropriate to the 1990s. The narrative addressed contemporary concerns over the role of the military and college in American life, particularly African-American life, by insinuating that they will allow rather than hinder Robinson's ability to succeed if he trusts in their authority. In the opening moments of the film, Robinson debated whether or not to remain in college; he intended to drop out in order to "give something back" to his mother by finding a job despite her vociferous objections. He changed his mind right after Pearl Harbor and decided to remain in college — but has his decision nullified upon receiving a draft letter. The filmmakers rearranged historical events, rewriting an American history, in order to give them more dramatic significance for contemporary viewers. Presumably, Robinson would be able to continue his college career and wind up in a better social position than his brother Mack — even though Mack has been identified already as "an Olympic winner, a college graduate," who nonetheless can only find a job sweeping streets.

Robinson's mistrust in the segregated Army, as well, appears ultimately misplaced. Robinson's refusal to move to the back of a bus, which Army policy had officially desegregated, leads to juridical problems and ultimately a court-martial. Viewers cannot miss the injustice of Robinson's arrest; the military police who accosted Robinson called him "sunshine," "boy," and other racist epithets. Yet even a white officer sympathetic to Robinson referred to the MPs as "a couple of bad apples," implying that they — rather than systemic segregation — created the problem. Robinson rejected the advice of his fellow black officers who advised him not to fight to his court-martial, telling them that he must "stand up for my rights as an officer and a man" and that if he does not he will have "no rights at all.... I gotta fight for this ... this [indicating his lieutenant's bars] is all I got." Robinson could not become an ideal American and gain his human rights unless he fought his court-martial on the terms laid down for him by the white Army of a white America. That system, and not Robinson, defined the desirable terms of identity, and he agreed to fight for those as his terms of inclusion; other definitions of "rights" (and who may obtain them) were incomprehensible, other terms impossible to understand. Robinson eventually won his court-martial, thanks to the assistance of a white lawyer who proved that the MPs have been lying. The white lawyer's success in acquitting Robinson implicitly demonstrated that Robinson's fellow black officers were incorrect in telling him that he could never achieve justice in a white system or by trusting a white lawyer; if Robinson's case could be pressed and won, so can all others. The system, according to the film, was not rigged and in fact lived up to its principles.

The closing moments of the film suggested that the institutionalized racism Robinson faced has been overcome. Robinson, having just accepted an offer to play for the Dodgers, emerges from the dark into the daylight and spreads his arms wide. The accompanying text[33] suggested that Robinson's efforts allowed the integration of not one but two intrinsically American institutions: major league baseball and the military. Both were portrayed as "integrated organizations" as a result, with their pervasive racism a thing of the past. Emulating Robinson by following the rules established by society would produce this desired integration; attempting to work outside their confines would not. The rehabilitation of Robinson also rehabilitated the military; while the latter was not necessarily romanticized, the events depicted in the film assuaged fears that racism might continue to exist in the 1990s Army.

Even when Robinson's story was used to discuss the failures of white baseball, the solution was to trust established institutional structures to effect legitimate change. In Ken Burns' *Baseball*, Robinson was concretely linked to America, held up as the mythic archetype who unified the country in theory and in at least one practice as well. Burns claimed that his film was "the story of race," though "Jackie Robinson's epic story is not the whole of it" and "the struggle did not stop, as it hasn't in the country at large"[34] — but the progress narrative underlying Burns' story suggests that success can only be achieved through a constrained, contained struggle that plays by the logic of paternalistic capitalism, rather than rejecting this logic itself as illegitimate. Defining the means of resistance in this manner precluded recourse to violent insurrection or uncontrollable, uncontainable actions: the violent rhetoric and struggles of the 1960s must be rejected as regressive, the nonviolent rhetoric and struggles of the 1950s and 1990s must have their progressive moments bridged by a figure such as Robinson. Robinson created a new time, claimed Gerald Early: "You can almost divide American history in the twentieth century, before Robinson and after Robinson ... Robinson coming in was enormous, because of the game being tied to the national character, in some sense to America's sense of mission and its destiny." That the inclusion of nonwhites in America's manifest destiny did not necessarily validate the mission itself was not considered; what mattered was that the post-Robinson era somehow contributed to American progress, irrespective of race.

Yet rather than focusing on Robinson's ultimate disillusionment with "the lack of progress in race relations," the need for the narrative in the present to provide a unifying sense of progress ultimately shaped Burns' interpretation of the past and Robinson's part in it. The documentary juxtaposed a passage from Robinson's posthumously published autobiography with scenes from his funeral: "'I cannot salute the flag. I know that I am a black man in a white world. In 1972, in 1947, at my birth in 1919, I know that I never had it made.'" Burns, however, chose to play "America the Beautiful" in the background of this scene, undercutting (if not repudiating) Robinson's statement about his ties with the American flag and the white world. His actions spoke louder than his words, with the resurrected Robinson portrayed as having symbolically achieved the American dream by working to be included and to change the system from within rather than attributing its problems to structural flaws or systemic racism. That "America the Beautiful" was also the closing tune of *The Jackie Robinson Story* provides an unconscious yet significant connection between the political exigencies and sensibilities of the 1950s and of the 1990s.

One other significant pattern could be seen in narratives about Robinson in the 1980s and 1990s. When the media addressed a white or mixed audience, they often implied that blacks alone faced difficulty assimilating into America. If Robinson "was [not] only a hero for blacks. He was a hero for mankind,"[35] the black population generally and black ballplayers in particular apparently forgot his heroic sacrifices. In 1985, a *Times* article about the World Series contrasted blacks like Kansas City's Frank White, who described Robinson as "my role model," with the likes of St. Louis' Vince Coleman, who reportedly "snapped" and "glared when asked about Jackie Robinson."[36] In 1987, the fortieth anniversary of Robinson's first appearance in the majors, *Sport* magazine conducted a poll of black athletes, many of whom expressed no knowledge of who Robinson was. Whites did not have to prove that they belonged in the major leagues by expressing respect for Robinson — blacks alone had that responsibility, and needed to prove that they could be "civilized" by accepting Robinson and what he stood for. In 1992, *Ebony* acknowledged the double standard of the 1940s, claiming that Robinson had to be "a better man ... as honest as Jesus, as clean as laundered white-on-white, as pure as Ivory ... merely to get a chance to play a mere sport which had, before him, boasted of all sorts of people of foreign extraction, rowdies, drunkards ... and called them heroes."[37] Yet *Ebony* also suggested that Robinson's quest had succeeded: that by changing the minds of millions of white Americans, he necessarily changed the system that created this racism in the first place. The double standard implicit in the *Sport* survey remained unexplored.

More recently, a *Philadelphia Inquirer* writer likened the ungrateful, un-American stance of racist ballplayers who threatened to strike in 1947 because of Robinson's presence to the ungrateful, un–American stance of modern ballplayers who struck in 1994 and 1995 for money. Titled "First Among Equals," the piece noted that Robinson was paid just $5000 for his nation-building sacrifices. The writer interspersed quotations from modern players — each identified as an "African-American ballplayer" whose salary ranged from $350,000 to $7,000,000 — throughout the text. These quotations indicated ignorance of Robinson's struggle or the significance attached to him by the primarily white media. The paucity of knowledge about Robinson thus appeared to be a deficiency of individual black players. In the writer's words, Robinson forced "open the minds of millions of white Americans" and inspired Lou Brock's "dream of playing that great American pastime in stadiums before big crowds" rather than being "just a dirt farmer" while the contemporary black players cited were implicitly closed-minded with petty, selfish dreams.[38] The role of white players in the strike was ignored; all the selfish players cited in the article were black, suggesting that race was somehow a primary catalyst behind the 1994-1995 strike. The system, it appeared, succeeded *in spite* of being integrated — not because of it.

This perspective is not monolithic, of course; at least one paper, the *Philadelphia Tribune*, rebuked baseball for maintaining "the system of exclusion that [Al Campanis] represents" rather than vent its anger solely on Campanis. A writer for that paper three years later compared Robinson's integration to "the settling of America where whites, for the most part, came to America and took the land under the guise of civilizing the natives" — obliterating or co-opting rival nonwhite institutions.[39] Yet these messages are overwhelmed by the more positive mythicization of Robinson that has been used more often to coopt and constrain social pressures that strive to change racial progress.

Conclusion

In conclusion, much as we might like to think of him otherwise, Robinson's image has always been politically contested terrain. We need to remember to celebrate the man for his character and his strength, yet also remain aware of who and what we support when commemorating him. Bruce Lincoln wrote that words, images and myths "may be strategically employed to mystify the inevitable inequities of any social order and to win the consent of those over whom power is exercised."[40] The stability in media images of Robinson across the decades, and the waxing and waning of his presence in the media, suggest that he, like every myth, is strategically employed to maintain social order and cohesion across racial lines, to disseminate an ideology that naturalizes human inequality while professing human equality.

As we remember Robinson, we should recall his pride and his strength, his accomplishments and his dedication. But we cannot let our memories of Robinson, brilliant as they may be, blind us to the inequities of the present — particularly when these memories are so malleable and can be rewritten, when this history of the past becomes indistinguishable from the politics of the present. The story of Robinson's inclusion should not be taken as the beginning or the end of our self-definition, but as one significant moment in a necessarily continuous process. We can view Robinson as an agent for positive change in the present, or as a symbol of a status quo with which we can be content. I believe Robinson would have preferred the former.

Notes

1. Burns, Ken. *Baseball*. Copyright 1994, The Corporation for Public Broadcasting.

2. Dundes, Alan. "Introduction" in *Sacred Narrative: Readings in the Theory of Myth*, edited by Alan Dundes. Berkeley: University of California Press, 1984. p. 1.

3. Fontenrose, Joseph. *The Ritual Theory of Myth*. Berkeley: University of California Press, 1971. pp. 57–58.

4. Lincoln, Bruce. *Discourse and the Construction of Society: Comparative Studies of Myth, Ritual, and Classification*. New York: Oxford University Press, 1989.

5. van Baaren, Theodore. "The Flexibility of Myth," pp. 217–224 in *Sacred Narrative: Readings in the Theory of Myth*, edited by Alan Dundes. Berkeley: University of California Press, 1984.

6. Firth, Raymond. "The Plasticity of Myth: Cases from Tikopia," pp. 207–216 in *Sacred Narrative: Readings in the Theory of Myth*, edited by Alan Dundes. Berkeley: University of California Press, 1984.

7. These sources have been chosen, in part, because they arrive at their conclusions from relatively different perspectives and fields: Barthes from semiotics, Goethals from art and religion, Carey from functionalist media studies. See Barthes, Roland. *Mythologies*. Translated by Annette Lavers. New York: The Noonday Press, 1990; Goethals, Gregor T. *The TV Ritual: Worship at the Video Altar*. Boston: Beacon Press, 1981; and Carey, James. *Communication As Culture*. New York: Routledge, 1992.

8. Battema, Doug. "Playing Inside the Lines: The Jackie Robinson Mythology as a Discourse of Cultural Power." Unpublished M.A. thesis, The Annenberg School for Communications, University of Pennsylvania, 1995.

9. "Montreal Signs Negro Shortstop." The *New York Times*, 23 October 1945, p. 17.

10. Young, Frank A. "JIM CROW LINE DENTED: Major League Points Way to Democracy." *The Chicago Defender*, 27 October 1945, p. 1.

11. Wilson, W. Rollo. "Through the Eyes of W. Rollo Wilson." The *Philadelphia Tribune*, 3 November 1945, p. 14.

12. "Family Man Jackie Robinson." *Ebony* vol. 2 no. 11 (September 1947), pp. 15–16.

13. Robinson, Jackie. "What's Wrong with Negro Baseball." *Ebony* vol. 3 no. 8 (June 1948), p. 16.

14. "Text of Jackie Robinson's Statement to House Unit." The *New York Times*, 19 July 1949, p. 14.

15. Daley, Arthur. "Sports of the *Times*: The Passing Baseball Scene." The *New York Times*, 13 May 1947, p. 32.

16. "This Picture." The *New York Times*, 14 May 1950, section 2, p. 3.

17. Crowther, Bosley. "The Screen in Review." The *New York Times*, 14 May 1950, p. 36.

18. "Robinson Story on Earle Screen." The *Philadelphia Tribune*, 27 May 1950, p. 11.

19. Gay, Eustace. "Facts and Fancies: The Jackie Robinson Story." The *Philadelphia Tribune*, 23 May 1950, p. 4.

20. Lincoln, *op. cit.*, pp. 24–5.

21. Young, A.S. "Doc." "The Jackie Robinson Era." *Ebony*, vol. 11 no. 1 (November 1955), p. 152.

22. "A Pioneering Athlete: Jack Roosevelt Robinson." The *New York Times*, 14 December 1956, p. 38.

23. Nordheimer, Jon. "Flag on July 4: Thrill to Some, Threat to Others." The *New York Times*, 4 July 1969, p. 23.

24. Anderson, Dave. "Jackie Robinson, First Black in Major Leagues, Dies." The *New York Times*, 25 October 1972, p. 1.

25. "All-American." The *New York Times*, 25 October 1972, p. 46.

26. Harrison, Claude, Jr. "Jackie Robinson Paved the Way for Black Professional Athletes." The *New York Times*, 28 October 1972, p. 21.

27. Broun, Heywood Hale. "Gallant Was the Word for Him." The *New York Times*, 29 October 1972, sec. 4, p. 3.

28. Anderson, Dave. "Sports of the *Times*: When the Dodgers Ignored Robinson." The *New York Times*, 15 April 1987, p. B9.

29. Ferretti, Fred. "A Musical Celebrates an Athlete." The *New York Times*, 8 October 1981, sec. 2, p. 1. The words are those of the musical's producer, describing

how the show had originally been centered around the personal interaction between Branch Rickey and Jackie Robinson, and specifically why the Dodger executive had tapped Robinson as the first black player. "The First," however, eventually "'became more compressed. What developed was what made Jackie tick.'"

30. Kerr, Walter. "A Libretto Has to Face the Music." The *New York Times*, 13 December 1981, sec. 2, p. 3.

31. Durso, Joseph. "40 Years Ago in Brooklyn, Robinson's Crusade Began." The *New York Times*, 12 April 1987, sec. 5, p. 1.

32. Safire, William. "View from the Grandstand." The *New York Times*, 13 April 1987, sec. 1, p. 19.

33. The text I refer to reads as follows: "In 1947, Jack Roosevelt Robinson became the first black man to play major league baseball, and in 1962 was inducted into the Baseball Hall of Fame. He devoted the rest of his life to the civil rights movement and the equality of all men [sic]. President Harry S. Truman signed an Executive Order on July 26, 1948, prohibiting racial segregation in the Armed Forces. Today, the Army is considered one of the most integrated organizations in the United States."

34. Burns, Ken. "Baseball: A Mirror of the Country." *USA Today*, 13 September 1994, p. 13A.

35. Anderson, Dave. "Sports of the *Times*: 'Jack Loved Playing in St. Louis.'" The *New York Times*, 24 October 1985, p. B17.

36. Anderson, Dave. "Sports of the *Times*: 'Jack Loved Playing in St. Louis.'" The *New York Times*, 24 October 1985, p. B17.

37. Young, A.S. "Doc." "Jackie Robinson Remembered." *Ebony*, vol. 42 no. 10 (August 1992), pp. 36–42.

38. Ecenbarger, William. "First Among Equals." The *Philadelphia Inquirer Magazine*, 29 January 1995, p. 13.

39. Smith, Jim. "The Black and White on Baseball." The *Philadelphia Tribune*, 5 October 1990, p. 3B.

40. Lincoln, Bruce. *Op. cit.*, p. 4.

The Influence of Jackie Robinson on the Serious Baseball Novel

Richard F. Peterson

A few years after Jackie Robinson crossed Organized Baseball's color line, the baseball novel began a dramatic change that opened its pages to racial integration. While Robinson's dramatic appearance and performance on the playing field forced baseball to confront its long standing policy and practice of racial intolerance and exclusion, the baseball novel, by shifting to a more serious and adult perspective, created its own opportunity to dramatize baseball's racial discrimination and its slow movement toward tolerance and integration. Yet, just as Organized Baseball struggled to achieve complete integration on the playing field, and fifty years later, still appears reluctant to grant African-Americans a central role in baseball management, the serious baseball novel has also struggled to make the African-American experiences central to its narrative. Still echoing the moral romances and rags-to-riches stories of dime novels and series books, the adult baseball novel, with a few notable exceptions, has portrayed the African-American ballplayer as relevant, not in himself, but in his ability to provide a moral or historical lesson for the white community or as validation that baseball for all its faults, still embodies the American dream of equal opportunity and fair play.

In the standard view of the history of baseball fiction, the serious or adult baseball novel did not begin its development until the *annus mirabilis* of 1952 with the publication of Bernard Malamud's *The Natural*, followed a year later by Mark Harris' *The Southpaw*. A more revisionist history of baseball fiction would include the efforts, as early as 1948, of Ed Fitzgerald and Frank O'Rourke to write serious baseball novels, the appearance in 1950 of Lucy Kennedy's *The Sunlit Field*, probably the first adult baseball novel written by a woman, and the publication in the 1950s of several important baseball novels besides *The Natural*, *The Southpaw*, and *Bang the Drum Slowly* (1956), including Douglas Wallop's *The Year the Yankees Lost the Pennant* (1954), Eliot Asinof's *Man on Spikes* (1955), and Charles Einstein's *The Only Game in Town* (1955).

For Mark Harris, the appearance of *The Southpaw*, more so than *The Natural*, was the important moment in the literary history of baseball because his book signified the beginning of "the realistic tradition of the baseball novel" (8). *The Natural* had angered Harris because "Malamud just wasn't realistic baseball" (9). Rather than pioneering realism in the baseball novel, *The Natural* encouraged baseball readers to believe that for baseball to be treated seriously as a literary topic it had to be symbolic and mythic. Eventually, Harris, prompted by the publication of Philip Roth's outrageously satirical *The Great American Novel* in 1973, decided that what he and Malamud had done twenty years earlier, despite their radically different approaches, was to liberate novelists to write seriously about baseball. With the Baseball Joe of juvenile fiction banished to biography, the Horatio Alger tradition was now replaced in the serious novel by "fantasy sometimes, realism sometimes, problem solving, ventures into myth, symbolism, baseball futurism, baseball science-fiction, into the very homosexuality for which Horatio Alger was condemned and fired from his ministry only 125 years earlier, drugs and other illegal or shadowy activities which make the alleged thievery of Baseball Joe seem tame indeed" (11).

Though not included in Harris's catalogue of subjects for the serious baseball novel, America's racial intolerance and discrimination also became a topic once baseball fiction began its realistic tradition. Reduced to harsh racial stereotypes and excluded from America's literary playing fields by dime novels and series books, African-Americans finally became integrated within the pages of baseball novels once Jackie Robinson crossed Major League Baseball's color line in 1947 and baseball writers, practically at the same historical moment, brought a more realistic perspective to writing fiction. While still excluded from symbolic and mythic baseball novels like Malamud's *The Natural*, African-American ballplayers finally began to cross the color line in baseball's fictional landscape with the publication of *The Southpaw* and the beginning of what Harris has claimed to be the realistic tradition of the baseball novel.

The influence of Jackie Robinson on the writing of *The Southpaw* becomes evident as soon as Henry Wiggen leaves home and heads south to his first professional training camp. When he arrives late at night and asks the security guard if anyone else is in camp yet, the guard tells him: "No ... There is one n — r. He is in the same barrackses as you" (83). Wiggen's meeting with Perry Simpson, also in his first professional season with the New York Mammoths, sets the stage in *The Southpaw* for Wiggen to learn something about racial discrimination as part of his education into manhood. As Wiggen and Simpson develop a close friendship at training camp, are assigned to the same minor league team, and, the following year, become roommates, at least for a while, in their first big league season, Wiggen as narrator, observes the discrimination directed at Simpson and, on a few occasions, finds that discrimination directly aimed at him.

At training camp, Wiggen notes that once workouts started Simpson "did not go out and eat on account of the regulations," which Wiggen regards as "pretty damn scurvy" (85). When the Mammoths play in Washington, a city Wiggen hates, he loses a roommate because "Perry must go sleep in Howard University" (247). Wiggen also notes that it "would have been the same in St. Louis" (248), if the Mammoth manager had not known the owner of the hotel where the team was staying. While Wiggen is willing to room with the "first colored Mammoth" (199) since 1947 and does not mind posing with his arm around Simpson for a colored photographer from a Harlem newspaper, he runs into some heckling on the field because he "rooms with the n — r" (207). Wiggen, however, who possesses a kind of innate or innocent tolerance, either ignores the taunts or, when they become too vicious, gives the opposing bench "the old sign, a finger up" (222).

As for Perry Simpson, he is clearly modeled after Jackie Robinson, though, unlike Robinson, he becomes a bench player, used mostly as a pinch runner, in his first season with the Mammoths. Like Robinson, Simpson was born in Georgia, but moved to the Far West for a better life. He plays a solid defensive game at second base, but his real strength is the way he rattles the other team's pitcher when he gets on base: "You can't judge Perry by averages. The way you judge him is by the way he gets on base, whether bunting or drawing a walk or beating out a roller that on most fellows would be an out, and you got to judge him by the way he keeps the opposition worried" (172).

As for Simpson's friendship with Henry Wiggen, it is actually modeled more after the literary relationship between the runaway slave Jim and Huck Finn than any real-life relationship. While Simpson experiences some of the same racial hatred and discrimination encountered by Robinson in his first major league season, his primary role in *The Southpaw* is to serve as a sidekick and moral conscience to Wiggen. The incidents of racial bigotry in *The Southpaw* are real enough, but they serve only as part of the moral education of Wiggen who grows into manhood by novel's end. Simpson's role is so secondary and expendable in *The Southpaw* that when the narrative reaches the climactic last month of the pennant race, Mark Harris brings up another African-American from the minors to replace Wiggen as Simpson's roommate: "Perry and Keith went their own way, and off the field I almost never seen them" (295). With Perry Simpson now segregated from the narrative of *The Southpaw*, the last chapters, without the distraction of racial intolerance and injustice, play out the Mammoths' championship season as Wiggen overcomes his moral mistakes and his errors of judgment, learns something about human nature and himself, and wins his manhood as well as Most Valuable Player and Player of the Year honors.

When Mark Harris disposes of Perry Simpson as Henry Wiggen's roommate, the plot contrivance echoes beyond *The Southpaw* because Simpson is replaced by Bruce Pearson, the athlete dying young in Harris' next novel. In *Bang the Drum Slowly*, Wiggen, now more Fitzgerald's Nick Carraway in manly concerns and responsibilities than Twain's Huck Finn, learns from a dying teammate with far less talent and intelligence something about the moral value of team camaraderie and personal loyalty and friendship. *Bang the Drum Slowly*, often praised as Harris' best work and as one of baseball's best novels, continues the moral education of Henry Wiggen but, without the social realism provided by a character like Perry Simpson, the novel, like its predecessor, never really strays far from the genre of the moral romance. Emotionally sentimental and morally instructive, *The Southpaw* fails to sustain and *Bang the Drum Slowly* avoids altogether the social realism that would have made the novels more convincing as fiction. Harris' sequel to *The Southpaw* would have been far different and perhaps far more realistic if it had returned to the relationship between Henry Wiggen and Perry Simpson and focused its theme of personal responsibility and loyalty on race relations in the 1950s within the context of America's National Game.[1]

The problem in *The Southpaw* is that the personal relationship between Henry Wiggen and Perry Simpson and Simpson's presence in the Mammoth clubhouse are never a part of the conflicts or challenges Wiggen faces on his way to manhood. The moral education of Henry Wiggen simply does not include facing his own ignorance of race relations or defending Simpson against the racial bigotry of their teammates. In Eliot Asinof's *Man on Spikes*, however, the issue of race does become a crucial part of a remarkably balanced and intimate study of the various forces at play in the life and career of a professional ballplayer. A much more realistic novel than *The Southpaw*, *Man on Spikes*, instead of moral romance, offers baseball readers a sharply focused, uncompromising view of the short-sightedness and narrow-mindedness, the petty jealousies and arbitrary judgments that are at the heart of professional baseball. Rather than finding innate goodness and hard work rewarded, readers witness the best years of a baseball career lost to military service and the difficulties of regaining a career undermined by the pettiness of the press, the prejudices within the game itself, the cowardice of baseball management, including the commissioner, and the financial and emotional struggle of surviving one more off season and one more poor contract just to keep alive the fading dream of playing baseball one day in a major league uniform.

For Mike Kutner, a short, slight, bespectacled center fielder who is no Roy Hobbs or Henry Wiggen in stature, the racial integration of baseball, and its inherent prejudices and hypocrisy, becomes yet another obstacle in his sixteen-year quest to play in the major leagues. In a chapter titled "The Negro," Kutner is forced to move from center field to left field for his Triple A Minneapolis team because the parent Chicago club wants to advance Ben Franks —"Move the big nigger in there and see what he can do" (155)—and cash in on Brooklyn's success: "Up in Chicago, Jim Mellon had his eyes on Brooklyn, shifting from the gate receipts to Robinson's ability and back to the gate receipts. The black man was being accepted and the ball club was making a fat dollar for its crusade. So Jim Mellon had to get himself a black man" (161).

Asinof's chapter is particularly striking and insightful because its narrative reflects Ben Franks' perspective rather than Mike Kutner's. From Franks' perspective, the reader of *Man on Spikes* encounters far more than Kutner's reaction to Franks' presence on the team. Asinof's narrative records the "hoarse, rasping voice of hate" (156) heard from the stands and the opposing bench and the deeply felt and expressed resentment of Franks' teammates. It also captures Franks' own feelings as he endures viciousness on the field and ostracism in the clubhouse. As Franks tries to cope with the "monster of hate and pressure" (159), he thinks about "Jackie Robinson up there breaking in with Brooklyn" and realizes that a black man "would have to be pretty terrific to stick, not just good enough" (158). He also realizes that his own owner, up in Chicago, believes that "Robinson was the wrong kind of black boy to bring up. Too smart, too aggressive, too tricky. His feet were too small. The public might not like too much of that. But a big, lumbering quiet boy who can blast that long ball. The crowds would really go for that" (161).

Knowing he is hated and exploited, Franks struggles to be good enough on the field and, when given the brief opportunity off the field, is capable of expressing his gratitude for the Negro league players who, while denied the opportunity, prepared the way to the major leagues for others. He remembers Josh Gibson — "ten times the ballplayer Ben was" (165) — and how badly Gibson wanted to play in the majors. He also tells Kutner and one of his teammates about the wonderful skills and accomplishments of Satchel Paige, who "left a trail of goose eggs across a good slice of the country" (166) despite the difficult playing conditions in the Negro leagues and the remarkable talent of some of the players.

What Franks finally realizes, however, is that Kutner and his teammates, rather than hating him because of his race, resent him because they are afraid of the black players "coming up, wondering if there was a mess of them who might beat [them] out" (166). Franks even reaches an understanding and acceptance of sorts with Kutner. When confronted by Franks for showing him up in the outfield, Kutner first tells Franks that he was due to go up to the majors next spring until he was forced to move from center field to left field to make room for Franks. When Franks bitterly complains that he is not being treated fairly as a ballplayer because of the color of his skin, Kutner takes off his glasses and tells Franks: "See these stinking things ... I got troubles of my own" (170).

Franks' understanding that Kutner has struggled throughout his career against another kind of prejudice changes nothing in the rivalry between the two, but when they finally and literally collide in the outfield, Kutner defends Franks by telling their teammates the collision was his fault. This crucial act of responsibility on the field drains the hatred, at least for the moment, from the faces of the other players and draws Franks and Kutner together as they walk off the field. When Franks hands Kutner his bent, but unbroken glasses, the two appear to have reached some level of acceptance by recognizing each other's determination to overcome the prejudices that would deny or exploit their dreams of playing in the major leagues.

While Asinof never wrote a sequel to *Man on Spikes*, he did write a later novel which has an African-American ballplayer as its central character. Unfortunately, *The Bedfellow*, published twelve years after *Man on Spikes*, has little to offer about baseball. When the novel begins, Mike Sorrell has quit the game in his prime rather than accept a trade that would have sent him from New York to Atlanta and undermined his planned interracial marriage. With Sorrell retired, the only opportunities in *The Bedfellow* for insights into the racial tensions in baseball and the status of black ballplayers in the 1960s come about through Sorrell's recollections. At an early point in the novel, for example, Sorrell recalls how African-Americans "were an integral part of every club, traveled together, dressed in the same locker room, played together, showered together. But off the field, we remained separate. An integrated-segregated split-screen colorvision show. We ate separately, roomed separately, socialized separately. And though it was not a necessity, essentially, that was the way it was. Baseball had broken the color line, but it couldn't abide Brotherhood" (58).

The problem in *The Bedfellow* is that the reader never experiences baseball's "integrated-segregated split-screen colorvision show." Instead the narrative follows Sorrell through a series of miscalculations and misadventures as he travels through the sophisticated white man's world of Madison Avenue and upper-crust New York society. The only time Sorrell plays ball is at a pick-up softball game in Central Park that turns into a mockery of Sorrell's baseball talent and career when he is given a second chance to hit the game-winning home run and act out the adolescent fantasy for the "Sunday morning athletes" (118) in attendance of "laughter and cheers, hero-worship and triumph, and the amusement of seeing the anticipated actually happen, I suppose, a big free bubbly show with celebrities and folklore and happy ending, all wrapped up into one lusty climax" (123).

Other than visits to ex-teammates, one a bigoted white, the other his black former roommate, Sorrell's journey focuses on his rebellion against the corruption and deception of the liberal white world that has embraced him and on his eventual acceptance, signified by his decision not to return to playing baseball, of hypocrisy and duplicity as the inherent conditions of integration: "So, the great conspiracy is all rounded out. Its power seems almost without limit, complete with all races and creeds, all moralities, legal and otherwise, and, that, I suppose, is the essence of integration" (222). Its power is also too much for Mike Sorrell who surrenders his dreams and his pride for a chance to return to the good life: "Then I weaved over all the debris, thankful for the destruction of that mirror, for the last thing I want to do is look at myself" (223).

The missed opportunities of Mark Harris and Eliot Asinof to write novels that do more than use the African-American ballplayer to embellish the moral education of a white ballplayer or to use baseball merely as a narrative contrivance to draw attention to the societal and political conditions of black/white relationships in America are typical of the serious or adult baseball novel. In Martin Quigley's *Today's Game* (1965), a novel that focuses on one day and one crucial mid-season game in the life of a baseball manager, Barney Mann has placed his job and career in jeopardy by trading Jerry Adams, his best friend and "most effective right-handed pitcher in baseball ... for a young Negro outfielder who still had his ability and himself to prove" (7). Rather than focusing on the racial implications of the resistance of the "Old Liners" to the trade and the pressures on the newly acquired Bill Wellington, the narrator focuses on the unorthodox strategies used by Mann to defeat his old friend. While Mann knows and regrets "that baseball is a game in which personal and even racial and religious hatreds were factors" (99) and recognizes the dissension race has caused in his own clubhouse, his attention is on winning today's game and using the skills of his players — Wellington ends the game with a wall-crashing catch — to achieve that end.

In John Hough, Jr.'s *The Conduct of the Game* (1986), the African-American ballplayer is more angry, aggressive, and outspoken, but his role in the narrative is secondary, only a part of the moral education of first-year major league umpire, Lee Malcolm. Appearing at the mid-point of the novel, Ron Chapman, also in his first season in the major leagues, is a Jackie Robinson for the Sixties. Educated at UCLA, arrested in Montgomery, Alabama "for sitting in the whites-only section of a city bus" (155) and a personal friend of Martin Luther King, Jr., Chapman forces Malcolm to recognize the racism that exists in baseball and influences decision making on and off the field. This recognition, however, like Malcolm's coming to terms with the homosexuality of one of his fellow umpires, is played out in the conventional coming-of-age narrative of baseball as a moral and emotional testing ground. In Hough's novel, Malcolm, a talented rookie umpire in love with baseball and devoted to his profession learns, like the Henry Wiggen of *Bang the Drum Slowly*, something about the value of camaraderie and friendship, in this case, from a homosexual rather than a fatally ill roommate. Once he learns the truth about those who play and control baseball, he actually gives up his career after his friend commits suicide because Malcolm now believes that the conduct of his own life is more important than the political positioning and posturing of those responsible for the conduct of the game.

In Barry Beckham's *Runner Mack* (1972), often designated as the only serious or adult baseball novel written by an African-American, the political awakening and education of Henry Adams, an African-American ballplayer who dreams of playing in the major leagues, is the essence of the narrative. In Beckham's novel, the African-American experience is central to the narrative as Henry Adams learns from the black militant Runner Mack that he will never realize his dream as long as American society is controlled by whites. The problem in *Runner Mack*, however, is that, like Asinof's *The Bedfellow*, baseball becomes secondary, more a source for metaphors in a narrative much more concerned with raising social and political consciousness than with racial issues inside baseball itself. The only time Henry Adams plays baseball is at a tryout with "the Stars, the

American baseball team" (86). In a surrealistic episode, Adams is forced to hit against a pitching machine turned up to 150 miles-per-hour and field against another machine that fires howitzer shots into the outfield. Even though Adams manages to hit and field impressively, the episode itself is so unreal that the baseball field merely becomes a symbol for an American society that turns dreams into nightmares for African-Americans. Heavily symbolic and surrealistic, *Runner Mack* is more an attempt to rewrite Ellison's *Invisible Man* for the postmodern era than a realistic portrait of the African-American ballplayer.

Ironically, in the postmodern era, several baseball novels written about African-Americans, rather than offering a portrait of black players in the post–Robinson world of baseball, have focused upon the Negro barnstorming teams in the pre-Robinson era of baseball. With the exception of *The Bingo Long Traveling All-Stars and Motor Kings* (1973), the novels use the experiences of Negro barnstorming teams to teach a white character something about racial intolerance and bigotry. In Martin Quigley's *The Original Colored House of David* (1981), the narrative follows a white youth, frustrated by his family's and the town's unwillingness to treat him as a grown up, as he goes on the road to prove himself. As Speedy, the deaf-dumb albino, he faces the same prejudices as his teammates, though in Quigley's coming-of-age novel there are no real violent confrontations. Speedy's real lesson is that, while he may play for the Original Colored House of David, he knows little about the life of the Negro in America and even less about the history of Negro baseball. In another moral romance about a Negro barnstorming team, John Craig's *Chappie and Me* (1979), a white young adult catches on with Chappie Johnson and His Colored All-Stars when the team comes up short of players. While there is one serious racial confrontation in the novel and a bit of unnecessary melodrama when a tornado injures a few of the players, the narrative, told by Joe Gillen who first wears black shoe polish, then lampblack, when he plays first base, is a bittersweet, often nostalgic retrospective of the All-Stars' "family feeling and the closeness and what we shared" (196). The novel ends only when the All-Stars head south and the narrator, a Canadian, decides that, with the outbreak of the Second World War "it was time to go home" (233).

In Jay Neugeboren's *Sam's Legacy* (1973) and Jerome Charyn's *The Seventh Babe* (1979), the narratives become much more symbolic and ambitious, but the role of Negro barnstorming remains essentially the same. In *Sam's Legacy*, the interior narrative, titled "My Life and Death in the Negro American Baseball League: A Slave Narrative," is a radical, revisionist memoir of Mason Tidewater's turbulent years as the "Black Babe" of Negro baseball, his obsession and eventual love affair with Babe Ruth, and his subsequent flight from baseball after he strangles to death a teammate who had been taunting Tidewater because of his light skin and had deliberately cost Tidewater a perfect no-hitter against an All-Star team of white major leaguers. Tidewater's memoir, written in a basement room used in the past to hide runaway slaves, is itself encased within the larger narrative of Sam Berman's struggle against his unlucky streak as a gambler and his legacy of stories and memories from his Jewish father and grandfather. While Tidewater's own story is the most compelling part of *Sam's Legacy*, Tidewater's role in the novel is to offer himself up as a surrogate father and to give Sam Berman an alternative legacy, one which Sam ultimately rejects because he believes that Tidewater, unlike Sam's own father, has made a text out of his loss of faith and his flight from himself, his people, and his world. At novel's end, Sam Berman imagines that soon after Mason Tidewater vanishes again, "a group of elderly black men" will appear to say "they had been looking for a man whom they believed had once been their teammate" (370).

In *The Seventh Babe*, Negro barnstorming once again plays a significant role in the narrative, but only as a subterranean world for Babe Ragland, cursed for being the seventh Babe to play for the Boston Red Sox after Babe Ruth and eventually banned by Judge Landis for unwittingly consorting with a gambler. Once Ragland joins the Cincinnati Colored Giants, however, he leaves history behind and enters a talismanic and timeless world where, accompanied by a hunchback dwarf, he encounters magical events and legendary players like Pharaoh Yarbull. Eventually Ragland, a left-handed third baseman of unlimited range, becomes primordial in appearance and wizard-like in skills, the stuff of myth himself and, while Negro barnstorming begins "to suffocate" (327), Ragland and his team, now "baseball dinosaurs" (327) continue to play baseball, which has now become more imagined than real in the narrative, an incurable "disease in the magician's head" (328).

Unlike *The Seventh Babe* William Brashler's *The Bingo Long Traveling All-Stars and Motor Kings* is grounded in the history of Negro barnstorming. The novel's main characters, Bingo Long and Leon Carter, are modeled after Negro League greats Josh Gibson and Satchel Paige. Its detailed description of the All-Stars' clowning to compensate for inferior competition and their ability to survive unbearable road conditions and intolerant racial attitudes also gives an air of credibility to the narrative. Even the break-up of the outlaw All-Stars is grounded in baseball history as the team's best young players are signed to minor league contracts in anticipation of the integration of Organized Baseball. Yet, Brashler's novel, for all its historical underpinnings, remains a picaresque tale of roguish heroes and vagabond adventures. And, while there is no white narrator or central figure to reduce the novel to a moral romance, the narrative celebrates the camaraderie of the All-Stars and closes on a clearly sentimental and nostalgic note as Bingo Long wistfully regrets that he "was born too quick" (244) to play in the major leagues.

This narrative tendency to incorporate and subsume the experiences of African-American ballplayers into revisionist histories or moral romances has continued in baseball fiction with the recent publications of Mark Winegardner's *The Veracruz Blues* (1996) and Peter Hamill's *Snow in August* (1997). In *The Veracruz Blues*, the inside narrative of Theolic "Fireball" Smith, a proud and bitter Negro League star pitcher who dreamed of being the first African-American to cross baseball's color line, serves the main narrative effort to transform the Mexican League's raid on the Major Leagues into the historical precursor to the unionization of baseball and the elimination of the reserve clause as well as a reminder of the exclusion of black ballplayers from baseball history and its traditional narratives. In *Snow in August*, Jackie Robinson's crossing of baseball's color line merely embellishes the coming-of-age narrative of the friendship between Michael Devlin, an Irish Catholic youth, and Rabbi Hirsch, a friendship that overcomes cultural and religious barriers as well as an anti-Semitic gang of local toughs. While the novel clearly displays Robinson as a guiding light for tolerance and understanding, the fight that breaks out between racist fans and union workers at Ebbets Field and the physical force conjured up to dispatch the anti-Semitic toughs suggest that something more than goodness of heart and spiritual enlightenment are needed in a world in which racial, ethnic, and religious understanding is as rare as snow in August.[2]

Fifty years after Jackie Robinson crossed Organized Baseball's color line, his historical act still influences the baseball novel, but the results of that influence remain as unsatisfactory as Robinson's impact on baseball itself. While numerous African Americans have now appeared on the playing fields of baseball and baseball fiction, their experiences have often been perceived as important or as valuable, not in themselves, but as moral or historical lessons for whites. Part of the problem in baseball fiction, of course, is the almost total absence of baseball novels written by African-Americans, but equally problematic is the expropriation and exploitation of African-American ballplayers, from Negro League barnstormers to Jackie Robinson, to serve baseball's self-congratulatory perception of itself as representing the best qualities of American society, its democratic spirit, its fundamental goodness and rightness of character, and its innate sense of fair play. This perception of baseball as synonymous with the American dream seems, however, oddly out of focus for those excluded or segregated from the baseball dream for so long and who still wait for a more realistic lens to give the proper perspective and rightful place to their experiences in the history of baseball.

Notes

1. Perry Simpson, listed in *Bang the Drum Slowly* as wearing number 42 in a special opening day score card, does appear in the novel, but in his only significant scene the hard feelings between Simpson and Wiggen over Bruce Pearson, a white southerner, lead to a complete severing of their relationship.

2. Hamill's *Snow in August* is reminiscent of an earlier coming-of-age novel, Robert Mayer's *The Grace of Shortstops* (1984), which, set in 1947, also exploits Jackie Robinson as an inspiration for racial and ethnic tolerance and understanding. Its young hero, Peewee Brunig, takes heart from Robinson's integration of baseball because he wants to be the "first Jewish shortstop in the majors" (6). Robinson's presence in the novel, however, fades out very early as Peewee, whose role model obviously is Peewee Reese, survives several family crises by acting with the grace of shortstops and the courage of catchers, but not with the character of second basemen.

Bibliography

Asinof, Eliot. *Man on Spikes*. New York: McGraw-Hill, 1955.
_____. *The Bedfellow*. New York: Simon and Schuster, 1967.
Beckham, Barry. *Runner Mack*. New York: William Morrow, 1972. Rpt. 1983.
Brashler, William. *The Bingo Long Traveling All-Stars and Motor Kings*. Harper and Row, 1973.
Charyn, Jerome. *The Seventh Babe*. New York: Arbor House, 1979. Rpt. 1996.
Craig, John. *Chappie and Me*. New York: Dodd, Mead, 1979.
Hamill, Peter. *Snow in August*. New York: Little, Brown, 1997.
Harris, Mark. *The Southpaw*. Indianapolis: Bobbs-Merrill, 1953. Rpt. 1984.
_____. *Bang the Drum Slowly*. New York: Knopf, 1956. Rpt. 1984.
_____. "Horatio at the Bat, or Why Such a Lengthy Embryonic Period for the Serious Baseball Novel," *Aethlon*, V:2 (Spring 1988), 1–11.
Hough, John Jr. *The Conduct of the Game*. New York: Harcourt, Brace, 1986.
Mayer, Robert. *The Grace of Shortstops*. New York: Doubleday, 1984.
Neugeboren, Jay. *Sam's Legacy*. New York: Holt, Rinehart, and Winston, 1973.
Quigley, Martin. *Today's Game*. New York: Viking, 1965.
_____. *The Original Colored House of David*. Boston: Houghton Mifflin, 1981.
Winegardner, Mark. *The Veracruz Blues*. New York: Viking, 1996.

Jackie Robinson and the National Baseball Hall of Fame

David W. Findlay and
*Clifford E. Reid**

There is always a fear that subtle racism will affect the voting, and maybe it does. Although he was extremely well liked, sportswriters didn't connect with Luis [Tiant] (or almost any black or Latin player) the way they did with Hunter and Gaylord Perry, good old boys from North Carolina, or the big, handsome blond guy, Drysdale. — Bill James, The Politics of Glory: How Baseball Hall of Fame Really Works, *p. 263*

Introduction

On Saturday, April 12, 1997, America celebrated the fiftieth anniversary of Jackie Robinson's historic entrance into organized white baseball, an event which foreshadowed the full social and racial integration of American life. On Thursday, June 12, 1997, the National Baseball Hall of Fame

We would like to thank several Colby College students for collecting the data. Bill Deane, former Research Associate, William J. Guilfoile, Vice President, Jeff Idelson, Director, Public Relations, Ralph Insinga, Research Associate (all of The National Baseball Hall of Fame) and Steven Gietschier, Director of Historical Records for The Sporting News *provided useful information at several stages of the study. An earlier version of this paper was presented at the Ninth Cooperstown Symposium on Baseball and American Culture, Cooperstown, NY, June, 1997. We alone, however, are responsible for any errors or omissions.*

and Museum celebrated the opening of "Pride and Passion: The African-American Baseball Experience," a permanent exhibit which highlights the important role of African-Americans in the long history of baseball.

While many of the chapters in this book explore the historical and social significance of these events on American society, we focus our attention on a long neglected aspect of Robinson's breaking of the color barrier in professional sports, namely, what effect did Jackie Robinson have on the racial and ethnic composition of the National Baseball Hall of Fame? To be more precise, we investigate the possible effects of race and ethnicity on Hall of Fame voting by members of the Baseball Writers' Association of America.

There are two separate paths to Cooperstown's Hall of Fame. The first path is by election for induction into the Hall of Fame by the Baseball Writers' Association of America (BBWAA). The voters, consisting of ten-year active and honorary members of the BBWAA, may vote for up to ten eligible candidates each election. To be eligible for election a player must have played at least ten seasons in the major leagues, have been an active player within twenty years of election, and have been retired for five years. In order to be elected for induction into the Hall, the player must receive votes on 75 percent of the returned ballots.

The second path to Cooperstown is by election into the Hall of Fame by the Committee on Baseball Veterans. For players who have played at least ten seasons and have been retired for at least 23 years, there is an 18-member Committee on Baseball Veterans which considers "old-timers" and uses the same 75 percent figure for induction. Both groups of voters have separate screening committees which prepare ballots of eligible candidates.[1] In 1971, a nine-member Baseball Hall of Fame Committee on Negro Baseball Leagues was established to consider players who played at least ten seasons in the pre–1946 Negro Leagues and/or the major leagues but who were not eligible to be elected into the Hall of Fame by members of the Baseball Writers' Association of America. In 1977, after the induction of nine players from the Negro Leagues, the special Committee on Negro Baseball Leagues was absorbed into the Committee on Baseball Veterans. Since 1978, four players from the Negro Leagues have been elected for induction into the Baseball Hall of Fame by the Committee on Baseball Veterans.

The need for careful analysis of potential racial and/or ethnic discrimination by baseball writers has become increasingly important as a larger number of players' contracts specifies incentive clauses based on, among other things, awards received; several of these awards are determined by the voting of the baseball writers.[2] More importantly, if discriminatory voting occurs as a result of, for example, writers indulging their biased preferences, such voting and the preferences it reveals could have effects beyond election to the Hall of Fame. First, race/ethnicity-based voting by the baseball writers could make it more difficult for fans to identify black and Latin stars by perpetuating the idea that these players are less deserving than their white counterparts. Indeed, Harry Edwards argues that "because of the subordinate position and status of blacks in the larger society, the role of blacks in the achievement of athletic victories may be covertly understated, or even omitted altogether."[3] Second, race/ethnicity–based voting might reveal preferences of writers which could indirectly affect fans' perceptions of minority players. If fans' perceptions of players are influenced by the writers' reporting, fans' perceptions of race and ethnicity might be indirectly (and unknowingly) influenced by the racial and ethnic preferences of the writers. Along these lines, Andersen's (1992) study on fan balloting for major league baseball All-Star games suggests that black players and, to a lesser extent, Latin players receive fewer votes than white players of equal performance. Finally, race/ethnicity-based voting and its indirect effect on fans could explain some of the discrimination found by Andersen and La Croix (1991) and by Nardinelli and Simon (1990) in their examination of customer discrimination in the market for major league baseball cards.

The principle focus of this paper is an investigation of possible voting bias against black and Latin major league baseball players by members of the Baseball Writers' Association of America. While published voting data allow us to undertake such an investigation, such data do not exist from the proceedings of the Committee on Negro Baseball Leagues or the Committee on Baseball Veterans. Nonetheless, we detour briefly to make some speculative comments concerning the impact or legacy of Jackie Robinson on those black and Latin players elected into the Hall of Fame by the Committee on Negro Baseball Leagues or the Committee on Baseball Veterans.

Hall of Fame Selections: Negro Baseball Leagues Players

Table 1 lists the thirteen players from the Negro Baseball Leagues who have been elected into The National Baseball Hall of Fame by either the Committee on Negro Baseball Leagues or the Committee on Baseball Veterans. We also include the year of their Hall of Fame induction, their primary playing position, and their lifetime batting average in the Negro Baseball Leagues.[4] We also include the same information for Jackie

Robinson who was inducted into the Baseball Hall of Fame in 1962 by vote of the Baseball Writers' Association of America. Jackie Robinson played one year for the Kansas City Monarchs in the Negro Baseball League before he was signed by the Brooklyn Dodgers in 1945 to play the following season for the Montreal Royals of the International League.

TABLE 1

HALL OF FAME INDUCTEES FROM THE NEGRO BASEBALL LEAGUES

Player	Year	Position	Batting Average
Robinson, Jackie	1962	SS	.345
Paige, Satchel	1971	P	
Gibson, Josh	1972	C	.354
Leonard, Buck	1972	1B	.341
Irvin, Monte1	1973	CF	.346
Bell, Cool Papa	1974	CF	.341
Johnson, Judy	1975	3B	.309
Charleston, Oscar	1976	CF	.357
Dihigo, Martin	1977	P	
Lloyd, Pop	1977	SS	.368
Foster, Rube	1981	P,M	
Dandridge, Ray	1987	3B	.355
Day, Leon	1995	P	
Wells, Willie	1997	SS	.334

Robinson's one year in the Negro Baseball League probably provided the necessary link for other Negro Baseball League stars to be considered for induction into the Baseball Hall of Fame by first the Committee on Negro Baseball Leagues and now the Committee on Baseball Veterans. While records from the Negro Baseball Leagues are spotty and incomplete, with eyewitnessed accounts and oral histories they necessarily provide Hall of Fame voters a reference with which to make their selection decisions.[5] For example, many observers of black baseball generally acknowledged that Jackie Robinson was only slightly above average in comparison with many of the existing Negro Baseball League stars. Jules Tygiel writes that "neither Rickey's scouts nor other black players considered Robinson the best player in the Negro Leagues."[6] Fairness would suggest that if Jackie Robinson was of Hall of Fame caliber, certainly some of those Negro Leaguers who did not have the opportunity to play major league baseball would also have had Hall of Fame careers. Furthermore, Robinson's breaking of the color barrier allowed other former Negro Leagues players to play in the major leagues. The major league success of these players (e.g. Hank Aaron, Ernie Banks, Roy Campanella, Larry Doby, and Willie Mays) and, just as importantly, their performance in the Negro Leagues provided the Committee on Negro Baseball Leagues and now the Committee on Baseball Veterans with additional information with which to assess the relative performance of those players who played exclusively in the Negro Leagues. This additional information enabled the committee members to make better informed and, we believe, fair decisions about those players who did not have the opportunity to play in the major leagues. Thus, one legacy of the Jackie Robinson phenomenon is the increased number of black and Latin players who are in the National Baseball Hall of Fame but who would not have been considered for induction if Jackie Robinson had not broken the major league baseball color barrier.

The second path to Cooperstown's Baseball Hall of Fame is by vote of members of the BBWAA. Have black and Latin major league baseball players been discriminated against in voting by these baseball writers? In the next section, we address this important question.

Hall of Fame Selections:
Baseball Writers' Association of America

In the first path to Cooperstown's Baseball Hall of Fame, racial and ethnic discrimination can occur at two separate stages: the nominating process and the voting process. The first possible source of racial/ethnic bias can emerge through the nominating and screening process if some members of the screening committee are racially or ethnically biased because some minority players will be excluded from the ballot and, therefore, never have an opportunity to receive votes from the baseball writers. While we are presently gathering all of the information we need to investigate analytically this first possible source of discrimination, we as yet have nothing meaningful to report. We thus turn our attention to the second possible source of discrimination, namely, racial or ethnic voting bias by members of the Baseball Writers' Association of America.

We examine first the changing racial and ethnic composition of the eligible players for election into the Hall of Fame during the 1962–1996 period. Second, we examine, for eligible players, the estimated effects of the player's race or ethnicity on: (1) the probability the player ever receives at least one Hall of Fame vote during his years of eligibility; (2) the percentage of Hall of Fame votes received; and (3) the probability the player is ever elected to the Hall of Fame.

Since we want to investigate possible voting bias against black and Latin players, we begin our sample for hitters in 1962, the year in which

Jackie Robinson was first eligible for election into the Hall. We begin our sample for pitchers in 1966, the year in which Don Newcombe, the first minority pitcher to appear on the ballot, was first eligible for election.[7]

Table 2 contains a summary of the racial and ethnic composition of the 455 players in our two study samples who were on a Hall of Fame ballot between 1962 and 1996.[8] The sample of 296 hitters and 159 pitchers concludes

---

TABLE 2
MINORITY COMPOSITION OF THE ELIGIBLE CANDIDATES FOR ELECTION TO THE NATIONAL BASEBALL HALL OF FAME
1962–1996

Year	Players on ballot	Players with yes votes	Players with no votes	Hitters	Black hitters	Latin hitters	Pitchers	Black pitchers	Latin pitchers	Voters
1962	32HH	32	–	7	1H	0	25	0	0	160
1964	46H	36	10	19	1	0	27	0	0	201
1966	55H	38	17	35	2	2	20	1	0	302
1967	50H	37	13	32	2	0	18	1	0	292
1968	33H	33	0	16	1	0	17	1	0	283
1969	35HH	35	0	18	1H	0	17	1	0	340
1970	35H	35	0	18	0	0	17	1	0	300
1971	43	41	2	23	1	1	20	1	0	360
1972	40HHH	40	0	23	0	1	17	1	0	396
1973	39H	39	0	20	0	0	19	1	0	380
1974	42HH	41	1	26	1	0	16	1	0	365
1975	37H	37	0	23	2	0	12	1	0	362
1976	30HH	30	0	20	2	0	10	1	0	388
1977	33H	33	0	23	4H	0	10	1	1	383
1978	36H	34	2	22	3	0	14	2	2	379
1979	37H	37	0	23	5H	1	14	1	0	432
1980	62HH	31	31	43	5	6	19	2	1	385
1981	37H	30	7	22	5	3	15	1H	1	401
1982	36HH	31	5	26	10HH	5	10	0	1	415
1983	44HH	29	15	27	7	5	17	1	3H	374
1984	27HHH	25	2	16	3	3H	11	0	0	403
1985	38HH	35	3	23	9H	4	15	1	0	395
1986	39H	37	2	24	11H	4	15	1	0	425
1987	26HH	24	2	17	7H	2	9	0	0	413
1988	43H	28	15	27	12H	4	16	1	1	427
1989	38HH	27	11	24	7	4	14	2	1	447
1990	42HH	32	10	27	11H	3	15	2	1	444
1991	43HHH	32	11	28	9	3H	15	1H	1	443
1992	33HH	27	6	23	8	5	10	1	1	430
1993	29H	24	5	23	11H	3	6	1	1	423
1994	34H	29	5	23	8	5	11	1	2	455
1995	35H	31	4	20	5	4	15	1	2	460
1996	34	30	4	22	10	3	12	1	0	470

Notes:
1. *Each H represents a player in that category who was elected to the Hall of Fame in that election.*
2. *In March, 1973, Roberto Clemente was elected to the Hall of Fame in a special election.*
3. *There are 455 players in our sample: 296 hitters and 159 pitchers. Of the 296 hitters, 186 received at least one vote. Of the 159 pitchers, 89 received at least one vote.*
4. *We calculate the above numbers based on our sample of players who were on the ballot between 1962 and 1996. We have, for reasons described in the paper, excluded some players from our sample who were on the ballot during these years.*

---

with the 1996 election in which, for the first time since 1971, no one was elected into the Hall of Fame by the BBWAA. A casual inspection of Table 2 yields several observations. First, since the late 1970s, the number of black and Latin hitters on the ballot has increased substantially which reflects the effects of the gradual integration of major league baseball during the late 1940s and early 1950s. Prior to 1979, the ballot never included more than four black and/or Latin hitters. Since 1979, the ballot has included fewer than eight black and/or Latin hitters only twice. Second, the number of black and/or Latin pitchers on the ballot has remained relatively low for the entire sample period which might reflect positional segregation by race or ethnicity. Recently, there does seem to be an influx of Latin pitchers in the major leagues; consequently, we can expect to see more Latin pitchers on Hall of Fame ballots in the near future. Third, the number of eligible voters has increased during the entire period. Finally, prior to the 1980 election virtually all players on the ballot received at least one vote from the baseball writers. The only notable exceptions occurred in the 1964, 1966, and 1967 elections. Starting with the 1980 election, however, the number of players who did not receive a vote has increased. Indeed, since 1980 there has never been a year when all of the players have received at least one vote.

The rules for election to membership into The National Baseball Hall of Fame state that "[V]oting shall be based upon the player's record, playing ability, integrity, sportsmanship, character, and contributions to the team(s) on which the player played ... No automatic elections based on performances such as a batting average of .400 or more for one (1) year, pitching a perfect game or similar outstanding achievement shall be permitted."[9] We thus assume that each voting member of the BBWAA bases his or her evaluation of an eligible player's qualification for election into the Hall of Fame on the player's career statistics, career accomplishments, and on the player's racial or ethnic status. For each Hall of Fame election, the secretary of the BBWAA reports the total number of ballots returned and the number of yes votes received by each eligible candidate.

In order to continue with the analysis of voter discrimination by members of the BBWAA, we discuss first the hitters sample and then the pitchers sample. For each group, we examine: (1) the probability the player ever received at least one Hall of Fame vote during his years of eligibility; (2) the percentage of Hall of Fame votes received; and (3) the probability the player is ever elected to the Hall of Fame.

The Hitters Sample

In order to determine which playing statistics are important in capturing playing ability and contributions to the team(s) on which the hitter was a member, we use as our guide one of the two recent articles which investigates customer discrimination in the market for major league baseball cards. Nardinelli and Simon (1990) use individual performance measures to capture a player's offensive capabilities. Andersen and La Croix (1991), on the other hand, use a performance index to capture a player's offensive ability. Since the use of the performance index does not alter the results we discuss below, we do not report the performance index results.

In the first stage of our statistical analysis, we determine the probability that the eligible hitter ever received at least one vote during his years of Hall of Fame eligibility. The results of our analysis allow us to consider whether the decision to cast *any* vote for a hitter is based on his race or ethnicity. In this first stage of our analysis, we use the following explanatory variables.

HITS equals the number of career hits. DOUBLES equals the number of career doubles. TRIPLES equals the number of career triples. HOMERS equals the number of career home runs. STOLEN equals the number of career stolen bases. SEASONS equals the number of major league seasons the player played. GOLD equals the number of Gold Gloves the player received during his career. WORLD equals the number of World Series games played by the eligible player. BOTH captures whether the player played at least ten percent of his career games in both leagues. LEAGUE captures whether the player played more than 50 percent of his career games in the National League. MGRCOACH captures whether the player was ever a manager and/or coach after his playing career. Finally, BLACK captures whether the player is a black North American player while LATIN captures whether the player was born in a Latin American country.

The interested reader can find the results of the statistical analysis in Appendix A. We find that the probabilities that a Latin and white player with identical career performances will ever receive a Hall of Fame vote by members of the BBWAA are the same. We also find, however, that the probabilities that a black and white player with identical career performances will ever receive a Hall of Fame vote are *not* the same. That is, the analysis indicates that the probability that a player will ever receive a vote is negatively affected if he is black. The estimates imply that the mean or average probability of a black player ever receiving at least one Hall of Fame vote, *ceteris paribus*, during his years of eligibility is 15.2 percent less than that of his white counterpart.[10]

We can use the results of our first-stage statistical analysis to obtain the predicted probabilities of ever receiving at least one Hall of Fame vote for all 72 black players in our hitters' sample. We do not present the analysis for the Latin players in our sample because the results, as we mentioned earlier, indicate that the predicted probabilities for Latin and white players are the same.

Table 3 contains for each of the 72 black players the years they were on a Hall of Fame ballot, the predicted probability of ever receiving at least one Hall of Fame vote from the baseball writers, the numerical rank for each of the players, the predicted probability of ever receiving at least one vote if the player was white (instead of black), the numerical rank if the player was white (instead of black), and the number of Hall of Fame votes received by the player on the first ballot.

TABLE 3
PREDICTED PROBABILITIES OF BLACK HITTERS
RECEIVING AT LEAST ONE HALL OF FAME VOTE

	Years on Ballot	Predicted Probability	Rank	Predicted Probability if White	Rank if White	Votes on First Ballot
H. Aaron	82	1.00	3	1.00	2	406
D. Allen	83–96	.861	128	.973	95	14
D. Baker	92	.985	76	.999	48	4
E. Banks	77	1.00	13	1.00	9	321
D. Baylor	94–95	.976	82	.998	56	12
P. Blair	86	.712	154	.919	120	8
B. Bonds	87–96	.998	47	1.00	33	24
J. Briggs	81	.128	256	.386	217	0
L. Brock	85	.9998	33	1.00	17	315
G. Brown	81	.100	264	.333	227	1
B. Bruton	71	.734	152	.929	117	1
A. Bumbry	91	.155	249	.429	208	0
R. Campanella	64–69	.659	164	.894	129	115
D. Cash	86	.358	208	.684	172	2
C. Chambliss	94	.470	189	.779	158	0
H. Clarke	80	.040	276	.181	257	0

	Years on Ballot	Predicted Probability	Rank	Predicted Probability if White	Rank if White	Votes on First Ballot
C. Cooper	93	.601	174	.864	138	0
T. Davis	82	.987	73	.999	47	5
L. Doby	66–67	.911	113	.986	84	7
C. Flood	77–96	.903	116	.984	87	16
G. Foster	92–95	.884	124	.979	90	24
O. Gamble	91	.089	266	.309	233	0
T. Harper	82	.168	246	.452	201	0
J. Hart	80	.164	247	.444	202	0
G. Hendrick	94	.692	158	.910	124	0
L. Hisle	88	.046	273	.206	253	0
W. Horton	86	.980	80	.999	54	4
E. Howard	74–88	.997	49	1.00	37	19
R. Jackson	93	.996	58	1.00	39	396
S. Jackson	80	.677	160	.903	127	1
A. Johnson	82	.163	248	.444	204	0
C. Jones	82	.201	240	.500	198	0
H. Lanier	79	.686	165	.894	132	1
C. Lemon	96	.290	220	.614	183	1
J. Leonard	96	.185	244	.480	199	0
G. Maddox	92	.758	147	.938	112	0
B. Madlock	93	.570	175	.847	142	19
G. Matthews	93	.768	145	.942	110	0
C. May	83	.039	277	.179	258	0
L. May	88	.992	63	.999	45	2
J. Mayberry	88	.142	252	.409	210	0
W. Mays	79	1.00	1	1.00	1	409
B. McBride	89	.203	239	.504	197	0
W. McCovey	86	.969	89	.997	60	346
H. McCrae	93	.390	201	.712	168	0
J. Milner	88	.076	268	.278	241	0
J. Morgan	90	.998	45	1.00	31	363
A. Oliver	91	.911	112	.986	82	19
A. Otis	90	.486	187	.791	155	0
V. Pinson	81–96	1.00	21	1.00	12	18
J. Ray	96	.137	253	.401	212	0
J. Rice	95–96	.929	106	.990	78	137
M. Rivers	90	.397	200	.719	167	2
B. Robinson	89	.098	265	.326	228	0
F. Robinson	82	1.00	7	1.00	4	370
J. Robinson	62	.841	131	.967	101	124
G. Scott	86	.939	99	.992	71	1
T. Scott	90	.011	290	.076	273	0
K. Singleton	90	.547	180	.832	144	0
R. Smith	88	.843	130	.968	99	3
W. Stargell	88	.9995	40	1.00	23	352
A. Thornton	93	.231	233	.540	190	2
B. Tolan	85	.213	237	.520	194	0
E. Valentine	91	.040	278	.179	259	1
C. Washington	96	.405	197	.726	165	0
B. Watson	90	.930	105	.990	76	3
F. White	96	.985	77	.999	49	18
R. White	85	.429	194	.745	161	0
W. White	75–77	.902	117	.983	88	7

	Years on Ballot	Predicted Probability	Rank	Predicted Probability if White	Rank if White	Votes on First Ballot
B. Williams	82–87	1.00	19	1.00	11	97
M. Wills	78–92	1.00	11	1.00	8	115
J. Wynn	83	.613	172	.871	137	0

Notes:
1. There are 296 hitters who were on the ballot between 1962 and 1996.
2. There are thirteen hitters in the sample whose predicted probability (unadjusted for the effects of race) is 1.00.
3. The mean predicted probability (unadjusted for the effects of race) of receiving at least one vote is .631.
4. The median predicted probability (unadjusted for the effects of race) of receiving at least one vote is .751.

The mean or average predicted probability of ever receiving at least one Hall of Fame vote is 63.1 percent for the entire sample of 296 eligible hitters. In order to place these predicted probabilities in some perspective, we rank each black player based on his predicted probability because this ranking represents one measure of the baseball writers' assessment of each player's accomplishments. For example, Hank Aaron had a 100 percent probability of ever receiving at least one Hall of Fame vote which ranked him 3rd among all 296 hitters in the sample. Dick Allen had an 86.1 percent probability of ever receiving at least one Hall of Fame vote which ranked him 128th in the sample. Dusty Baker had a 98.5 percent probability of ever receiving at least one vote which ranked him 76th in the sample. Each black player's probability and rank can be read accordingly.

We highlight the results for Gary Maddox and Gary Matthews who have predicted probabilities of 75.8 percent and 76.8 percent, respectively. When we glance at the last column of Table 3 we see that these two players have the highest predicted probabilities among black players who never received a Hall of Fame vote from the baseball writers! The following black players never received a Hall of Fame vote despite having predicted probabilities of receiving at least one vote greater than 50 percent: Cecil Cooper, George Hendrick, Ken Singleton, and Jim Wynn.

We also obtain estimates of the predicted probabilities of receiving at least one vote assuming each black player was white by eliminating the estimated negative effects of the player's race on the predicted probability. When we do so, for example, the probability that Gary Maddox and Gary Matthews receive at least one vote increases to 93.8 percent and 94.2 percent, respectively. Gary Maddox's rank increases from 147th in the sample to 112th while Gary Matthews' rank increases from 145th to 110th. Furthermore, the elimination of the negative effects of the players' race on the predicted probabilities causes the estimated probabilities of the following players (who initially rank in the bottom half of the distribution) to increase above the median probability (75.1 percent) of the entire sample: Paul Blair, Bill Bruton, Roy Campanella, Chris Chambliss, Cecil Cooper, George Hendrick, Sonny Jackson, Hal Lanier, Bill Madlock, Amos Otis, Ken Singleton, and Jim Wynn.

There are two reasons why we focus initially on the probability of a player ever receiving at least one Hall of Fame vote by members of the Baseball Writers' Association of America. First, since we observe that the decision to cast a vote for a hitter appears to be affected by his race (but not by his ethnicity), black hitters on Hall of Fame ballots may be disproportionately limited for future Hall of Fame consideration given the current 5 percent minimum vote rule. Prior to 1981, an eligible player could remain on the ballot for a maximum of 15 years. Starting in 1981, however, candidates had to receive 5 percent of the votes to remain on the ballot. The failure to reach the 5 percent minimum can have real consequences because as Bill Deane notes "fortunately for many, this rule has not always been existent; more than seventy current Hall of Famers received less than 5 percent of the vote in their first tries!"[11] Thus, the probability of a player ever receiving at least one vote by members of the Baseball Writers' Association of America may affect the racial composition of subsequent ballots and the racial composition of the membership of the Baseball Hall of Fame.

Second, if a sufficient number of baseball writers base their decision to cast a vote on the hitter's race, the number of votes a black hitter receives and, consequently, his probability of election to the Hall of Fame may be affected. We turn now to an extended analysis of this second issue for hitters.

In the second stage of our statistical analysis we formulate four different dependent variables to investigate whether any racial or ethnic bias exists in the percentage of votes received by eligible baseball players or in the probability that eligible players are ever elected into the Baseball Hall of Fame. We argue below that the four different dependent variables complement each other because each might represent a different dimension of the voting process.

We define the voting percentage in any year as the ratio of the number of yes votes to the total number of ballots cast. A player is elected to the Baseball Hall of Fame if his voting percentage is equal to or greater than 75 percent. We define the first dependent variable, FVOTES, as the voting percentage in the first year the player received votes. The second dependent variable, HIVOTES, is the highest voting percentage received by a player during his years of eligibility. The third dependent variable, LVOTES, is the voting percentage received in the last election the player received votes. The final dependent variable, ELECTED, is a variable which indicates whether the player was ever elected into the Hall of Fame by the BBWAA. In our sample of 186 (296) hitters who received at least one vote (were eligible to receive votes), 29, or 16 percent (10 percent), were elected into the Hall of Fame by the BBWAA.[12]

We thus start with the voting percentage from the initial year of eligibility and conclude with the last voting percentage the player received. We also include the highest voting percentage ever received and whether the player was ever elected into the Hall of Fame by the BBWAA. We argue that it makes more sense to investigate the historical voting record because voting percentages do fluctuate and the elected/not elected dichotomy may not adequately capture all of the dynamics of the voting process. For example, voting results from the initial year of eligibility may be important because this election *may* allow writers to exercise their racial or ethnic prejudice (or any other bias writers might have concerning a particular player) without later preventing a deserving player from ultimately being inducted into the Hall of Fame.

For example, Steve Wulf (1988) notes that Maury Allen, a columnist for the *New York Post*, has written that some writers "use the ballots vindictively 'paying back certain players for personal slights by withholding their votes.'" Likewise, Jackie Robinson said before his election into the Hall of Fame that "I'm positive I won't be accepted into the Hall of Fame this year. Maybe some day, but regardless of what my achievements were, many writers are going to disregard this because of Jackie Robinson, Negro outspoken."[13] Despite his predictions, Jackie Robinson was elected on the first ballot in 1962.

The issue of player ethnicity has also been discussed by a number of individuals. For example, Peter Gammons (1994) has commented that Latin players have not received the same recognition as their peers. These observations are echoed by James (1994) when he examines the Hall of Fame candidacy of Latin pitcher Luis Tiant. James notes that "although he was extremely well liked, sportswriters didn't connect with Luis (or almost any black or Latin player) the way they did with Hunter and Gaylord Perry, good old boys from North Carolina, or the big, handsome blond guy, Drysdale." Concerns about the effects of ethnicity on Hall of Fame voting were most recently stated by former player and current Hall of Fame candidate Tony Perez who notes that "it might be just because my last name is Perez. I'm not only speaking for myself. What about Luis Tiant, Dave Concepcion, Tony Oliva and all the other guys?" In response to this claim, Jack

Lang, assistant secretary of the BBWAA, argues that "the writers have given so many Latin players the MVP, Cy Young and Rookie of the Year awards, you can't find fault with us."[14]

To continue our investigation of racial/ethnic bias in Hall of Fame voting, we use many of the explanatory variables that we used in the first stage of our statistical analysis. For example, we continue to use HITS, HOMERS, STOLEN, GOLD, WORLD, SEASONS, BOTH, BLACK, and LATIN. We include two additional explanatory variables: MIDINF and TIME(T). MIDINF, which accounts for the defensive capabilities of players, captures whether the player played a middle infield (Catcher, Second Baseman, or Shortstop) position.

TIME(T) corresponds to the year of the relevant vote and is included to examine whether the standards of the baseball writers have changed over time. There are several factors that may have affected the composition of the voters, the voting process, and, subsequently, the vote totals of players during the period. These factors, therefore, may have affected the standards for election to the Hall. If, for example, the standards have declined, we would expect that a player on the 1962 ballot would receive a lower voting percentage than a pitcher with identical statistics on, say, the 1996 ballot. While it is possible that an individual writer's standards might change with age, it is more likely the case that the changing *composition* of the voters will affect the overall standards of the voters. In the 1962 election, 160 writers cast votes while in the 1996 election, 470 writers cast votes. Even if we assume (unrealistically) that the 160 writers who voted in the 1962 election also voted in the 1996 election, the remaining 'new' 310 voters may have standards different from their colleagues.[15] The introduction of a time variable enables us to determine whether the standards of this ever-changing group of voters have changed.

Several aspects of the eligibility requirements and the nomination and voting processes have changed since 1962. First, the use of a screening committee between 1968 and 1978 and from 1981 to the present to limit the number of candidates on the ballot may have affected the voting behavior of writers. Second, there also existed different minimum vote requirements for a player to remain on subsequent ballots during the sample period. Third, based on our inspection of several sample ballots, we observed that the format of the ballot has changed over time.

An additional reason for including a time variable is to capture the possible effects of changes in the game itself on voting behavior. As Roger Barry (1982) notes, "[t]he game has expanded, contracted and expanded while wars have been fought, moving indoors, from grass to artificial turf, from day to night. Playing tactics and styles have changed, new equipment has been developed, new positions created." Although some of the changes mentioned by Barry occurred before 1962, innovations to the game of baseball continue today. For example, we have recently witnessed changes in the size of the strike zone and changes in the height of the pitching mound.

Finally, some of the recent eligible candidates believe that the standards have changed. For example, after finishing second but still falling short of the required 75 percent threshold in the 1996 election, Tony Perez commented that "I think it's getting harder and harder every year. The Baseball Hall of Fame is hard to get into right now. You have to have really super numbers or whatever; you've got to be Babe Ruth or Hank Aaron."[16]

Appendix B contains the results from the four different dependent variables we use to investigate whether any racial or ethnic bias exists in the percentage of votes received by eligible baseball players or in the probability that eligible players are ever elected into the Baseball Hall of Fame for our sample of 186 hitters.[17]

Since many readers will be unfamiliar with interpreting this form of statistical analysis, we present our conclusions in summary form only.[18] The results for the FVOTES, HIVOTES and LVOTES equations are basically the same and generally consistent with what one would expect. We observe that increases in hits, home runs, stolen bases, the number of Gold Glove awards won, and the number of world series games played have a positive effect on all three voting percentages. We also note that players who played a middle infield position receive a higher voting percentage than do players who played an outfield or corner infield position. Players who played in both leagues, despite any additional media exposure they might have gained from this, receive a significantly lower voting percentage than do players who played over 90 percent of their games in one league. Increases in the number of seasons played do not have an effect on any of the voting percentages.

A casual observation of the remaining results for the FVOTES, HIVOTES and LVOTES equations yields two final conclusions. First, given the negative and significant coefficient on the time variable, the standards of the voters appear to have increased over time. Second, we observe that the coefficients on the race and ethnicity variables are statistically insignificant. Therefore, we obtain no statistical evidence that the hitter's race or ethnicity affects the hitter's voting percentages.

For the ELECTED equation, increases in hits, home runs, stolen bases, and the number of Gold Glove awards won increase the probability the player will be elected to the Hall of Fame. Once again, we observe that Hall of Fame voters appear to take into account the defensive capabilities of players who play a middle infield position. Unlike the results of the three voting percentages equations, we observe that the number of world series games played and whether the player played at least 10 percent of his games in both leagues have no effect on the probability of a hitter being elected to the Hall of Fame.

We do observe, however, that the effects of time, race and ethnicity on the probability of being elected to the Hall of Fame are the same as those observed for the voting percentages equations. First, the negative and significant coefficient on the time variable indicates that the standards for election into the Baseball Hall of Fame have increased over time. For the ELECTED equation, this result indicates that the probability a player will be elected to the Hall will be lower, for example, in 1996 than it would be for a player with identical career statistics who appeared on, say, the 1962 ballot. Finally, the insignificance of the coefficients on the BLACK and LATIN variables indicates that the hitter's race or ethnicity has no effect on the probability of being elected to the Hall.[19]

At the beginning of the chapter, we indicated that we wanted to examine: (1) the probability the player ever received at least one Hall of Fame vote during his years of eligibility; (2) the percentage of Hall of Fame votes received; and (3) the probability the player is ever elected to the Hall of Fame. For hitters, we find that members of the Baseball Writers' Association of America discriminate against black hitters only when determining the probability the player ever received at least one Hall of Fame vote during his years of eligibility. There appears to be no voting bias against Latin hitters.

While Jackie Robinson would applaud, as we all do, the general absence of Hall of Fame voting bias against black and Latin hitters, the exclusion of black and Latin players prior to the 1947 baseball season has had a subtle effect on the racial composition of the National Baseball Hall of Fame for at least two reasons. First, the number of eligible black and Latin players would have been greater in the absence of the general ban against black and Latin players. Second, the increased standards (which apply to all players) that we find make it more difficult for all players now to be elected to the Baseball Hall of Fame. We thus observe that as more black and Latin players become eligible for Hall of Fame membership the standards for induction have also increased. We turn now to our sample of black and Latin pitchers.

THE PITCHERS SAMPLE

Recall that our sample for pitchers begins with the 1966 election in which Don Newcombe was first eligible for induction into the Baseball

Hall of Fame and includes all pitchers whose first year of eligibility was 1966 or later. In our sample of 89 (159) pitchers who received at least one vote (were eligible to receive votes), 16, or 18 percent (10 percent), were elected into the Hall by the BBWAA.

As before, in the first stage of our statistical analysis, we determine the probability that the eligible pitcher ever received at least one vote during his years of Hall of Fame eligibility. The results of our analysis allow us to consider whether the decision to cast *any* vote for a pitcher is based on his race or ethnicity. In this first-stage analysis, we use the following explanatory variables.

The first group of explanatory variables measures various aspects of the player's pitching ability. WINS equals the number of career wins. LOSSES equals the number of career losses. SAVES equals the number of career saves. COMPGAMES equals the number of career complete games. ERA equals the pitcher's career earned run average. STRIKES equals the number of career strike outs. HITS equals the number of career hits allowed.

The second group of explanatory variables represents the pitcher's special achievements. WIN20 equals the number of 20-win seasons a pitcher achieved during his career. NOHIT equals the number of career no-hit games.[20] WSINNINGS equal the number of career innings pitched in World Series games.

The third group of variables includes two variables we used in our sample of hitters. SEASONS equals the number of major league seasons the player played while BOTH captures whether the player played at least ten percent of his career games in both leagues. SIZE equals the population of the city in which the player played the majority of his career and is the only variable that we could construct which might serve as a proxy for the characteristics of the writers. As we mentioned before, we attempted to obtain additional information about the writers, but the policies of the BBWAA prevent the release of any such information.

The final category of explanatory variables refers to the racial classification or ethnicity of the pitcher. BLACK captures whether the pitcher is a black North American pitcher while Latin captures whether the pitcher was born in a Latin American country.

Once again, the interested reader can find the results of the first stage of our statistical analysis in Appendix A. While the results allow us to determine which factors affect the probability that a pitcher will ever receive at least one Hall of Fame vote by members of the BBWAA, we are most interested in the effect a pitcher's race or ethnicity has on that probability.[21]

The statistical insignificance of the coefficient for BLACK indicates that the probability that a black pitcher and white pitcher with identical career performances will ever receive a Hall of Fame vote is the same. We do find, however, that the probability a pitcher will ever receive at least one vote during his years of eligibility is negatively affected if he is Latin. The estimates imply that the mean or average probability of a LATIN pitcher ever receiving at least one vote, *ceteris paribus*, is 29.9 percent less than that of his white counterpart.[22]

A quick comparison of the careers of Mike Cuellar (born in Cuba) and Don Drysdale provides additional, anecdotal evidence of the possible effects of ethnicity on whether the pitcher ever receives at least one vote. Cuellar had four 20-win seasons compared to Drysdale's two. While Cuellar had fewer wins (185 compared to Drysdale's 209), he also had 36 fewer losses than Drysdale's 166. Thus, Cuellar's winning percentage of .587 was greater than Drysdale's .557. Both pitchers won a Cy Young award.

Drysdale, whose predicted probability of receiving at least one vote is .95, was elected to the Baseball Hall of Fame by the BBWAA in 1984. Cuellar, whose predicted probability of receiving at least one vote is .88, never received a Hall of Fame vote! We do not intend to argue here that Cuellar should have been elected to the Hall, nor do we even argue that he was a better pitcher than Drysdale. We simply point out that ethnicity might explain why the player (Cuellar) with the forty-sixth highest predicted probability of receiving at least one vote (in our sample of 159 pitchers) did not receive even one vote on the 374 returned ballots in 1983. Cuellar, by the way, also has the highest predicted probability of receiving at least one vote among all pitchers who never received a vote.

We use the results of our first-stage statistical analysis to obtain the predicted probabilities of receiving at least one vote for the nine Latin pitchers in our sample. We do not present the results for the black pitchers in our sample because the analysis indicates that the predicted probabilities for black pitchers and white pitchers are the same.

Table 4 contains for each of the Latin pitchers in the sample the years they were on a Hall of Fame ballot, the predicted probability of ever receiving at least one Hall of Fame vote from the baseball writers, the numerical rank for each of the players, the predicted probability of ever receiving at least one vote if the player was white (instead of Latin), the numerical rank if the player was white (instead of Latin), and the number of Hall of Fame votes received by the player on the first ballot. As we mentioned previously, the predicted probabilities for each of the pitchers in our sample can be used as a rough guide of the BBWAA's evaluation of each player.

TABLE 4
PREDICTED PROBABILITIES OF LATIN PITCHERS
RECEIVING AT LEAST ONE HALL OF FAME VOTE

	Years on Ballot	Predicted Probability	Rank	Predicted Probability if White	Rank if White	Votes on First Ballot
M. Cuellar	83	.876	46	.993	29	0
W. Hernandez	95	.468	91	.894	45	2
J. Marichal	81–83	.996	25	1.00	11	233
C. Pasqual	77–78	.277	113	.770	61	3
J. Pizzaro	80	.181	133	.663	69	0
P. Ramos	78	.017	157	.215	126	0
D. Sequi	83	.045	153	.359	105	0
M. Soto	94	.014	159	.195	145	0
L. Tiant	88–96	.965	35	.999	21	132

Notes:
1. There are 159 pitchers who were on the ballot between 1966 and 1996.
2. There are nine pitchers in the sample whose predicted probability (unadjusted for the effects of ethnicity) is 1.0.
3. The mean predicted probability (unadjusted for the effects of ethnicity) of receiving at least one vote is .562.
4. The median predicted probability (unadjusted for the effects of ethnicity) of receiving at least one vote is .525.
5. Luis Tiant received votes in the 1997 election and is eligible to receive votes until 2002 unless he is elected into the Hall or receives fewer than 5 percent of the total vote from voting members of the BBWAA.

The mean or average predicted probability based on the sample of 159 eligible pitchers is .562. In order to place these predicted probabilities in some perspective, we rank each pitcher based on his predicted probability of ever receiving at least one Hall of Fame vote. For example, as discussed previously, Mike Cuellar had an 87.6 percent probability of receiving at least one vote which ranked him 46th among all 159 pitchers in the sample. Willie Hernandez had a 46.8 percent probability of receiving at least one vote which ranked him 91st in the sample. Juan Marichal had a 99.6 percent probability of receiving at least one vote which ranked him 25th in the sample of pitchers. Each of the remaining Latin pitchers' probability and rank can be read accordingly.

We also calculate the predicted probabilities of receiving at least one vote after eliminating the negative effects of the pitcher's ethnicity on the predicted probability. For all nine Latin pitchers, both the predicted probability and rank are higher after eliminating the negative effect of their Latin birth. For example, Willie Hernandez's probability increases from

46.8 percent to 89.4 percent while his rank increases from 91 to 45. Furthermore, we observe that the elimination of the negative effects of ethnicity causes Willie Hernandez, Camilo Pasqual, and Juan Pizzaro now to be ranked in the top half (above .525) of the distribution of 159 pitchers.

We offer the same two observations we provided when discussing the hitters' sample. First, since the decision to cast a vote for a pitcher appears to be affected by the pitcher's ethnicity, Latin pitchers on the ballot in any year may be disproportionately limited for future Hall of Fame consideration given the current 5 percent minimum vote rule. Second, if a sufficient number of baseball writers base their decision to cast a vote on the pitcher's ethnicity (or race), the number of votes a player receives and, consequently, whether the player is ever elected to the Hall of Fame may also be affected by the player's ethnicity (or race). We now turn our attention to the effects of the pitcher's race or ethnicity on the percentage of Hall of Fame votes received and on the probability of being elected to the Hall of Fame.

In the second stage of our statistical analysis for pitchers we, again, formulate our four different dependent variables, though we only report results from the FVOTES and HIVOTES specifications.[23] We include the following explanatory variables which were also included and defined in the first-stage analysis: WINS, LOSSES, SAVES, ERA, STRIKES, HITS, SEASONS, NOHIT, BOTH, SIZE, BLACK, and LATIN.

We add the following explanatory variables. GOLD equals the number of Gold Gloves the pitcher received during his career and is thus a measure of the pitcher's defensive ability. LCTEAM equals the number of seasons the pitcher played on a team that appeared in the World Series and thus represents not only a measure of post-season play and the relative success of the pitcher's teams but also the increased media exposure the player would receive during his career in these games.

Finally, since we have a reduced number of performance variables, we construct two types of interaction terms. First, we include race/ethnicity-WINS and race/ethnicity-SAVES terms to examine whether racial or ethnic discrimination varies by level of performance. Second, we include race/ethnicity-time interaction terms to examine whether any racial or ethnic discrimination varies over time.[24]

Appendix C contains the results from the two different dependent variables we use to investigate whether any racial or ethnic bias exists in the percentage of votes received by eligible baseball players or in the probability that eligible players are ever elected into the Baseball Hall of Fame for our sample of 159 pitchers. Once again, we present our conclusions in summary form only.

We examine first whether the effect of the pitcher's performance on the first-year voting percentage and the highest voting percentage varies by race or ethnicity when we assume that any effects of race or ethnicity do not change over time; see the first and third columns of Appendix C. First, the two most frequently discussed measures of pitcher performance and, coincidentally, the two variables for which the coefficient estimates are always statistically significant are WINS and SAVES. Second, the estimated coefficients on BLACK and LATIN suggest that the pitcher's race or ethnicity, independent of the level of performance, has a negative effect on the first-year voting percentage. Third, the estimated coefficients on BLACK suggest that the pitcher's race (but not ethnicity) has a negative effect on the highest voting percentage.

Fourth, the positive and statistically significant coefficients on the BLACK-WINS, BLACK-SAVES, LATIN-WINS and LATIN-SAVES interaction variables indicate that the discrimination we observe *decreases* as the pitcher's productivity, as measured by career wins and saves, increases. Finally, the negative coefficient on TIME (T) suggests that the standards for admission to the Hall of Fame as determined by the voters of the BBWAA have increased over time.

The second and fourth conclusions indicate that for the first-year voting percentage racial and ethnic bias exists but that this bias disappears the more productive (in terms of wins and saves) the black and Latin pitcher. The third and fourth conclusions indicate that for the highest voting percentage racial bias exists but that this bias disappears the more productive (in terms of saves) the black pitcher. Ethnic bias does not exist for the highest voting percentage.

The final conclusion indicates that today's writers simply have higher standards than those of their predecessors. Another plausible explanation is that the expansion in the number of games and in the number of teams has made it easier for a player to obtain a given level of performance. Writers, recognizing this possible dilution of talent, respond by adjusting how they evaluate players' career statistics. Moreover, as the number of players increases over time, it may become more difficult for a player to reach the top category of his generation. Since writers may vote for no more than 10 players, the standards will rise as the number of players increases, assuming that the distribution of talent is stable.

We examine second whether the effect of the pitcher's performance on the first-year voting percentage and the highest voting percentage varies by race or ethnicity when we allow any effects of race or ethnicity to vary over time; see the second and fourth columns of Appendix C. First, we continue to observe the statistical importance of WINS and SAVES. Second, the estimated coefficients on BLACK and LATIN suggest that the pitcher's race or ethnicity, independent of the level of performance, has a negative effect on the first-year voting percentage. Third, the estimated coefficients on BLACK and LATIN suggest that the pitcher's race has a negative effect on the highest voting percentage. Fourth, the positive and statistically significant coefficients on the BLACK-WINS, BLACK-SAVES, LATIN-WINS and LATIN-SAVES interaction variables indicate that the discrimination we observe *decreases* as the pitcher's productivity, as measured by career wins and saves, increases.[25] Fifth, the negative coefficient on TIME (T) suggests for the first time that the standards for admission to the Hall of Fame as determined by the voters of the BBWAA have not increased over time. Sixth, given the insignificant coefficient on the BLACK-TIME variable, the negative effects of the pitcher's race on the first-year and highest vote percentages do not change over time. Finally, the negative and statistically significance coefficient of the LATIN-TIME interaction variable indicates that the negative effects of the player's ethnicity (on either the first-year voting percentage or the highest voting percentage) *increase* over time. The time dimension of this increased discrimination against Latin pitchers could potentially explain the declining voting percentage received by Luis Tiant during his years on the ballot.

Conclusion

The initial idea for our study came after we read a *Sports Illustrated* article about Henry Aaron who was elected to the Hall of Fame in 1982.[26] The article mentions a newspaper story kept by Aaron which "decries the terrible injustice that nine voters somehow thought Aaron wasn't worthy of Cooperstown, keeping the Home Run King from entering by unanimous vote." We pondered how a writer could not vote for the player who hit more home runs than any other player in the history of the game.

On April 15, 1947, Jackie Robinson broke the color line in major league baseball. Fifteen years later his impact on the history of the game continued when he became the first black player included on a Hall of Fame election ballot; the vote results of that same election also made Robinson the first black player inducted into the Baseball Hall of Fame. Robinson's impact on the integration of major league baseball has been well documented. Our analysis of Robinson's direct and indirect impact on the racial and ethnic composition of the Hall of Fame elections and on the number of minority players inducted to the Hall of Fame suggests that Robinson's legacy has also affected the National Baseball Hall of Fame.

Robinson's successful integration of major league baseball opened the doors for other highly qualified black and Latin players. As the number of black and Latin players has increased, we have witnessed an increase in the number of minority players on Hall of Fame ballots and an increase in the number of minority players elected to the Hall of Fame. Robinson's own participation in the Negro Leagues combined with his successful integration of major league baseball also facilitated an analysis of the careers of those players who played exclusively in the Negro Leagues. This comparison of the performances of Negro League players with the performances of Jackie Robinson and other black players who later played in the major leagues, we argue, contributed to the Hall of Fame induction of many of these Negro League players.

These increases in the participation of black and Latin players in major league baseball, the increases in the representation of black and Latin players on Hall of Fame ballots, and the increases in the number of black and Latin players inducted to the Hall of Fame do not, however, guarantee that a player's race or ethnicity does not affect his chances of being elected to the Hall of Fame.

In this paper, we investigate a largely unexplored source of potential bias, that is, racial or ethnic discrimination by the Baseball Writers' Association of America. Specifically, we use statistical analysis of baseball writers' voting behavior to determine whether black, Latin, and white major league baseball players receive the same consideration for membership to the Hall of Fame.

We find that a player's racial or ethnic status may have a significant effect on his vote outcomes at various stages of his eligibility. When conducting the first stage of our analysis, we obtain evidence that black hitters and Latin pitchers have a significantly lower probability of ever receiving at least one Hall of Fame vote. In the second stage of our analysis, we find that the hitter's racial or ethnic status does not affect the voting percentage or the probability that the hitter will be elected to the Hall of Fame. We do obtain evidence, however, which indicates that the race and ethnicity of the pitcher can affect the pitcher's voting percentage. We also find that discrimination against Latin pitchers has increased over time. In short, the results suggest that race and ethnicity sometimes matter.

It is beyond the scope of this paper to investigate the effects of race/ethnicity–based voting on baseball fans. At the same time, we would argue that if race/ethnicity–based voting has occurred, the race or ethnicity of a player may have influenced how some writers described the abilities and accomplishments of players. Writers who indulged in racial or ethnic preferences in their columns could then influence fans' perceptions of minority players and, therefore, indirectly influence the amount of customer discrimination. In addition to these observations, there is some other evidence that broadcast sports journalists harbor many of the racial and ethnic stereotypes that are common among the general public.[27]

Appendix A: Probit Estimates of the Probability the Player Ever Received at Least One Hall of Fame Vote During His Years of Eligibility

A. First-Stage Analysis for Hitters

Vote= - 2.95*** + .0023 Hits*** - .006 Doubles* + .012 Triples* + .0042 Homers***
     (4.53)   (2.88)   (1.55)   (1.53)   (2.50)

    + .0003 Stolen - .039 Seasons + .113 Gold** + .035 World*** + .006 Both
     (0.19)   (0.72)   (1.81)   (2.43)   (0.03)

    + .531 League** + 1.50 Mgrcoach*** - .841 Black*** - .182 Latin
     (2.43)   (5.23)   (2.78)   (0.47)

N = 296
Percent Correct Predictions = .84
Log of Likelihood Ratio = -96.3

B. First-Stage Analysis for Pitchers

Vote= - 6.856*** + .0267 Wins** - .0126 Losses + .0167 Saves***
     (2.88)   (2.00)   (0.90)   (3.06)

    | .0058 Compgames + 1.1586 ERA* + .0006 Strikes - .0013 Hits
     (0.74)   (1.96)   (1.02)   (1.22)

    + .0686 Seasons + .3019 Win20* + .9483 Nohit***
     (0.85)   (1.50)   (2.40)

    + .0304 Wsinnings** - .1182 Both + .00102 Size*
     (2.02)   (0.42)   (1.53)

    - .3349 Black - 1.329 Latin**
     (0.68)   (1.99)

N = 159
Percent Correct Predictions = .78
Log of Likelihood Ratio = -64.1

*Notes: The absolute value of the t-statistics are in parentheses. * indicates $p < 0.10$; ** indicates $p < 0.05$; and *** indicates $p < 0.01$. We use one-tail significance tests for each of the estimated coefficients except for the coefficients of the sample selectivity bias (λ), Both, Seasons, Black and Latin variables.*

Appendix B: Second-Stage Results for Hitters

Independent Variables	FVOTES	HIVOTES	LVOTES	ELECTED
INTERCEPT	-58.48***	-49.78***	-51.33***	20.97***
	(6.56)	(4.22)	(4.40)	(3.44)
HITS	.0142***	.0301***	.02994***	.0063***
	(3.17)	(5.91)	(5.98)	(2.41)
HOMERS	.1037***	.0877***	.0885***	.0370***
	(7.23)	(4.71)	(4.74)	(3.42)
STOLEN	.0348**	.0209*	.0203*	.0080**
	(2.25)	(1.45)	(1.40)	(1.69)
MIDINF	11.64***	12.17***	13.26***	6.686***
	(3.62)	(3.28)	(3.60)	(2.81)
GOLD	1.352**	.9099*	.9863*	.2660*
	(1.99)	(1.49)	(1.60)	(1.31)
WORLD	.4102***	.3485***	.3465***	-.0621
	(3.93)	(2.58)	(2.69)	(1.00)
SEASONS	.9463	.054	.1986	.0215
	(1.49)	(0.06)	(0.25)	(0.04)
BOTH	-7.498***	-9.59***	-8.798***	-3.14
	(2.85)	(2.96)	(2.78)	(1.11)
BLACK	3.222	.0335	1.073	2.078
	(0.81)	(0.01)	(0.25)	(1.28)
LATIN	4.077	4.53	5.299	1.229
	(0.86)	(0.81)	(0.96)	(0.51)
TIME(T)	-.4337***	-.799***	-.9058***	-.3839***
	(3.12)	(4.67)	(5.22)	(3.00)
λ	16.62***	12.99***	13.85***	2.788
	(5.34)	(3.28)	(3.51)	(0.76)
$\overline{R^2}$	.63	.60	.61	.86

Independent Variables	FVOTES	HIVOTES	LVOTES	ELECTED
F	26.75	23.88	24.83	
s_ε	16.97	20.48	20.11	
N	186	186	186	186
Predictions				.97
Log of Likelihood Function				-12.64

Appendix C: Second-Stage Results for Pitchers

Independent Variables	FVOTES	FVOTES	HIVOTES	HIVOTES
WINS (W)	.5524***	.5556***	.5156**	.5258**
	(4.42)	(4.35)	(2.33)	(2.36)
SAVES (S)	.2751***	.2735***	.2944***	.2895***
	(8.07)	(7.83)	(5.57)	(5.51)
BLACK	-35.167***	-34.863***	-28.787**	-30.206*
	(3.72)	(4.04)	(2.29)	(1.73)
LATIN	-176.589***	-198.261***	-189.083	-329.132***
	(4.50)	(6.16)	(1.63)	(5.68)
BLACK*W	.1181***	.1184***	.0919	.0909
	(2.77)	(2.91)	(1.57)	(1.56)
LATIN*W	.7782***	1.007***	.8400	2.193***
	(4.39)	(4.94)	(1.63)	(5.29)
BLACK*S	2.348***	2.334***	2.843***	2.839***
	(2.75)	(3.23)	(2.75)	(2.88)
LATIN*S	.6986***	1.106***	.7926	3.055***
	(3.78)	(4.17)	(1.39)	(5.32)
TIME (T)	-.1270	-.1182	-.4778**	-.4504
	(0.87)	(0.72)	(1.68)	(1.46)
BLACK*T		-.0190		.0579
		(0.06)		(0.07)
LATIN*T		-1.731**		-9.230***
		(2.08)		(4.68)
$\bar{R}^2$	.71	.84	.75	.75
F	10.92	29.91	14.07	12.92
Independent Variables	**FVOTES**	**FVOTES**	**HIVOTES**	**HIVOTES**
s_ε	10.95	11.08	16.42	16.39
N	89	89	89	89

Note: Each of the above equations also includes the following variables: CONSTANT, LOSSES, ERA, STRIKES, HITS, SEASONS, GOLD, NOHIT, LCTEAM, BOTH, SIZE and λ.

Notes

1. The BBWAA screening committee existed from 1968 to 1978 and was revived in 1981. Starting with the 1996 election, Veterans Committee candidates must have received votes on at least 60 percent of the ballots in any given year or received at least 100 votes in any election prior to 1992. The Veterans Committee candidates are eligible for election three years after their BBWAA eligibility expires.

2. In his recent book, *Memories of Summer*, Roger Kahn indicates that in 1952 Joe Black should have been selected the Most Valuable Player in the National League. Kahn recounts that many white baseball writers, particularly from the Midwest, voted instead for Hank Sauer of the Chicago Cubs.

3. Harry Edwards, 1973, p. 255.

4. We obtain playing position and career batting average in the Negro Leagues from James A. Riley's *The Biographical Encyclopedia of The Negro Baseball Leagues.*

5. For example, although Jackie Robinson spent only one year in the Negro Leagues, different sources report different career batting averages for him!

6. See Jules Tygiel's *Baseball's Great Experiment: Jackie Robinson and His Legacy*, p. 64.

7. The first hitters born in a Latin American country to appear on the ballot were Bobby Avila and Chico Carrasquel in 1966. The first pitcher born in a Latin American country to appear on the ballot was Camilo Pasqual in 1977. We did not include in our pitcher's sample Dolph Luque, who was born in Cuba and who pitched in the major leagues between 1914 and 1935. Luque received votes between 1937 and 1939 and between 1952 and 1960.

8. Unfortunately, newspapers have only recently listed the players who do not receive votes. With the assistance of Jeff Idelson, Ralph Insinga, and Steven Gietschier, we have obtained the names of all voteless hitters who were on the ballot between 1964 and 1996 and the names of all voteless pitchers who were on the ballot between 1966 and 1996.

9. *Rules for Election to The National Baseball Hall of Fame by Members of The Baseball Writers' Association of America.*

10. We find that the negative and highly statistical significant coefficient on BLACK is insensitive to the use of alternative measures of career performance. When we estimate alternative specifications of our first-stage equation, the negative effect of the black player's race on his probability of ever receiving at least one Hall of Fame vote ranged between 11 percent and 19 percent.

11. Bill Deane, 1995, p. 242.

12. Although we include the BBWAA vote totals of any player elected into the Hall of Fame by the Committee on Baseball Veterans, these players are not classified as elected (by the BBWAA) into the Hall for this study.

13. The Jackie Robinson quotation comes from the 29 January 1962 issue of *Newsweek*.

14. The Perez and Lang quotations come from Goodwin (1997). Other members of the BBWAA have views similar to those of Lang. For example, as reported by Bass (1997), Jack O'Connell, secretary treasurer of the BBWAA, states, in response to Perez's comments, that "I've never heard of that kind of prejudice. There are Latin players in the Hall."

15. When we attempted to obtain information about Hall of Fame voters, Jack Lang, then-secretary of the BBWAA, informed us that it has been and will continue to be the policy of the BBWAA to maintain the anonymity of the vote decisions of each

writer. Lang also indicated that it would be against the policy of the BBWAA to provide any information about the voters.

16. The Perez quotation comes from Whiteside (1996).

17. This footnote contains technical information that will be of interest only to the statistical specialist. First, from 1960 to 1968, a "run-off" election was used if no eligible player received the necessary 75 percent of the votes. In those years when a "run-off" election took place, we include the vote totals from the first election. Second, several of the players in our sample are still eligible for election into the Hall. For these players, it is still possible that they may receive a higher voting percentage (or even be elected into the Hall) in a future election. Finally, we estimate the FVOTES, HIVOTES and LVOTES equations using Heckman's two-step procedure and White's procedure to obtain sample selectivity corrected estimates and heteroskedastic-consistent estimates of the standard errors. We estimate the ELECTED equations using the binary logic estimation procedure.

18. The interested reader can obtain from the authors an earlier version of the paper which goes into much more detail about the statistical procedures and the analysis of the statistical results.

19. We should note, however, that results obtained by Findlay and Reid (1997), who (in addition to examining alternative measures of the dependent variables) estimate non-linear specifications of the voting percentages equations, indicate that the race and ethnicity of the hitters do affect the voting percentages and the probability the player will be elected to the Hall. These equations, however, are beyond the scope of this paper.

20. We include only no-hitters of nine innings or more that are not shared with other pitchers.

21. The only surprising result is the positive and statistically significant coefficient on the ERA variable.

22. We find that the negative and statistically significant coefficient on LATIN is insensitive to the use of alternative measures of career performance. When we estimate alternative specifications of our first-stage equation, the negative effect of the Latin pitcher's ethnicity on his probability of ever receiving at least one Hall of Fame vote ranged from 26.1 percent to 33.8 percent.

23. The results for the LVOTES specification are similar to those for the FVOTES and HIVOTES specifications. In contrast to the results for FVOTES and HIVOTES, none of the race, ethnicity, and interaction variables is significant in the ELECTED equations. We, therefore, do not report the results for the ELECTED equations. Since our primary interest lies with the effects of race and ethnicity on voting behavior (and to save space), we only report the estimated coefficients for the WINS, SAVES, race, ethnicity, time, and interaction variables. As we mentioned earlier, the interested reader can obtain from the authors the complete results.

24. When we do not include these interaction terms, we find that the pitcher's race or ethnicity has no effect on the voting percentages and on the probability of being elected to the Hall.

25. The coefficient on BLACK*W in the HIVOTES specification is close to being statistically significant.

26. See Mike Capuzzo, "A Prisoner of Memory," *Sports Illustrated*, December 7, 1992.

27. For an excellent short book on racial bias by media and coaches, see Hoose (1989).

References

Andersen, Torben, "Race Discrimination by Major League Baseball Fans: Evidence from All-Star Voting Data," unpublished manuscript, 1992.

Andersen, Torben, and Sumner J. La Croix, "Customer Racial Discrimination in Major League Baseball," *Economic Inquiry*, Vol. 29, October 1991, pp. 665–677.

Banaian, King, and William Luksetich, "Sportswriters and Customer Discrimination in Major League Baseball: Evidence from Voting for the Hall of Fame," unpublished manuscript, 1994.

Barry, Roger, "Time to Restructure The Baseball Hall of Fame," *The Patriot Ledger*, January 21, 1982.

The Baseball Encyclopedia, Tenth Edition, New York: Macmillan Publishing Company, 1996.

Bass, Mike, "Team Report: Cincinnati Reds," *The Sporting News*, January 11, 1997.

Becker, Gary S., *The Economics of Discrimination*, 2nd edition, Chicago: The University of Chicago Press, 1971.

Capuzzo, Mike, "A Prisoner of Memory," *Sports Illustrated*, December 7, 1992.

Deane, Bill, "Awards and Honors," in *Total Baseball*, Fourth Edition, Edited by John Thorn and Pete Palmer with Michael Gershman, New York: Warner Books, Inc., 1995.

Deane, Bill, "Hall of Fame Election Rules," not dated.

Edwards, Harry, *Sociology of Sport*, Homewood, IL: The Dorsey Press, 1973.

Findlay, David W., and Clifford E. Reid, "Voting Behavior, Discrimination and the National Baseball Hall of Fame: An Examination of Pitchers," Working Paper, Colby College, 1996.

Findlay, David W., and Clifford E. Reid, "Voting Behavior, Discrimination and The National Baseball Hall of Fame," *Economic Inquiry*, Vol. XXXV, 1997, July 1997, pp. 562–578.

Gammons, Peter, "Reaching out to Hispanics a Yankee Problem," *The Sunday Boston Globe*, July 17, 1994.

Goodwin, Peter, "Sports Log," *The Boston Globe*, January 8, 1997.

Heckman, James, "Sample Selection Bias as a Specification Error," *Econometrica*, Vol. 47, January 1979, pp. 153–161.

Hoose, Phillip M., *Necessities: Racial Barriers in American Sports*, New York: Random House, 1989.

James, Bill, *The Politics of Glory: How Baseball's Hall of Fame Really Works*, New York: Macmillan Publishing Company, 1994.

Kahn, Lawrence M., "Discrimination in Professional Sports: A Survey of the Literature," *Industrial and Labor Relations Review*, Vol. 44, April 1991, pp. 395–418.

Kahn, Roger, *Memories of Summer*, New York: Hyperion, 1997.

Lang, Jack, "BBWAA to Veterans: Don't Put Our Rejects in Hall," *The Sporting News*, February 19, 1990.

Nardinelli, Clark, and Curtis Simon, "Customer Racial Discrimination in the Market for Memorabilia: The Case of Baseball," *The Quarterly Journal of Economics*, Vol. 105, August 1990, pp. 575–595.

Total Baseball, Fourth Edition, edited by John Thorn and Pete Palmer with Michael Gersham, New York: Viking, 1995.

Tygiel, Jules, *Baseball's Great Experiment: Jackie Robinson and His Legacy*, New York: Oxford University Press, 1983.

Riley, James A., *The Biographical Encyclopedia of the Negro Baseball Leagues*, New York: Carroll & Graf Publishers, Inc., 1994.

White, Halbert, "A Heteroskedasticity-Consistent Covariance Matrix and a Direct Test for Heteroskedasticity," *Econometrica*, Vol. 48, 1980, pp. 721–746.

Whiteside, Larry, "Hall Voters throw a Shutout," *The Boston Globe*, January 9, 1996.

Wulf, Steve, "Pops, Yes ... but the Spaceman?", *Sports Illustrated*, January 25, 1988.

The Great Experiment
Fifty Years Later

Jules Tygiel

Fifty years have passed since Jackie Robinson boldly seized the conscience and imagination of the nation. More than a decade has transpired since my own rendering of this tale appeared in 1983. Mine was, of course, far from the first chronicle of this momentous epic. A *New York Times* reviewer referred to *Baseball's Great Experiment,* not unflatteringly, as the "three dozenth repetition" of the Robinson saga.[1] During the past thirteen years, there have been, in one form or another, dozens of additional retellings, a torrent which will turn into a flood during the coming fiftieth-anniversary commemorations.

As my friend and fellow historian Steve Riess has commented, the Jackie Robinson story is to Americans what the Passover story is to Jews: it must be told to every generation so that we never forget. But if this is true, and it most assuredly is, what is it that we must not forget? The subtitle for *Baseball's Great Experiment* was *Jackie Robinson and His Legacy.* What, however, is the legacy of Jackie Robinson fifty years after his triumph, in an America in which the Voting Rights Act, school busing, affirmative action, and other integration strategies find themselves increasingly on the defensive; an America in which black nationalism and separatism, the antithesis of Robinson's vision, win a welcome audience in African-American communities; an America in which the tenets of *Brown v. Board of Education*, the cornerstone judicial ruling of the civil rights era, are challenged by the sole African-American Supreme Court justice?

Ironically, amidst this growing retreat from integrationist values, Jackie Robinson has become, if possible, even more of a national icon, more firmly embedded in American culture than ever before. His name itself has long since entered our language as a synonym for the first to enter a field, the pathbreaker, the pioneer. At least three statues of Robinson have appeared: in Los Angeles, in Daytona Beach, Florida, and in Montreal, where a sculpted Robinson holds the hands of two children, one black and one white. Public schools, like the Jackie Robinson Academy in Long Beach, California, and the Jackie Robinson Junior High School in Brooklyn, bear his name. The Library of Congress lists fifteen books published about Jackie Robinson since 1983, thirteen of them addressed to juvenile and young adult readers.[2] Indeed, he has become a staple of social studies courses, usually segregated, ironically, into the annual celebration of African-American history month. There have been two television movies (including *The Court-Martial of Jackie Robinson*, in which Joe Louis and Dodger scout Clyde Sukeforth improbably wait outside a 1944 Texas military hearing room for the fateful verdict), a murder mystery (*The Plot to Kill Jackie Robinson*),[3] a mercifully short-lived Broadway musical entitled *The First*, and at least two itinerant one-man shows devoted to his life.

Just as each generation has retold the Jackie Robinson story, each has reinterpreted his character and contributions. From the start, Robinson has always assumed not just heroic but biblical proportions. In the 1940s and 1950s, many in both the black and white communities saw Robinson as a Moses, leading his people out of the wilderness to the promised land. In the years before Martin Luther King, Jr., Robinson, more than any other individual, personified the era's liberal optimism and reaffirmed the possibility of racial integration.

Historian Lerone Bennett has commented, "Integration has never been tried in this country. It has not even been defined."[4] But for millions of Americans the experiment launched by Branch Rickey and Jackie Robinson not only defined integration but created an allegory for the nation's future. Their bold enterprise rested on several fundamental, and soon to be widely shared, assumptions: discrimination, not racial inferiority, blocked African American advancement; the removal of discriminatory barriers would allow blacks to demonstrate their talents and prove their worth; white participants and observers, although initially resistant, would, in the words of Alexander Pope, often quoted by Branch Rickey, "first endure," but "then embrace" first the standard bearer and then the concept of integration; success would inspire (and indeed necessitate) emulation among rivals and embolden other African Americans to challenge racial strictures. These Joshuas, accepting the mantle of leadership from

Robinson's Moses, would bring the walls of Jim Crow tumbling down. Rickey and Robinson consciously crafted this parable; Robinson's charismatic dynamism infused it with substance. At least in its early stages, the Robinson saga offered a blueprint for liberal dreams of racial equality in post–World War II America.

Conservatives as well as liberals could embrace this allegory. This drama, after all, had been enacted by a pair of men usually identified as Republicans. Rickey, throughout his life, endorsed conservative causes.[5] Robinson endeared himself to Republicans by his ill-conceived 1949 denunciation of Paul Robeson and support for Richard Nixon in 1960. Even in Robinson's more characteristically moderate political mode, he maintained a Republican affiliation and advocated the virtues of American capitalism. More significantly, the integration of the Brooklyn Dodgers embodied several traditional conservative themes: individual achievement, meritocracy, and progress without government interference. As late as 1950, Rickey (who would later support civil rights laws) wrote, "As I see it, legislative force can delay rather than accelerate the solution" to the nation's racial problems.[6] The Robinson saga thus united people across a broad political spectrum. What other American fable could elicit encomiums over one four-day period, as Robinson's did in 1987, from George Will, William Safire, and the Communist *Daily Worker*?[7]

Robinson's triumph had a profound effect on African Americans, further cementing the dominance of integrationist values. Black nationalist and separatist visions had proliferated in the 1920s with Marcus Garvey and others and would resurface in the 1960s with Malcolm X. But these philosophies reached a nadir in public support in the post–World War II years.[8] Integrationist thought reigned virtually unopposed in black America in the 1940s and 1950s.

The strange career of Negro League historiography illustrates this phenomenon. In the 1960s most Americans had forgotten that the Negro Leagues had ever existed. As late as 1982, the essential Negro League library consisted of a handful of titles.[9] Recent years, however, have witnessed an unprecedented celebration of baseball in the Jim Crow era. Dozens of books, including general overviews, oral histories, encyclopedias, photo books, several excellent team histories, numerous biographies and autobiographies, reprints of long-out-of-print classics like Sol White's 1906 *History of Colored Baseball*, and many volumes devoted to a juvenile and young adult audience, have appeared.[10] Both the Macmillan *Baseball Encyclopedia* and *Total Baseball* now include Negro League sections. Several documentaries, including Ken Burns' *Baseball*, have described black baseball. August Wilson's Pulitzer Prize–winning play, *Fences*, employed the frustration of the Negro League star as its central motif. Major League teams host Negro League reunions, and former players are featured guests at card shows and autograph sessions. The sale of Negro League uniform replicas has become a flourishing business. In short, Jim Crow baseball has at long last been integrated into the American cultural mainstream.

The new Negro League history reminds us of the vitality of black baseball before Jackie Robinson and the dual tragedy often noted by Sam Lacey. "I felt that not only were blacks deprived of the opportunity to make some money," laments the great African-American sportswriter, "but that whites were being deprived of the opportunity to see these fellows perform.... Both were being cheated."[11]

But a revisionist streak that stands the traditional Robinson saga on its head runs through many of these accounts. In this version, Rickey and Robinson emerge as the villains who destroyed the Negro Leagues.[12] Rickey, motivated neither by idealism nor a desire to win pennants, selfishly sought to prevent Negro League teams from attracting potential Brooklyn Dodger fans. When his attempts to become the czar of an all-black United States League failed, according to one variation, he cut his losses by signing some of the players he had scouted. Even those who accept the United States League as a smokescreen see Rickey's primary goal as capturing the Negro League Market. Rickey compounded this strategy by raiding the black teams and refusing to pay, or underpaying, Negro League owners for rights to their players. Robinson receives credit for his courage and pathbreaking role but, because of his unflinching support of Rickey's strategies and his own pointed criticisms of the Negro Leagues, is cast as an ingrate to the institution which had kept baseball alive in black America.

Many of these studies take their lead from playwright Amiri Baraka, who recalled the Negro Leagues as "extensions of all of us, there, in a way that the Yankees and Dodgers and what not could never be ... the collective black aura that only can be duplicated with black conversation or music."[13] Sociologist Harry Edwards, questioning the process that Rickey employed, notes the great paradox of baseball integration: that by destroying the Negro Leagues, integration limited, rather than expanded, opportunities for blacks in baseball. Since organized baseball initially culled only the top African-American stars and for decades failed to hire blacks as managers, coaches, and scouts, far fewer blacks earned their living from baseball after 1950 than at any previous time in the twentieth century. Edwards argues that an alternative plan for integration that incorporated the Negro Leagues into organized baseball might better have served black America.[14]

A 1996 conference presentation asked: "Could the Negro Leagues

Have Been Saved?"[15] But what is significant is how seldom this question, or its corollary, "Should the Negro Leagues be saved?," was asked during the 1940s and 1950s. What distinguishes Baraka's paean to the spirit of the Negro Leagues is its rarity. While Baraka and others have crafted a nostalgia for black baseball, few in the 1940s posited it as a preferable alternative to major league integration. Edwards's proposition for prolonging the Negro Leagues, even in the unlikely event that it would have been feasible, is strikingly similar to that of obstructionist New York Yankee owner Larry MacPhail in 1946, who offered a similar suggestion as a means to forestall desegregation. MacPhail's solution was universally criticized by black and white advocates of equality.

The baseball model, fears Edwards, implied that "overall Black integration into the mainstream of American life [would] necessarily demand the denigration, abandonment and ultimate collapse of parallel Black institutions."[16] But unlike other African-American entities such as black churches, music, and colleges that survived and flourished after the civil rights years, the Negro Leagues lacked any legitimacy outside of a segregationist context. Robinson's critique of the Negro Leagues stemmed not from any personal hostility to African-American culture but from his perception of these teams as Jim Crow institutions. Most African Americans agreed. What killed the Negro Leagues was not Rickey's calculated callousness, nor Robinson's ingratitude, but the clearly stated preference of black fans for even the barest rudiments of an interracial alternative.

Thus, in the 1950s and early 1960s, integration became the only game in town. As professional and major college sports increasingly became dominated by African-American athletes and as the civil rights movement scored victory after victory in the courts, in the streets, and ultimately in the Congress, Americans celebrated Jackie Robinson as the prophet of these advances. A closer look at the racial realities of baseball, however, foretold the difficulties awaiting the broader society. Given the spectacular success of the first black players to reach the majors, desegregation of most clubs advanced with remarkable hesitancy. Many teams adopted a *de facto* quota system limiting black access and disproportionately relegating blacks to specific positions. While superstar African-American athletes experienced minimal difficulty reaching the major leagues, those of average and even above average talent often lost out to less-talented whites. Racism and discrimination plagued black players in spring training, off-field accommodations, fan reactions, salaries, and endorsement opportunities. Most tellingly, major league organizations made no efforts, and apparently gave minimal thought, to bring blacks into coaching, managing, front office, or ownership roles. Robinson's repeated critiques of these conditions won him further praise from some but a growing enmity and disdain from others. In a society experimenting with new visions of race relations, Robinson, and sports in general, continued to symbolize the possibilities, rather than the limitations, of integration.

In the 1960s, Robinson remained a heroic figure to the majority of Americans, both black and white. To a new generation of black national-ists and other 1960s radicals, however, he increasingly assumed the garb of a false prophet. In November 1963 Malcolm X savagely attacked Robin-son in an "Open Letter" in the *Amsterdam News*, as the creation of a suc-cession of "White Boss(es)," for whom he was "still trying to win 'The Big Game.'" Robinson, alleged Malcolm, had "never shown appreciation for the support given [him] by the Negro masses." Robinson had misled African Americans in the Robeson incident, the Nixon campaign, and now his alliance with Nelson Rockefeller. "Just who are you playing ball for today, good Friend?" taunted Malcolm.[17] Amiri Baraka would later deride Robinson as a "synthetic colored guy" who was "imperfected" at the "Cal-ifornia laboratories of USC" whose "ersatz 'blackness' could represent the shadow of the Negro integrating into America."[18]

It is not surprising that Robinson would become a target of radicals in the 1960s. The assault on Robinson by black nationalists reflected not merely his perceived political misdeeds or shift to the right but two fun-damentally different world views. Robinson had committed his life to a heartfelt belief in the malleability of United States society and the poten-tial inclusiveness of the American Dream. Malcolm X and others during the sixties had jettisoned these visions and rummaged through a stockpile of competing ideologies for alternatives.

Ironically, militant critics ignored how central Robinson had made the message of black pride and identification to his mystique. There was noth-ing "ersatz" about Jackie Robinson; he was the genuine article. he had been molded not at the "laboratories of USC" but on the mean streets of Pasadena, the uneven playing fields of UCLA, and the Jim Crow buses of the United States Army. At the core of Robinson's strength and image lay his ability to compromise and accommodate without losing his essential dignity and identity. Indeed, it was Robinson's unrelenting insistence on asserting his blackness that had elevated his athletic triumph into a soci-etal emblem.

To Robinson, integration always embodied equal participation in, rather than total submission to, American culture. In the heady integra-tionist atmosphere of the 1950s, Jackie and Rachel Robinson opted to reside in the white suburbs of Connecticut. But Jackie's primary energies and commitment always revolved around black America. Robinson countered the political goals of black separatism with a vision of black capitalism, in which African-American investors, helped by sympathetic whites and government assistance, would create black-owned businesses, employ black workers, generate demand among the black masses, and raise the general level of prosperity, education, and opportunity among the nation's black population. Unlike Marcus Garvey or Elijah Muhammed, who also advocated black enterprise, Robinson overoptimistically envisioned these undertakings as a wedge into full and equal participation in American society, rather than as the basis for a separate economy.[19] And, unlike some contemporary African-American conservatives, Robinson never lost sight of the need for government assistance to overcome the legacy of past discrimination to achieve these ends.

In the early 1970s Robinson assumed yet another biblical persona: that of Job, upon whom untold sufferings had descended to test his faith. His first-born son had succumbed to drug addiction and then met an untimely death. Robinson's body was wracked by diabetes and heart ailments, his hair snow white, his eyesight fading. Roger Kahn, in *The Boys of Summer*, which introduced the Robinson saga to yet another generation, memorably described having to slow his own pace "so as not to walk too quickly" for the ailing Robinson.[20]

Most dishearteningly, Robinson had come to realize that this Moses had gone to the mountaintop, but that neither he nor his people would be allowed to enter the promised land. The game in which he had placed his hopes still neglected blacks for managerial positions. The movement to which he had devoted his life seemed in disarray. His onetime political ally, Richard Nixon, now sat in the White House, the beneficiary of "white backlash" and suitor of a "Southern strategy." The limitations of black capitalism had grown apparent. While a significant number of African Americans had been able to take advantage of the opportunities that Robinson, in no small measure, had helped engender, the persistence of poverty and the bleak descent of black urban communities into drugs, crime, and violence had begun, claiming his namesake child as an early victim.

"I cannot possibly believe that I have it made while so many black brothers and sisters are hungry, inadequately housed, insufficiently clothed, denied their dignity as they live in slums or barely exist on welfare," he wrote in his angry 1972 autobiography. Yet if Robinson's trials and disappointments had sorely shaken his faith, they had not broken it. Amidst his disillusionment about the progress of the "great experiment" he had started, Robinson nonetheless professed his hope "that some day the pendulum will swing back to the time when America seemed ready to make an effort to be a united state."[21]

His death in 1972, at age fifty-three, completed the biblical cycle. To many, Robinson's youthful sacrifices, his role as standard bearer, and his unnatural pact with Rickey to withhold retribution had precipitated his physical decline and caused his premature passing. Jackie Robinson, they said, had died for our sins. Upon his death, Robinson ascended to the heaven reserved for the saints of American folklore. His faults and mistakes would be forgotten, his accomplishments repeatedly celebrated and romanticized. Even better, those who chose to honor him need no longer contend with his insistent voice reminding them that they had denied him his full testament, as did major league baseball at the 1972 World Series. Or so they thought.

On Opening Day 1987, major league baseball planned a fortieth-anniversary commemoration of Robinson's historic debut. Ceremonies would be held at each stadium to remind a new generation of his struggles and triumphs. Robinson's number, 42, would adorn the second-base bag prior to all games. But baseball learned, yet again, that the legacy of Jackie Robinson remained a double-edged sword. On the evening before the festivities, Los Angeles Dodger vice-president Al Campanis appeared on ABC's *Nightline* with Ted Koppel. Campanis had played shortstop alongside Robinson with the Montreal Royals in 1946 and now guided the team that had integrated the game. Yet when Koppel asked him, "Why is it that there are no black managers, no black general managers, no black owners?" Campanis responded, "I truly believe that they may not have the necessities to be, let's say, a field manager, or perhaps a general manager." When Koppel proffered Campanis "another chance to dig yourself out," the old shortstop buried himself deeper, describing African-American musculature and questioning the desire of blacks to assume leadership positions.

The Campanis debacle laid bare baseball's hiring practices in a manner that not even Robinson himself could have achieved. Only one team had a black manager, and only one African-American, Frank Robinson, had served a significant stint as a field manager. Among the top 879 administrative positions in baseball, blacks filled only seventeen; Hispanics held another fifteen. Four teams in California — the Dodgers, Giants, Athletics, and Angels — accounted for almost two-thirds of all minority hiring. Ten out of fourteen American League teams and five of twelve National League franchises had no African-Americans in management positions.[22] Although few major league executives would have been so intemperate as to state the obvious as Campanis, his comments clearly reflected a widely held sentiment.

Stunned by the national outcry evoked by the *Nightline* broadcast,

Baseball Commissioner Peter Ueberroth vowed to remedy the situation. Black and Latino former players and their allies within organized baseball formed a Minority Baseball Network to pressure clubs to hire more minorities for front office jobs. The National League named former St. Louis Cardinal star Bill White as president.

During the late 1980s these efforts bore little fruit, but the 1990s produced a more substantial harvest. By 1993 blacks and Hispanics held seven of twenty-eight major league managerial positions. The success of these pioneers as a group was phenomenal, dispelling lingering notions of African-American inadequacies and insufficient "necessities." Cito Gaston, in his first five years as manager of the Toronto Blue Jays, won four divisional championships, two pennants, and two World Series. Dusty Baker of the San Francisco Giants and Don Baylor of the Colorado Rockies both won manger-of-the-year awards. Progress extended into other areas of hiring as well. By 1995, 27 percent of all coaches were black or Latino. Minority hiring in the front office expanded to 17 percent in 1992, a level that held steady through 1994.[23]

Nonetheless, race relations in baseball remain far from ideal. As is characteristic of most American industries, minority ownership is nonexistent. All twenty-eight chief executive officers are white. Bob Watson, who guided the New York Yankees to the World Series Championship in 1996, is the sole minority general manager. African-American players still voice complaints about discriminatory treatment.

In addition, the spotlight on managerial positions masked an equally disturbing development: the decline of baseball as a force in the black community. Ironically, as African-American athletes came to constitute an overwhelming majority of players in college and professional football and basketball, the proportion of American-born black players in baseball's major leagues dropped from an estimated one in four in the late 1960s to only one in six in the late 1980s. The situation in the minor leagues and in college baseball, an increasingly important source of major league talent, was even worse.[24] Surveys indicated that African Americans, who had flocked to major league ballparks in the 1950s accounted for less than 7 percent of attendance by 1987. "It is clear," wrote *New York Times* reporter Brent Staples, "that black fans, after a romance with baseball that began at the turn of the century and flourished through the early 1950s, have abandoned the national pastime."[25]

Staples blamed the hostile reception that blacks received at many ballparks and the well-publicized patterns of hiring bias for this disaffection. Other observers noted the virtual absence of African Americans among the scouts who identified potential major leaguers. While other sports shared baseball's paltry front office and managerial hiring record, commented Staples, "in baseball, with its mystical grip on the imagination of America, this discrimination seems particularly heinous."[26] Organized baseball responded with youth programs like RBI, Reviving Baseball in Inner Cities, and in both 1994 and 1995 the percentage of American-born blacks in the majors actually rose.[27] Baseball, however, like American society, remains haunted by the persistence of racial inequalities.

Amidst these controversies, Americans continue to resurrect Jackie Robinson in a variety of often surprising symbolic forms. As the nation absorbs large numbers of their ethnic and racial groups, the Jackie Robinson model offers an inspirational example of assimilation to new groups of Americans. The modern children's classic *In the Year of the Boar and Jackie Robinson*, written by Chinese-American writer Bette Bao Lord, tells the story of Shirley Temple Wong, a Chinese immigrant girl, whose passion for Robinson and the 1947 Dodgers facilitates her entry into American life.[28] Two years after the Rodney King riots, which often pitted the Koreans of Los Angeles against the city's blacks and Hispanics, the Dodgers signed Korean pitcher Chan Ho Park. Reporter David Margolick speculated that Park, like Jackie Robinson five decades earlier, might help to heal the gaping racial wounds.[29]

More commonly, however, the Robinson saga has begun to take on an air of wistful nostalgia. In the film *Do the Right Thing*, Spike Lee's ambivalent hero, Mookie (named presumably for a lesser black New York baseball player), parades through the Brooklyn ghetto in a Jackie Robinson Brooklyn Dodger jersey. Unlike Robinson, who lived in a presumably less complicated era and for whom the "right thing" always seemed predetermined, neither Mookie, nor Lee, nor the audience can ever discern the appropriate course of action for a young black man in modern America. When television producer Gary Alan Goldberg attempted to re-create the life of a Jewish family in the 1950s in the series *Brooklyn Bridge*, Robinson was a constant presence in the cultural background of the program. Ken Burns, the preeminent American documentary filmmaker, consciously crafted his recent *Baseball* opus around the Robinson saga. Burns' opening narrative invoked the history of the Brooklyn Dodgers as a pastiche of the nation's history, highlighted by "baseball's finest moment — when a black man wearing number 42 trotted out to first base." In the offbeat movie *Blue in the Face*, the ghost of Jackie Robinson materializes in a Brooklyn cigar store, to reminisce about a simpler, and inferentially, better, world that we have lost.

Is this, then, to be the legacy of Jackie Robinson: to evoke an idyllic, if imaginary past, when Americans held higher hopes and greater optimism;

when the racial divide seemed bridgeable and our social problems solvable? Does Jackie Robinson, the standard bearer of mid-century liberalism, still have relevance as we approach the millennium, a more conservative and chastised nation?

It is important to remember that the 1940s and 1950s, as Edenic as they may now seem, held no such allure at the time. The problem of Jim Crow seemed unsolvable, the challenges insurmountable, and the path uncertain. White supremacy, although weakened, remained a mainstream, not a fringe, ideology. Advocates of racial division held positions of power throughout the nation. The attack against segregation, in baseball and in society, constituted an experiment in every sense of the word, and its outcome remained uncertain. Jackie Robinson and Branch Rickey, however, launched their experiment with one fundamental, and, at the time, revolutionary premise: that all Americans inhabit this nation together and that the key to our future prosperity and happiness rests in the elimination of *all* obstacles to full participation. The responsibility for achieving this goal, they demonstrated, required the initiative and sacrifice of blacks and whites alike. This vision never entailed a surrender of ethnic and cultural distinctiveness but rather a celebration of racial pride and an inspirational model for the future.

The target assaulted by Rickey and Robinson — the seemingly impregnable wall of traditional Jim Crow — has long been obliterated. African-Americans are no longer, to apply Ralph Ellison's memorable metaphor, invisible men and women. The black middle class has expanded dramatically in both size and influence. African-Americans hold thousands of elected offices and other public positions, many in predominantly white communities. African-American entertainers and athletes rank among our most celebrated and beloved national figures. A retired African-American general is the preferred presidential candidate of millions of Americans. These achievements reflect not merely black accomplishments but a profound transformation of racial attitudes in white America.

Nonetheless, we have been forced to acknowledge the naiveté of our earlier optimism. While millions of African-Americans have benefited from the dismantling of more rigid racial thought and strictures, conditions for millions of others in our inner cities have deteriorated. The economic heritage of slavery and segregation has proved enduring and, thus far, intractable. Integrationist strategies, adopted in the 1950s and now seemingly embedded in our lives, have failed to achieve many of their stated goals. Amidst a backdrop of economic contraction and dislocation, this reality has engendered disenchantment and disillusionment on all sides of the racial divide. Discrimination and hostility toward African-Americans and other minority groups remain persistent and growing realities. Politicians, mistaking the outcomes of poverty for the causes of decline, find convenient scapegoats in the embattled African-American community. Within that community, voices of hatred and division often drown out those of reconciliation. Reactions to racially charged episodes like the O.J. Simpson trial reveal the vastly different worlds and perceptions of white and black Americans.

Amidst this maelstrom we must rescue Jackie Robinson from the realm of nostalgia. We remain engrossed in the great social experiment that he began. But, as with all incomplete experiments, we must periodically reassess its progress and reinvigorate its promise. We must reinforce those strategies that work, reject those that have failed, and assay new initiatives. The Jackie Robinson saga, whether in myth or reality, has always appealed to "the better angels of our nature." Today, fifty years after he first graced us with his pride, his courage, his passion, and his vision, our nation, amidst our current failures, disappointments, and spiriting political drift, has yet to produce a more compelling prophecy of a just, interracial society than that which we envision when we invoke the memory of Jackie Robinson.

Notes

The author wishes to thank the following people for their critiques of earlier drafts of this piece: Luise Custer, Peter Dreier, Bill Issel, Michael Knight, Barbara Loomis, Sheldon Meyer, Mike Pincus, David Shipp, Eric Solomon, Naomi Weinstein, and Richard Zitrin.

1. *New York Times*, July 13, 1983.

2. While there is still no satisfactory biography of Jackie Robinson, two recent books shed further light on his life. See Maury Allen, *Jackie Robinson: A Life Remembered* (New York, 1987), and David Falkner, *Great Time Coming The Life of Jackie Robinson from Baseball to Birmingham* (New York, 1995).

3. Donald Honig, *The Plot to Kill Jackie Robinson* (New York, 1993).

4. Bennett quoted in Studs Terkel, *Race: How Blacks and Whites Think and Feel About an American Obsession* (New York, 1992), 380.

5. On Rickey's political views, see Stephen Fox, "The Education of Branch Rickey," *Civilization* (September/October, 1995), 52–57.

6. *Ibid.*, 55.

7. See *Newsweek* (April 13, 1987); Fort Lauderdale *Sun-Sentinel*, April 14, 1987; and *People's Daily World*, April 17, 1987. For more recent example of Robinson's appeal to conservatives, see Steve Sailer. "How Jackie Robinson Desegregated America," *National Review* (April 8, 1996), 38–41.

8. See Harvard Sitkoff, *A New Deal for Blacks* (New York, 1978), 252–53, 333–34.

9. Prior to 1983, the best available books on the Negro Leagues were Robert Peterson, *Only the Ball Was White* (Englewood Cliffs, 1970), and John Holway, *Voices from*

the Great Negro Baseball Leagues (New York, 1975). William Brashler's novel, *Bingo Long and His Traveling All-Stars and Motor Kings* (New York, 1978), and his biography, *Josh Gibson: A Life in the Negro Leagues* (New York, 1978), also helped fill the vacuum.

10. The outpouring of books on the Negro Leagues is far too voluminous to list here. However, the following studies are particularly noteworthy: Donn Rogosin, *Invisible Men: Life in Baseball's Negro Leagues* (New York, 1983); Janet Bruce, *The Kansas City Monarchs: Champions of Black Baseball* (Kansas, 1985); Rob Ruck, *Sandlot Seasons* (Evanston, Ill., 1986); James Overmyer, *Effa Manley and the Newark Eagles* (Metuchen, N.J., 1993); Neil Lanctot, *Fair Dealing and Clean Playing: The Hilldale Club and the Development of Black Professional Baseball, 1910–1932* (Jefferson, N.C., 1994). There are also several good reference books, including James A. Riley, *The Biographical Encyclopedia of the Negro Baseball Leagues* (New York, 1994), and Dick Clark and Larry Lester, eds., *The Negro Leagues Book* (Cleveland, 1994). Photo histories include Bruce Chadwick, *When the Game Was Black and White: The Illustrated History of the Negro Leagues* (New York, 1992), and Phil Dixon and Patrick J. Hannigan, *The Negro Baseball Leagues: A Photographic History* (Mattituck, N.Y., 1992). There are also many biographies and autobiographies of former Negro League stars now available.

11. Ron Fimrite, "Sam Lacy: Black Crusader," *Sports Illustrated* (October 29, 1994), 91.

12. For examples, see Rogosin, 208–10; Bruce, 111; and John Holway, *Blackball Stars: Negro League Pioneers* (Westport, Conn., 1988), xi–xvi.

13. Amiri Baraka, *Autobiography* (New York, 1984), 35.

14. See Edwards's review of *Baseball's Great Experiment and Invisible Men* in *Journal of Sport and Social Issues* (Winter/Spring, 1985), 41–43.

15. Lee Lowenfish, "Could the Negro Leagues Have Been Saved?" (Paper presented at the conference Breaking Baseball's Color Line: Jackie Robinson and Fifty Years of Integration, Daytona Beach, Florida, March 15, 1996).

16. Edwards, 43.

17. *New York Amsterdam News*, November 30, 1963.

18. Baraka, 35.

19. For Robinson's views, see Jackie Robinson with Alfred Duckett, *I Never Had It Made* (New York, 1972), especially Chapter 17.

20. Roger Kahn, *The Boys of Summer* (New York, 1971), 402.

21. Robinson, 247, 251.

22. *USA Today*, April 9, 1987.

23. See Richard E. Lapchick, *1995 Racial Report Card* (The Center for the Study of Sport and Society, Northwestern University, 1995).

24. For figures on the 1960s, see Jack Orr, *The Black Athlete: His Story in American History* (New York, 1969), 97. For late 1980 figures, see Richard E. Lapchick and Jeffrey R. Benedict, *1994 Racial Report Card* (The Center for the Study of Sport and Society, Northwestern University, 1994). Many newspaper articles from the late 1970s through the early 1990s commented on the decline of African-American baseball players. See, for example; "Black Supply Turns from Torrent to Trickle," *Sporting News*, February 19, 1977; "Blacks Not Making Gains; Is There a Quota System?," *San Francisco Chronicle*, June 22, 1982; "College Baseball Becomes Primarily a White Game," *Los Angeles Times*, May 22, 1990; "A Scarcity of Black Division I College Players Raises Concern," *New York Times*, June 11, 1990; "Fewer Blacks Participate in Baseball," *Washington Post*, July 7, 1991; and "Blacks in Baseball," *Boston Globe*, August 4, 1991. To some extent the declining percentage of American-born blacks stemmed from the rise in Latin-American players. But even when this is taken into account, the drop in the percentage of American-born blacks between the 1960s and late 1980s was dramatic.

25. Brent Staples, "Where Are the Black Fans," *New York Times Magazine* (May 17, 1987), 28. In addition, see *New York Times*, March 23, 1986; *Boston Globe*, August 4, 1991; and "Baseball in Inner Cities: Pastime Is Passed Over," *Washington Post*, July 6, 1990.

26. Staples, 28–32. On scouting, see *San Francisco Examiner*, June 24, 1982. Many people have argued that the phenomenal popularity of basketball in the black community accounts for the declining support for baseball, but it is difficult to see why this would be the case. Support for basketball has also risen in the white community, but baseball attendance among whites, at least prior to the 1994 strike, skyrocketed. There is no reason that the two cannot coexist.

27. Lapchick, *1995 Racial Report Cord*, 6.

28. Bette Bao Lord, *In the Year of the Boar and Jackie Robinson* (New York, 1984).

29. *New York Times*, April 10, 1994.

Index